INTIMATE FRONTIERS

HISTORIES OF THE AMERICAN FRONTIER

Ray Allen Billington, General Editor

William Cronon, Coeditor
Howard R. Lamar, Coeditor
Martin Ridge, Coeditor
David J. Weber, Coeditor

ALBERT L. HURTADO

Intimate Frontiers

SEX, GENDER, AND CULTURE
IN OLD CALIFORNIA

✛ ✛ ✛

University of New Mexico Press Albuquerque

Library of Congress Cataloging-in-Publication Data

Hurtado, Albert L., 1946–

Intimate frontiers : sex, gender, and culture in old California / Albert L. Hurtado. —
1st ed.

p. cm. — (Histories of the American frontier)

Includes bibliographical references and index.

ISBN 0-8263-1953-X. — ISBN 0-8263-1954-8 (pbk.)

1. California — Social life and customs — 18th century. 2. California — Social life and
customs — 19th century. 3. Sex role — California — History — 18th century. 4. Sex role —
California — History — 19th century. 5. Heterosexuality — Social aspects — California —
History — 18th century. 6. Heterosexuality — Social aspects — California — History — 19th
century. 7. California — Race relations. 8. Frontier and pioneer life — California.
I. Title. II. Series.

F864.H897   1999

305.3'09794 — dc21   98-47009

                                                                          CIP

For Jean, now and always

Contents

Illustrations

✠

✛

Tables

✠

✛

Foreword

When we first invited Albert Hurtado to write a book about sex and gender for the Histories of the American Frontier series, we imagined that he would cover much of the early West, as do many books in this series. Al persuaded us that it would be more sensible to narrow his focus to a smaller slice of geography. He was right. Concentrating on a single state freed him to tell richer stories, and early California, with its rich Native American, Hispanic, Anglo American, and Chinese populations, proved an exceptional setting to explore intimate cultural encounters in the contact zones that we think of as "frontiers."

Even by narrowing his focus, however, Hurtado still faced a daunting challenge for a book in a series aimed at general readers. What narrative lines might link sex, gender, and culture in a space as large as California over a time span that extends from the beginnings of European settlement in 1769 through the gold rush and its aftermath? Hurtado solved the problem brilliantly by drawing on illustrative moments or figures rather than attempting encyclopedic coverage of all aspects of his subject. His sparkling vignettes introduce us to the famous and the forgotten, from Junípero Serra to Amelia Kuschinsky, and illuminate three of California's historic eras: Spanish (1769–1821), Mexican (1821–1848), and early Anglo American (1848–1860). Hurtado lingers longest in California after the gold rush, when sources become more abundant and enable him to speak more assuredly about topics like abortion and divorce. In all three eras, however, he finds that outsiders brought their own cultural conceptions of sex and gender into a land new to them but old to Native Americans. As in many frontier settings, the newcomers were overwhelmingly male. Early California's extraordinary gender imbalances distorted gender roles for men and women alike of all cultures, who generally wished to replicate a traditional way of life in an untraditional setting. Hurtado makes fine use of secondary literature, but goes beyond mere synthesis. *Intimate Frontiers* contains new stories and insights drawn from his shrewd analysis of unpublished personal correspondence and official records, and from his fresh readings of published primary sources. By looking at the ways that sex, gender, and culture shaped individual and group behavior, Hurtado also makes us see old subjects in new ways. Familiar topics, from the Spanish missions to the Donner Party, and familiar individuals from Olive Oatman to Dame Shirley, take unfamiliar turns in *Intimate Frontiers*. The much-studied Anglo American males who led their families to California, for example, appear in these pages as men burdened with responsibility. In cases where males made the decision to move their families west, males believed they bore responsibility for the success or failure of the enterprise and defeats weighed heavily on them. Hurtado suggests that the fact that more men than women died during the Donner tragedy may be explained in part by severe depression brought on by the men's sense of failure.

Drawing from the literature of social science, Hurtado offers explanations for human behavior, including the actions of male rapists whose behavior is easier to blame than explain. His use of insights from the social sciences, however, rests on a solid foundation of historical evidence, as when he turns to an unpublished census to reveal that two-thirds of the prostitutes in the overwhelmingly white city of Sacramento in 1860 were women of color. Throughout this rich book, he is concerned with the interplay between sex, gender, race, ethnicity, and class — all "cultural" constructions. Written in limpid prose, Al Hurtado's concise and engaging book fits our series splendidly. It is a work of original scholarship built on solid evidence and informed by theory. His analysis of sex, gender, and culture flows from interesting stories about events and individual lives, and draws on the behavioral sciences to reveal deeper meanings within those stories. Hurtado also puts California in broad perspective, taking his readers on the overland trails to the gold fields, to the South, to Michigan, and even to Panama and Brazil, and the questions that he considers in early California have analogues in frontier settings everywhere.

A native son of California, Al Hurtado earned his B.A. and M.A. at California State University, Sacramento, and his Ph.D. at the University of California, Santa Barbara, where he worked under the direction of Wilbur Jacobs. His first book, *Indian Survival on the California Frontier* (Yale 1988), won the 1989 Ray A. Billington Prize, given every other year by the Organization of American Historians for the best book to appear on the American frontier in the previous two years. His scholarly articles have won prizes from the Pacific Coast Branch of the American Historical Association, the Western History Association, and the Montana Historical Society. He is coeditor with Peter Iverson of *Major Problems in American Indian History* (1994), and is completing a biography of the great historian of the Spanish frontier in North America, Herbert E. Bolton. In the autumn of 1998, after a twelve-year career at Arizona State University, Hurtado became the Paul H. and Doris Eaton Travis Professor of Modern American History at the University of Oklahoma.

Like other books in this series, *Intimate Frontiers* tells a complete story, but it is also intended to be read as part of the broader history of western expansion told in these volumes. Each book has been written by a leading authority who brings to his task both a deep knowledge of his subject and well-honed skill at narration and interpretation. Each provides the general reader with a sound, engaging account of one phase of the nation's frontier past, and the specialized student with a narrative that is integrated into the general story of the nation's growth.

The series, conceived by the distinguished historian Ray Allen Billington in 1957 as a multivolume narrative history of the American frontier in eighteen volumes, has expanded over the years to include topics and geographical units that Ray had not originally envisioned: Sandra L. Myres's *Western Women and the Frontier Experience, 1800–1915* (1982), Elliott West's *Growing Up with the Country: Childhood on the Far Western Frontier* (1989), Donald J. Pisani's *To Reclaim a Divided West: Water, Law, and Public Policy, 1848–1902* (1992), Duane A. Smith's *Rocky Mountain West: Colorado, Wyoming, & Montana, 1859–1915* (1992), and Arrell Morgan Gibson and John S. Whitehead's *Yankees in Paradise: The Pacific Basin Frontier* (1993). Meanwhile, titles that Ray Billington planned in 1957 continue to appear in forms that Ray could not have anticipated — as with Terry G. Jordan's multidisciplinary examination of *North American Cattle-Ranching Frontiers: Origins, Diffusion, and Differentiation* (1993). As the series enters its fifth decade, we will continue to explore old frontiers in new, and perhaps more intimate, ways.

William Cronon   University of Wisconsin
Howard R. Lamar   Yale University
Martin Ridge   The Huntington Library
David J. Weber   Southern Methodist University

Preface

In 1979, while looking for information about the Indians who had lived in the Shasta-Trinity National Forest, I quickly rummaged through the steel file cabinets that housed the old records of Shasta County. The Forest Service had hired my employer to write an historical overview of the forest and I was part of a research team making a search of the local archives. I wasn't having much luck finding anything about Indians, and didn't expect the local records to reveal much about people who had been forced to scatter in the face of white miners during the gold rush. Finally, I looked in the last cabinet with drawers marked "Coroner's Records." Since this had been a region where white "Indian hunting" expeditions had been at work in the 1850s and 1860s, there was a grim possibility that someone had actually recorded the deaths of some Indians in the official files. Sure enough, a couple of unidentified Indian corpses turned up in the record, dead from unknown causes. Not much to go on here, I thought.

Then I saw a thick wad of folded papers tucked amid the single-page forms. What might this be? I unfolded the document, and unwittingly began to work on this book. It was a detailed report of a coroner's inquest over the body of Amelia Kuschinsky, an unwed teenager who had evidently died from a botched abortion in 1860. She was a servant and her employer got her pregnant. Suspicious neighbors and physicians gave much testimony. I scanned the report in perhaps five minutes, picking up a few fleeting details while my colleague urged me to quit so we could move on to the next stop. Amelia Kuschinsky had nothing to do with our project, and less to do with the doctoral dissertation that I meant to write on California

Indians. So I folded and refiled the report, closed the door, and went on to other things.

But I couldn't forget Amelia. I finished my dissertation, some articles, then a book while doing my apprenticeship as a public historian and gypsy academic. Still she haunted me. Thoughts about her came to me late at night after I had finished my "real" work. Who was she? Why was her life and death so compelling? What did she have to do with large historical issues? As my work on California Indians evolved, I became more interested in the experiences of Indian women, marriage, the family, and reproduction. Eventually my examination of these matters provided a general context for Amelia, too. I decided that I wanted to write a book about the interplay of sex, gender, race, and culture. Surely Amelia's short, sad history spoke to some of these concerns.

In 1989 I sent a letter "to whom it may concern" at Shasta Community College in Redding, where I first saw the coroner's report. I explained a bit about what I was looking for and where it might be found. Could someone please send me a copy of the report? I would happily pay the bill. The report came by return mail, and with no bill! The story that is embedded in that long-forgotten report may be found in chapter 6 in the present volume.

In the course of completing this book I have dealt with many well-documented people and events, but it was always Amelia who reminded me of what I was really writing about: the intimate matters of ordinary people and everyday lives. Her story discloses how risky sex could be for a woman in the nineteenth century and furnishes an example of the handicaps of class and gender that could weigh down a young woman and sink her if she were unlucky. She also made me think about young men who outnumbered women in gold-rush California. What sort of chances did they have for courtship, marriage, and family life? How did that affect their relations with women? Fortunately, most women were not as unlucky as Amelia, and most men were not as abusive as the ones she had to deal with. Yet the account of her death illustrates the complications of sex and gender in her time and place. Amelia also reminded me of how little we can know about the intimate lives of most people in past times. It was only her untimely death that caused a record to be made and kept. Otherwise there is little doubt that she, too, would have remained anonymous. I hope that by revealing some things about the private lives of Amelia and other people that this book will give readers a keener appreciation of how the powerful undercurrents of sex and gender have helped to shape the history of the American frontier. If I succeed in this, then Amelia's haunting of me will have been for a good purpose.

I have incurred many personal and intellectual debts while writing this book. David Weber is my foremost creditor. He suggested that I write such a book for the Billington series, and I wrote chapter 2 of the present volume in his National Endowment for the Humanities summer seminar on borderlands history in 1986. David's generous support for this project has been continuous despite many delays on my part. He and the other series editors, Martin Ridge, Howard Lamar, and William Cronon, have made writing this book a genuine pleasure. I cannot imagine a more congenial and helpful band. Like scores of other historians, I have benefited from Martin Ridge's interest in my scholarship. I thank him here for the many kindnesses that he has extended to me over the years, and especially for his helpful suggestions about this book. In 1986 I proposed to write a book that covered the entire West, but this soon proved to be an overwhelming task. William Cronon suggested that I write a more focused book using California to illustrate the sex and gender frontier, and the present volume is the result.

My colleagues and graduate students at Arizona State University have helped me to refine my arguments and avoid error. Professors Rachel Fuchs, Susan Gray, Gayle Gullett, Asunción Lavrin, Vicki Ruiz, Lynn Stoner, and Sybil Thornton, and graduate students Claudine Barnes, Eve Carr, Margaret Lamphier, and Timothy Hogdon invited me to present my work in the women's studies seminar. Their suggestions have guided the writing and revision of this book. Stimulating and useful discussions with Rachel, Susan, and Vicki have extended over several years at lunches, parties, and casual campus encounters. All faculties should be blessed with such collegial coworkers and friends. Vicki, Professor Kenneth N. Owens, and Cindy Baker of California State University, Sacramento, generously shared their research materials with me. Two talented doctoral students, Jeffrey Pappas and Brian Frehner, helped me to compile and organize research materials. Kate Magruder, an independent scholar in northern California, generously shared her knowledge of Dame Shirley. Gary Krahenbuhl, dean of the College of Liberal Arts and Sciences, provided a generous grant to illustrate this work. While the book was in press, I accepted the Paul H. and Doris Eaton Travis Chair in Modern American History at the University of Oklahoma, which assumed the grant that Dean Krahenbuhl authorized. My thanks to Dean Krahenbuhl and Paul B. Bell, dean of the College of Arts and Sciences at the University of Oklahoma.

This work would not have been possible without the professional assistance of a host of librarians and archivists at the California State Library, Bancroft Library, Huntington Library, and the Hayden Library at Arizona

State University. And, of course, I thank the anonymous archivist at Shasta Community College who sent me the coroner's report on Amelia Kuschinsky. Thanks to David Holtby, the editor in charge of this project, and the University of New Mexico Press staff for easing the myriad burdens that attended the publication of this book.

Finally, I thank Jean, my wife and fellow traveler on the intimate frontier of marriage. Her love and support is constant and I return it in full measure.

Introduction

The Intimate Challenges of a Multicultural Frontier

Know that to the right hand of the Indies was an island called California, very near the region of the Terrestrial Paradise, which was populated by black women, without there being any men among them, that almost like the Amazons was their style of living. They were of vigorous bodies and strong and ardent hearts of great strength; . . . their arms were all of gold . . . in all the island there was no other metal whatsoever. . . . And . . . when they had peace . . . there were carnal unions . . . , and if they gave birth to a female they kept her, and if they gave birth to a male, then he was killed. . . .
Any male that entered the island was killed and eaten by them. . . .[1]

GARCI ORDOÑEZ DE MONTALVO, *1510*

This book examines the intersection of sex, gender, and culture on California's multicultural frontier. It pays special attention to heterosexuality, courtship, and marriage. I have chosen this focus because family formation had much to do with who would control California — Indians, Europeans, people of mixed blood, or Americans. This was a biological and cultural question as well as a political one. In the mid-eighteenth century, when this story begins, the answers were by no means settled. A century later Anglo Americans believed that they had attained a satisfactory outcome (with them in control), but today's Anglo Californians are less certain of their hegemony. With beaches on the Pacific and a border on Mexico it is likely that the state's demographic structure will always be in flux and that the state will cease to have an Anglo American majority.

The collision of nations and the mixture of cultures in California have made the identification of racial, cultural, and national status of individuals a tricky business. California Indians spoke scores of different languages and followed many different life ways before the arrival of Europeans, so the generic term *Indians* does little except distinguish California's native people from newcomers. Whenever possible, I have used particular tribal designa-

tions. Spain colonized California in 1769, and by definition the colonizers
were *Spanish*, a term that I have used to describe nationality, although many
of the Franciscan priests hailed from other nations and most of the first
pobladores (settlers) were born in Mexico of mixed parentage. In 1821 Mexico became independent from Spain and California's Spaniards became
Mexicans, regardless of their point of origin. While this was going on,
Spaniards and Mexicans in California created a distinctive pastoral way of
life and called themselves *californios* (women were called *californianas*). They
also used the term *gente de razón* (people of reason) to distinguish themselves from Indians who were not assimilated into Hispanic society. I have
used the term *Hispanic* to identify all people who spoke Spanish and had
accepted other aspects of Spanish life including the Catholic religion.

Race is an especially problematic category, and it was particularly perplex-
ing in Mexico with its mixture of European, Indian, and African blood. Most
californios were of mixed origin, although there were some who correctly
claimed Spanish ancestry. Spaniards kept a labyrinthine system of racial
classification that accounted for parentage, skin color, and behavioral characteristics that offspring of mixed parentage supposedly exhibited. Since
"pure" Spaniards were at the top of this color-conscious racial hierarchy,
many californios claimed to be white Spaniards who were, in reality, of
mixed blood. I have applied the term *white* to californios who claimed to be
entirely of Spanish blood, although this was not strictly true in every case.[2]

People of the United States called themselves "Americans," and most
people of other nations accepted this practice. Following the modern pattern, I have used the terms *American* and *Anglo American* more or less
interchangeably, although many Americans had no Anglo ancestry and
would have bristled at being associated with England in the first half of the
nineteenth century. Americans placed all people with white skin above
people of color, but whiteness alone was not a sure guarantee of acceptance
in American society. Many Americans looked down on the Irish, Jews,
Germans, Catholics, and recent European immigrants generally, even
though they were white.[3]

I have examined homosexuality only as it represented a threatening alternative to the Hispanic family model and Catholic norms. I have no doubt
that some Spanish and Mexican men and women had homosexual relationships. It seems likely that during the gold rush, when there were so few
women and so many men, that more men than usual established homosexual ties.[4] These are important areas of inquiry, but heterosexual relations
are the essence of this work. More than anything else, this is a study of the
relations of power among men and women and diverse cultures. Those

relations cluster around the issue of marriage, the formal institution where heterosexual intercourse was permitted and its biological consequences — children — were encouraged. Marriages are important because they form linkages between families, and exogamy — marriage outside of one's own group — is of particular interest. Although in-laws have been known to disagree, many links between families from different cultures should foster a deeper mutual understanding between the cultures. Conversely, fewer mixed marriages mean fewer opportunities to gain positive insights into the other group. California's rich medley of races and cultures provides a rich arena for the study of mixed marriages.

Prostitution, rape, divorce, and abortion are part of this story because they illuminate the status of women and provide additional context for courtship, marriage, and family formation. Women were a minority in frontier populations and were politically powerless. Laws that governed divorce, prostitution, and abortion were particularly important because they described the legal limits of control that women had over their own bodies, although plenty of women and men were willing to break these statutory boundaries. Rape, though illegal, also limited female freedom and reenforced the idea that safety was most likely to be found within the family and other structures of patriarchal authority.

Patriarchy was common to Hispanic, Mexican, and Anglo society. Here I rely on Gerda Lerner's definition of patriarchy, "the manifestation and institutionalization of male dominance over women and children in the family and the extension of male dominance over women in society in general."[5] Although patriarchy was a common thread in all of these cultures, each group manifested male dominance in particular ways, and men ordinarily followed the customs that were specific to their cultures. Nor did patriarchy mean that women were utterly bereft of personal rights and remedies under the law if they had suffered abuse at the hands of men. Under the civil law of Spain and Mexico, for example, married women possessed rights to property, wages, and other legal rights as an individual. Most American wives were subject to common law that did not recognize community property rights in marriage and that made them inferior legal appendages of their husbands.[6] On the other hand, in the nineteenth century American women were not ordinarily subject to arranged marriages as were Hispanic women.

The term *social construction* is a key concept for understanding the intersection of people, time, and place. It means that each society construes gender, what it means to be a "man" or a "woman," and defines what kind of behavior is acceptable and desirable. Gender signifies far more than sexual difference; it is a condition that determines power relationships in society. As historian Joan Wallach Scott has put it, "gender is a constitutive element in social relationships based on perceived differences between the sexes, and gender is a primary way of signifying relationships of power."[7] Likewise, sexuality is a social construction that varies among cultures. Thus, gender and sexuality are fluid conditions of human life and their manifestations — such as heterosexual monogamy — are not "natural" biological consequences, but constructions that manipulate the range of biological and social possibilities and that change over time.[8] California is an especially interesting place to look at such matters because Indian, Hispanic, and Anglo cultures had distinctive ideas about sex and gender as well as different rules of sexual conduct, courtship, and marriage. Such differences left much room for misunderstanding if everyone played by their own society's rules.

The French philosopher Michel Foucault has shaped modern inquiry into the history of sexuality more than any other scholar. He argues that in the modern age Western societies have supported public discourses about sexuality that are meant to sustain structures of power within those societies. The state, church, and science collaborated in this. The Catholic Church contributed much to the evolution of discourses on sexuality by expanding the scope of sexual interrogation during confession. While ecclesiastical authorities cautioned priests against discussing sexual acts too candidly with penitents, confessors were supposed to inquire into "all insinuations of the flesh: thoughts, desires, voluptuous imaginings, delectations, combined movements of the body and the soul," Foucault explains, and "all this had to enter, in detail, into the process of confession and guidance."[9] The Catholic ritual confession of sexual sins even influenced the publications of libertines like Marquis de Sade, who urged his readers to narrate "the most numerous and searching details; the precise way and extent to which we may judge how the passion you describe relates to human manners and man's character."[10] The church required confessions of illicit sexual behavior in order to redeem the penitent and to modify future behavior, and the process — when it was successful — had the added benefit of regulating sexuality so that it was beneficial to the state. Sex within marriage produced legitimate children who were most likely to contribute to the economy, pay taxes, staff the military, and support the state.

According to Foucault, Western institutions have compelled "everyone to transform their sexuality into a perpetual discourse, to the manifold mechanisms which, in the areas of economy, pedagogy, medicine, and justice, incite, extract, distribute, and institutionalize the sexual discourse, an immense verbosity is what our civilization has required and organized."[11]

During the nineteenth century, Foucault says, such diverse influences as the church, psychoanalysis, eugenics, hygiene, demography, and police powers were employed to politicize sexuality for "the harnessing, intensification, and distribution of forces, the adjustment and economy of energies." Simultaneously, politicized sex regulated "populations, through all the far reaching effects of its activity."[12]

Some readers may judge Foucault's analysis to be too general, sinister, and conspiratorial for their taste. Yet they are likely to hear clear echoes of Foucault when they read about the missionaries' efforts to control Indian sexuality in chapter 1, and Alexander Everett's attempts to incite a confessional discourse in Louise Clapp, better known as Dame Shirley, the famous author of letters that described the gold rush. So, too, we may imagine hearing Foucault's analytical voice commenting on the life and death of Amelia Kuschinsky in chapter 5.

Looking backward, we easily recognize the relations of power and the discourses that supported them. In their own time and place, most people who wrote of intimate matters did not consider the political ramifications of their discourse. They believed that their sexuality and genders were not malleable conditions, but ordained by God and nature. In expressing their emotional and erotic needs, they often used the sentimental language of the heart. "You say in your letter that you would very much like to know what it is that I have to tell you so very sweet," Mary Shannon gently teased her beloved Johnson Beal.[13] "As I said in the last letter I wrote you, it is something that you must make haste to come down to hear." She closed her letter with a poem:

> To love is panefull that is true
> not to love is panefull to
> (But oh) it gives the greatest Pain
> to love and not be loved again

Ann Stevens expressed her carnal need for her lover more succinctly. "If you was here," she wrote to Walter Knight, "I suppose we should do some tall fucking."[14] Discourses of power were also dialogues of the heart and of the loins.

The intricacy of current ideas about sexuality and gender matches the complexity of California's history. For Spaniards, California was an idea long before it was a place on a map, and a complicated idea at that. Garcí Ordóñez de Montalvo's novel *Las Sergas del muy esforzado caballero Esplandian* — quoted at the head of this chapter — provided a name and a romantic land for Spaniards to seek. His book also explicates Spanish ideas about sex and gender constructions during the age of exploration. Women of color ruled on Montalvo's mythical island and complacently copulated with or cannibalized the men who came their way. This state of affairs represented for sixteenth-century Spaniards a perverse distortion of the social world, gender roles, and relations that they knew and valued. Montalvo eventually put things right by having Queen Calafía, the island's ruler, become a Christian and marry a Spaniard, thus properly domesticating and subordinating the obstreperous woman.[15]

Montalvo could not have known it, but his fictitious tale both prefigured and distorted the gender dynamics of California history. At the most general level Montalvo got it right. Spaniards were determined to reorder California's social world so that it conformed to Spanish and Roman Catholic norms. Montalvo cannot be expected to have predicted the course of history that occurred two hundred years after his death, but he knew his own people well. Marriage brought Queen Calafía to heel as a wife who was properly submissive to male authority (although she may have fantasized about making a tasty pâté of her husband's liver when she chafed under the marriage yoke). In the long run, men on the mythical island of California would cohabit with native women under Spanish rules, and so it was in reality. The Spanish impulse in this regard was conservative to the core, and it is one of the themes of this book. Nor were Spaniards alone in establishing familiar patterns of sex and gender relations. Not surprisingly, Mexicans—who of course had been Spaniards until 1821—carried on Spanish traditions and prejudices. The Americans and Europeans who followed them also longed for customary practices and partners that they had known at home, with two short-lived exceptions that are the subject of chapter 2.

Montalvo erred in representing native California women as aggressive cannibals who threatened men. If anything, history inverted Montalvo's plot. Native women were threatened by Spanish, Mexican, and Anglo men. The century that encompassed the mission, Mexican, and gold-rush eras saw the number of Indian women decline more rapidly than the numbers of Indian men while the total native population dropped from about 300,000 to 30,000.[16] There were marriages between Indians, Spaniards, and Mexicans, but they were not the norm that may be inferred from the queenly marriage in Montalvo's book. Even though Indians far outnumbered the Hispanic population, Spanish and Mexican men preferred to marry women from their own caste, class, and race. Here is another theme that I pursue throughout this book and that applies to Americans as well.

Montalvo's story foreshadows another of California's historical realities:

it was racially and culturally diverse. California was a multicultural frontier long before Spaniards sailed over the horizon. For thousands of years scores of tribes had occupied the land, and their cultures and languages varied, perhaps as dramatically as those of the nations of Europe. They coexisted peacefully for the most part, but at times they violently clashed.[17] In 1769 Spain planted and incubated its colonial mission outposts among Indians who were then urged to abandon tribal ways that were repellent to the Catholic Church and Spanish sensibilities. By the nineteenth century a distinctive *californio* culture had emerged in time for European and American visitors to observe and record it. The cultural heart and soul of the californio was Mexican—an amalgamation of Hispanic and Indian life ways. Californio food, folkways, religion, hospitality, prejudices, and aspirations were essentially those of their forebears from the south. The differences between californios and *mejicanos* were regional variations that evolved due to time, distance, isolation, and historical circumstances.[18]

Americans and Europeans began to arrive after the establishment of Mexican independence and liberalization of trade and immigration laws in 1821. The addition of these men (and a few women) added to California's cultural and racial mix. Most of them were white, and many of them married into californio families before the advent of American sovereignty and the gold rush. With the gold rush came an influx of people from all over the world, but Americans dominated the scene because they formed (in most places) a majority of the new population and because they controlled the new state and local governments that they established under American law. Violence erupted frequently amidst this volatile mixture of people as they struggled to control California. Wars, Indian resistance, committees of vigilance, and the administration of criminal law illustrate the underlying current of violence that suffused the state's early history.

Demographic conditions were among the driving forces of California history. Californios were always a tiny minority in a vast—though shrinking—Indian majority. Indians may have been numerous, but to most californios they were not desirable marriage partners. From 1769, when Spanish missionaries and soldiers first settled California, through the end of the gold rush in 1860 there were too few women, or at least there were too few of the *right* women, given the racial preferences of the non-Indian men at the time. Looked at in another way, one could argue that there were too many men. The californio minority tended to marry within its own ranks rather than seeking marriage partners from the Indian majority. The influx of Americans did not help much, for they, too, preferred to mate with women of their class and caste. Moreover, the gold-rush immigrants were mostly men. For nearly one hundred years after Spain colonized California, there was intense competition among men for suitable marriage partners. This condition created a century-long crisis in the marriage market that influenced social life among all classes of Californians.

The oversupply of men enabled some women to make more socially and financially advantageous marriages than they otherwise might have, if they had the requisite racial qualifications, but it also inflated the demand for prostitutes and — arguably — increased the incidence of rape of women of color, especially Indians. Chapters 1 and 4 especially speak to this issue. Poor white women were also subject to sexual abuse, as the sad case of Amelia Kuschinsky shows in chapter 5.

The book follows the general chronology of California history from the foundation of the missions through the gold rush. Its focus on sex, gender, and culture gives a new perspective on familiar episodes like the Donner Party tragedy and famous personalities like Dame Shirley. The emphasis on intercultural relations widens the angle of vision on such well-known events as the founding of the Franciscan missions and the gold rush.

As a work in the social history of the American West, this book augments the path-breaking work of a generation of scholars who have renewed and reinvigorated the field as an important area of historical research.[19] The historians who have pioneered this new approach to western history have challenged the idea of the frontier that previous generations of historians adhered to, arguing that this outmoded vision of the frontier was ethnocentric, nationalistic, and sexist.[20] The present volume is part of the Histories of the American Frontier series, but it examines a decidedly different sort of frontier than some of its distinguished predecessors. This book explores a multicultural frontier, a place where several distinctive peoples met who possessed dissimilar histories, discordant goals, and uncertain futures. California was the sort of place that David Weber had in mind when he wrote of "the drama of life on the *edges* where people and places meet."[21] There was plenty of drama when ordinary people me. on the fragile edge of the North American continent where ideas about sex, gender, courtship, and marriage seemed to be in flux.

Carlos Fuentes, the great Mexican novelist, wrote of frontiers in *The Old Gringo*. In this fictionalized account of the last days of Ambrose Bierce, the famous California writer who disappeared in Mexico during the revolution in 1913, Fuentes characterized Bierce and other gringos. "They spent their lives crossing frontiers, theirs and those that belonged to others," and Bierce had gone to Mexico "because he didn't have any frontiers left to cross in his own country." An American woman asked a Mexican general, her lover, if the frontier was "in here?" touching her forehead. He answered with a question, "and the frontier is in here?" while touching his heart. Then Fuentes offers Bierce's imagined opinion. "There's one frontier we only dare to cross at night. The frontier of our differences."[22] These are the intimate frontiers that this book explores — frontiers of the mind, frontiers of the heart, frontiers of difference.

ONE

Sexuality in California's Franciscan Missions:

Cultural Perceptions and Historical Realities

At one of these Indian villages near this mission of San Diego the gentiles therein many times have been on the point of coming here to kill us all, [because] some soldiers went there and raped their women, and other soldiers who were carrying mail to Monterey turned their animals into their fields and they ate up their crops. Three other Indian villages about a league or a league and a half from here have reported the same thing to me several times. For this reason on several occasions when Father Francisco Dumetz or I have gone to see these Indian villages, as soon as they saw us they fled from their villages and fled to the woods or other remote places, and the only ones who remained in the village were some men and some very old women. The Christians here have told me that many of the gentiles of the aforesaid villages leave their huts and the crops which they gather from the lands around their villages, and go to the woods and experience hunger. They do this so the soldiers will not rape their women as they have already done so many times in the past.[1]

FATHER LUÍS JAYME, 1772

Before Father Junípero Serra founded California's Franciscan missions, he led a religious revival in Mexico's Oaxaca region. Francisco Palóu, Serra's companion and biographer, approvingly reported that Serra's religious work produced concrete results. He reformed an adulteress who at the tender age of fourteen had begun to cohabit with a married man whose wife lived in Spain. This sinful arrangement had lasted for fourteen years, but on Serra's order she left the house of her lover. The man was desolate. He threatened and begged, but to no avail. Then "one night in desperation," Palóu related, "he got a halter, took it with him to the house where she was staying, and hung himself on an iron gate, giving over his soul to the demons." At the same moment a great earthquake shook the town, whose inhabitants trembled with fear. Thereafter, the woman donned haircloth and penitential garb and walked the streets begging forgiveness for her shameful past. "All were edified and touched at seeing such an unusual conversion and subsequent penance," the friar wrote. "Nor were they less fearful of divine Justice," he added, "recalling the chastisement of that unfortunate man." Thus, Palóu believed, the tragedy brought "innumerable conversions . . . and great spiritual fruit" to Serra's Oaxaca mission.[2]

This story was a kind of parable that prefaced Palóu's glowing account of Serra's missionary work in California. It demonstrated not only the presence of sexual sin in Spain's American colonies—which is not especially surprising—but that priestly intervention could break perverse habits, and that public exposure and sincere repentance could save souls. This incident is especially important because Palóu linked Serra's Mexican missionary triumph with the rectification of sexual behavior on the eve of his expedition to California. Thus, a discussion of sexuality in the California missions is not merely a prurient exercise, but goes to the heart of missionaries' intentions. While errant sexuality was not the only concern of priests, the reformation of Indian sexual behavior was an important part of their endeavor to Christianize and Hispanicize native Californians. Their task was fraught with difficulty, peril, and tragedy for Indians and Spaniards alike.

Native people, of course, already behaved according to sexual norms that, from their point of view, worked perfectly well. From north of San Francisco Bay to the present Mexican border, tribes regulated sexual life so as to promote productive family relationships that varied by tribe and locality. Everywhere the conjugal couple and their children formed a basic household unit, sometimes augmented by aged relatives and unmarried siblings. Indian families, however, were not merely a series of nuclear units, but were knit into sets of associations that comprised native society. Kinship defined the individual's place within the cultural community, and family associations suffused every aspect of life.

Indian marriages usually occurred within economic and social ranks and tended to stabilize economic and power relationships. Chiefs (who were occasionally women) were usually from wealthy families and inherited their positions. Since secure links with other groups provided insurance against occasional food shortages, chiefs frequently married several elite women from other *rancherías* (a Spanish term for small Indian communities). Diplomatic polygyny provided kinship links that maintained prosperity and limited warfare that could result from poaching or blood feuds. In the event of war, kinship considerations helped to determine who would be attacked, as well as the duration and intensity of conflict.[3]

Given the significance and intricacy of kinship, marriage was an extremely important institution, governed according to strict rules. Parents or respected ranchería elders often arranged marriages of young people and even infants. California Indians regarded incest — defined according to strict consanguinial and affinal rules — as a bar that prohibited marriage if a couple was related within three to five generations, depending on tribal affiliation. Consequently, men had to look for eligible wives outside their tribelet. Since most groups had patrilocal residence customs, women usually left their home communities, thus strengthening the system of reciprocity that girded native California.

The bride price symbolized women's place in this scheme. The groom gave his parents-in-law a gift to recognize the status of the bride's family, demonstrate the groom's worth, and compensate her family for the loss of her labor. The bride price did not signify that the wife was a chattel. No husband could sell his spouse, and an unhappy wife could divorce her husband. Even so, men were considered to be family heads, descent was usually through the male line, and residence in the groom's ranchería.[4]

California's native household economy was based on hunting and gathering according to a sexual division of labor. Men hunted and fished, and — after the advent of white settlement — raided livestock herds. Women gathered the plant foods that comprised the bulk of the Indian diet — acorns, seeds, roots, pine nuts, berries, and other staples. All California tribes prized hardworking, productive women.[5] Women's material and subsistence production was of basic importance to Indian society, but they made another crucial contribution as well — they bore children, thus creating the human resources needed to sustain native communities. When populations suffered significant reductions, the lack of fertile women meant that the capacity to recover was limited.

Re-creating the sexual behavior of any people is a difficult task, but it is especially difficult in societies that lacked a written record. Still, modern anthropology and historical testimony make possible a plausible — if partial — reconstruction of intimate native life. California Indians regulated sexual behavior in and out of marriage. Premarital sex does not seem to have been regarded as a matter of great importance, so virginity was not a precondition in a respectable mate. After marriage spouses expected fidelity from their husbands and wives, possibly because of the importance of status inheritance. Consequently, adultery was a legitimate cause for divorce and husbands could sometimes exact other punishments for the sexual misbehavior of their wives. Chumash husbands sometimes whipped errant wives. An Esselin man could repudiate his wandering wife, or turn her over to her new lover who had to pay the cuckold an indemnity, usually the cost of acquiring a new bride. Wronged Gabrielino husbands could retaliate by claiming the wife of his wife's lover, and could even go so far as to kill an adulterous spouse, but such executions were probably rare.

Women were not altogether at the mercy of jealous and sadistic spouses, for they could divorce husbands who mistreated them, a circumstance that probably meant they could leave if their husband committed a sexual indiscretion. In Chumash oral narratives, women often initiated sex and ridiculed inadequate partners. Some women even killed their husbands. It is impossible to know how frequently adulterous liaisons and subsequent divorces took place, but anthropologists characterize the common Gabrielino marital pattern as serial monogamy with occasional polygyny, indicating that separations were common. It is not unreasonable to suppose that because so many marriages were arranged in youth some California Indians subsequently took lovers after meeting someone who struck deeper emotional chords than their initial partners had. Nor is it implausible to speculate that some grievances were overlooked completely in the interest of maintaining family harmony and keeping intact the economic and diplomatic advantages that marriage ties were meant to bind. Prostitution was extremely rare in California, and was noted only among the Salinan Indians before the arrival of the Spanish. The lack of a flesh trade may indicate that such outlets were simply not needed because marital, premarital, and extramarital associations provided sufficient sexual opportunities.[6]

There was one other sexual practice common among California Indians — male homosexual transvestism, or the so-called berdache tradition which was evident in many North American tribes. The berdache dressed and acted like women, but they were not thought of as homosexuals. Instead, Indians believed that they belonged to a third gender that combined both male and female aspects. In sex they took the female role, and they often married men who were regarded as perfectly ordinary heterosexual males. Sometimes a chief took a berdache for a second wife because it was believed that they worked harder. Moreover, the berdache were thought to have special spiritual gifts that made them especially attractive spouses.[7]

Serra and the secular colonizers of Spain's northern frontier based their familial concepts on a narrower Spanish model that was in some respects contradictory. The state regarded marriage as a contract that — among other things — transferred property and guaranteed rights to sexual service.

On the other hand, the church regarded marriage as a sacrament before God and sought to regulate alliances according to religious principles.[8]

In theory, although not always in practice, Spanish society forbade premarital sex and required marital fidelity. Marriages were monogamous and lasted for life; the church granted divorces only in the most extraordinary cases, although remarriage of widows and widowers was permitted. The church regarded all sexual transgressions with a jaundiced eye, but held some acts in special horror. By medieval times Christian theologians had worked out a scheme of acceptable sexual behavior that also reflected their abhorrence of certain practices. Of course, fornication, adultery, incest, seduction, rape, and polygamy were sins, but far worse than any of these were the execrable sins "against nature," which included masturbation, bestiality, and homosexual copulation. The church allowed marital intercourse only in the missionary position; other postures were unnatural because they made the woman superior to her husband, thus thwarting God's universal plan. Procreation, not pleasure, was God's purpose in creating the human sexual apparatus in the first place. Therefore, to misuse the instruments of man's procreative destiny was to subvert the will of God. Medieval constraints on intimate behavior began to erode in the early modern period, but Catholic proscriptions against what the church defined as unnatural sexual behavior remained a part of canon law when Spain occupied California.[9]

This was the formal sexual ideology that Franciscans, soldiers, and pobladores brought to California. They also brought sinful lust. Maintaining sexual orthodoxy in the remotest reaches of the empire proved to be a greater task than Franciscan missionaries and secular officials could accomplish. Spaniards also brought to California an informal sexual ideology rooted in Mediterranean folkways that often ran counter to the teachings of the church. In this informal scheme, honor was an important element in determining family and individual social ranking and male status was linked to sexual prowess. To seduce a woman was to shame her and to dishonor her family while her consort acquired honor and asserted his dominant place in the social hierarchy. Women were thought to be sexually powerful creatures who could lead men astray, and more importantly, dishonor their own families. Society controlled female sexual power by segregating women, sometimes going so far as to sequester them behind locked doors to assure that they would not sully the family escutcheon with lewd conduct.[10] Catholic priests labored to restrict sexual activity in a world of philanders, concubines, prostitutes, and lovers.

Thus California's Spanish colonizers brought with them formal and informal ideas about sexuality that were riven with contradictions. The conquest of the New World and its alien sexual conventions made the situation even more complicated, but did not keep Spaniards from intimate encounters with native people. From the time of Cortés the crown and the church encouraged intermarriage with native people, and informal sexual amalgamation occurred with great regularity. Throughout the empire interracial sex resulted in a large mixed-race, *mestizo* population. Ordinarily, the progeny of these meetings attached themselves firmly to the religion and society of their Spanish fathers. Thus, sexual amalgamation was an integral part of the Spanish colonial experience that served to disable native society and strengthen the Hispanic population as it drew Indians and their children into the colonial orbit.[11] This was the world that Serra had tried to reform in Oaxaca; it was a world that he and fellow Spaniards would unwittingly replicate in California.

In 1775 Father Serra wrote thoughtfully to the viceroy of New Spain about interracial marriages in California. Three Catalán soldiers had already married neophyte women and three more were "making up their minds to marry soon."[12] Serra approved of new Spanish regulations that subsidized such marriages with a seaman's salary for two years, and provided rations for the mixed-race couple for five years. Such families should be attached permanently to the wife's mission and receive some livestock and a piece of land from the royal patrimony, provided the husband had "nothing else to fall back upon."[13] To Father Serra, these marriages symbolized the foundation of Spanish society. The new families formed "the beginnings of a town" because all the families lived in "houses so placed so as to form two streets." The little town of Monterey, Serra observed, also included the mission buildings and "all together make up a square of their own, in front of our little residence and church."[14] Happily, children were already beginning to appear in Monterey, thus assuring that the community would have a future.

Serra's idealistic vision of colonization incorporated Spanish town building and Catholic marriages that tamed the sinful natures of Spaniards and Indians and harnessed them to Spanish imperial goals.[15] If he could have had his way, the only sexual activity in California would have occurred in the few sanctified marriage beds that were under the watchful eye of the friars. But that was not to be.

Serra recognized that Spanish and Indian sexual transgressions occurred, and they troubled him. Common Indian sexual behavior amounted to serious sins that merited the friars' solemn condemnation. Perhaps the worst cases were the berdache, who seemed ubiquitous in California. Their so-called sins against nature challenged religious and military leaders alike. While Serra extolled the virtues of marriages, Captain Pedro Fages, in 1775, reported that Chumash Indians were "addicted to the unspeakable vice of sinning against nature," and that each ranchería had a transvestite "for common use."[16] Fages, reflecting Spanish and Catholic values, apologized for even mentioning homosexuality because it was "an excess so criminal that it seems even forbidden to speak its name."[17] The missionary Pedro Font observed "sodomites addicted to nefarious practices" among the Yuma and concluded that "there will be much to do when the Holy Faith and the Christian religion are established among them."[18]

Civil and church officials agreed on the need to eradicate homosexuality as an affront to God and Spanish men alike. At the Mission Santa Clara the fathers noticed an unconverted Indian who, though dressed like a woman and working among women, seemed to have undeveloped breasts, an observation that was made easier because Indian women traditionally wore only necklaces above the waist. The curious friars conspired with the corporal of the guard to take this questionable person into custody, where he was completely disrobed confirming that he was indeed a man. The poor fellow was "more embarrassed than if he had been a woman," said one friar. For three days the soldiers kept him nude — stripped of his sexual identity — and made him sweep the plaza near the guardhouse. He remained "sad and ashamed" until he was released under orders to abjure feminine clothes and stay out of women's company.[19] Instead, he fled from the mission and reestablished a berdache identity among gentiles.[20]

The Spanish soldiers thoroughly misconstrued what they were seeing and what they had done. The soldiers no doubt thought they had exposed an impostor who was embarrassed because his ruse had been discovered. They did not realize that their captive — and his people — regarded himself as a woman and reacted accordingly when stripped and tormented by men.

Humiliated beyond endurance and required to renounce a sexual orientation that had never raised an eyebrow in Indian society, the Santa Clara transvestite was forced to flee, but perhaps he was more fortunate than he knew. Father Francisco Palóu reported a similar incident at the Mission San Antonio, where a berdache and another man were discovered "in an unspeakably sinful act." A priest, a corporal, and a soldier "punished them," Palóu revealed, "although not as much as they deserved."[21] When the horrified priest tried to explain how terrible this sin was, the puzzled Indians told him that it was all right because they were married. Palóu's reaction to this news was not recorded, but it is doubtful that he accepted it with equanimity. After getting a severe scolding the homosexual couple left the mission vicinity. Palóu hoped that "these accursed persons will decrease, and such an abominable vice will be eradicated," as the Catholic faith increases "for the greater Glory of God and the good of those pitiful, ignorant people."[22]

The revulsion and violence that ordinary Indian sexual relations inspired in the newcomers must have puzzled and frightened native people. Formerly accepted as an unremarkable part of social life, berdache faced persecution at the hands of friars and soldiers. To the Spaniards homosexual behavior was loathsome, one of the many traits that marked California Indians as a backward race. In a word, they were "incomprehensible" to Father Gerónimo Boscana. The "affirmative with them, is negative," he thought, "and the negative, the affirmative," a perversity that in the priest's mind was clearly reflected in Indian homosexuality. In frustration, Boscana compared the California Indians "to a species of monkey."[23]

For Spaniards and California Indians alike, the early days of colonization created a confused sexual landscape, but Spanish intolerance of homosexuality was not the only cause of this. In order to convert Indians, the Franciscans had to uproot other aspects of the normative social system that regulated Indian sexuality and marriage. At the very least, missionaries meant to restructure Indian marriage to conform to orthodox Catholic standards of monogamy, permanence, and fidelity, changes in intimate conduct that engendered conflict on the California frontier.

At the outset, friars had to decide what to do about married Indians who became mission neophytes. Even the acerbic Father Boscana believed that monogamous Indian marriages were lawful and should be permanently binding on neophytes, except for couples who were united against their will.[24] But what about marriages where one partner became a Christian while the other remained a heathen? And what should be done about polygynous unions? Missionaries worked out the answers according to canon law and its application to Indian converts in Mexico. Neophyte couples remarried in the Catholic Church, and when indigenous marriages were divided by religious beliefs the Christian partner was permitted to take a new Christian spouse. Plural marriages presented a knottier problem for married Indians because the church required the husband to recognize only his first wife while renouncing the others, a decision that necessarily depended solely on Indian testimony. This requirement sometimes led to convoluted explanations from a husband who claimed to have married his youngest wife first. The desire to retain a particular wife among several may have reflected economic as well as sexual preferences since a young wife would probably produce more children than her older counterpart, work longer, and be able to care for her husband in his old age.[25]

Franciscans applied these Christian marriage rules to California. Records from seven missions in northern California show that between 1769 and 1834 the church remarried 2,374 Indian couples.[26] This practice was wise, for it permitted thousands of native couples to retain family and emotional attachments while taking up Catholic and Spanish life. The retention of conjugal connections eased the Indian transition to mission authority and no doubt encouraged some Indians to convert.

Not all Indian marriage customs were admissible under Catholic scrutiny, however. Father Francisco Palóu, generally sympathetic to Indian marriage customs, unfortunately found that the Chumash were inclined to wed "their sisters-in-law, and even their mothers-in-law," thus adding incest to the sin of polygamy.[27] Chumash widows and widowers remarried within their deceased spouse's family, a practice that the church prohibited. Indian spouses with such ties who wished to enter the mission had to abandon established marriages, lie about their relationships, or reject conversion.[28]

The road to imposing a new sexual orthodoxy in California was a hard one. Christian ceremonies did not automatically eliminate older cultural meanings of Indian marriage, nor did they necessarily engender Catholic values in the Indian participants. Dissident neophyte runaways sometimes abandoned their old wives and took new ones according to tribal custom.[29] When the fathers forbade specific neophyte marriages, unhappy Indians found ways to insist on having the relationship that they preferred. In 1816, for example, an Indian man, probably Chumash, left the Mission San Buenaventura to be with the woman he wanted at Santa Barbara. "This happens," Father José Señan revealed, "every time his shackles are removed."[30] It is not clear if the missionaries had shackled the man for previously running off to his lover or for some other offense, but Señan allowed that it would be best to permit the couple to wed quietly. If, however, the Indian made mischief, "send him back to us."

All Christian marriages, of course, were not blissful, nor did they all reflect the wifely obedience that Hispanic society celebrated. Sometimes, dissatisfied Indian wives used traditional kinship links to solve domestic problems. The inherent possibilities of such arrangements were revealed in 1795, after a skirmish between unconverted Chumash Indians near Mission San Buenaventura. Almost immediately after the fight — and perhaps related to it — the priests found a dead neophyte in the mission garden. His Christian wife, her neophyte brother, and two other neophytes had decapi-

I. DANSES DES HABITANS DE CALIFORNIE A LA MISSION DE SAN FRANCISO.
Indians dance under the watchful eyes of Franciscans in front of the Mission San
Francisco de Asis (popularly known as the Mission Dolores). In the background
seminude women look on. Priests were determined to convert Indians to the Catholic religion and Spanish cultural norms, but it was a slow process. Indians were
determined to maintain their customs despite the friars' importunities. Engraved
from a 1816 painting by Louis Choris.
Courtesy of the Bancroft Library.

tated him.[31] Their motives are not known, but it is clear that neophytes who
wanted to violate Christian precepts — or observe Indian concepts of justice — could enlist traditional kin to do so.

Spanish attempts to reform Indian behavior caused many problems
among the tribes of California. Costanoans near Mission Santa Cruz became restive because of Spanish interference with Indian marriages. In
1794, a traditional Costanoan man organized some Christian and gentile
Indians who attacked the mission guards, wounded two soldiers, and burned
two buildings. The motive for this assault, Father Fermin Francisco de Lasuén explained, was that the soldiers had taken the Costanoan leader's wife to
the San Francisco presidio along with some other neophyte runaways.[32]
Evidently, the Spaniards ran risks when they separated Indian couples. A few
years later the Santa Cruz friars claimed that sexual restrictions caused

Costanoan neophytes to flee from the mission. Indians who could not "entirely gratify their lust because of the vigilance of the missionaries," they reckoned, decamped "in order to give full sway to their carnal desires."[33]

The missionaries simply could not accept that Indians adhered to a different set of sexual rules than did Spanish Catholics. Nor did they understand Indians' kinship practices. Instead, Franciscans like Father Lasuén thought of California Indians as people utterly without "government, religion, or respect for authority" who "shamelessly pursue without restraint whatever their brutal appetites suggest to them." They were "people of vicious and ferocious habits who knew no law but force, no superior but their own free will, and no reason but their own caprice." Father Lasuén evidently believed that sex was high on the list of brutal native appetites for he thought that Indians were inclined to "lewdness."[34]

What is lewd in one culture, however, is not necessarily lewd in another. Conflicting Indian and missionary attitudes about the human body are a case in point. California Indian men were customarily nude, and the women wore only skirts of bark or skins. Missionaries wondered that nudity did not embarrass the Indians, who "showed not the least trace of shame" even though the natives saw that Spaniards wore clothes.[35] A Spaniard who went about naked would not have been allowed to run loose in Spanish society for very long, and the Franciscans regarded undress as a mark of uncivility and paganism. Consequently, missionaries devoted much time and energy to clothing the neophytes. Indians and missionaries were caught in a classic case of cultural misunderstanding. The missionaries could not accept Indian sexual attitudes and practices because they contravened a sacred sexual ideology and Spanish cultural norms. Indians could not comprehend the need for such strict rules.

Caught in this conflict, missionaries demanded that Christian Indians adopt formal Spanish attitudes about sex and punished them when they did not. Within the mission they tried to achieve this goal by segregating the Indians by sex at night, a policy that—as we shall see—was not altogether successful.[36] Neophytes who failed to live up to Catholic standards ran afoul of the missionaries who imposed corporal punishment. When, for example, Chumash neophytes at Mission Santa Barbara reverted to polygyny—which the friars evidently regarded as concubinage after Christian conversion—Father Esteban Tapis first admonished the offenders. On the second offense Tapis laid on the whip, and when this did not convince the Indians of the error of their ways he put them in shackles.[37]

Franciscans believed they had a right to use corporal punishment to correct unruly Indians. Indeed, the lash was used throughout Spanish society.

2. MONJERIO, MISSION LA PURÍSIMA CONCEPCIÓN.
Padres locked unmarried women in this barracklike building at night to keep them
from having illicit affairs. The priests were not successful in preventing sexual
liaisons, as their frank complaints and mission birth records show. The sequestering
of Indian women had an unforeseen effect on the inmates. Deadly communicable
diseases spread quickly among the women in the closed, fetid environment. Mission
statistics show that Indian women died at higher rates than Indian men, a trend that
mission living conditions probably exacerbated. Photograph by Richard Orsi 1992.
Courtesy of California History.

Eighteenth-century Spanish parents whipped children; teachers whipped
pupils; magistrates whipped civil offenders; pious Catholics whipped themselves as penance. Neophytes accepted the lash as a fact of mission life when
their sexual transgressions caught the watchful eyes of the friars, but the
Spanish and Catholic understanding of the whip as an instrument of correc-
tion, teaching, mortification, and purification probably eluded them.[38]
In Indian society, corporal punishment as a means of social control was

rare. Some tribes permitted husbands to physically punish adulterous wives, but Indians saw punishment as a husband's right because adultery threatened the economic and diplomatic role of the family, not because sex was wrong or sinful.[39]

Indian sexuality was not the only carnal problem that the fathers had to contend with in California. Civilians and soldiers brought to California sexual attitudes and behavior that were at odds with Catholic and Indian values. Rape was a special concern of friars, who monitored Spanish deviant sexual behavior in California.[40] As early as 1772 Father Luís Jayme complained about some of the soldiers, who deserved to be hanged for "continuous outrages" on the Kumeyaay women near the Mission San Diego.[41] "Many times," he asserted, the Indians were on the verge of attacking the mission because "some soldiers went there and raped their women." The situation was so bad that the Indians fled from the priests, even risking hunger "so the soldiers will not rape their women as they have already done so many times in the past."

Father Jayme thought Spaniards' assaults were all the worse because the Kumeyaay Indians had become Christians and given up polygyny and incestuous marriages. Married neophytes did not commit adultery and bachelors were celibate. Kumeyaay sexual behavior was not only the result of the missionaries' teaching, but a reflection of their traditional belief that adultery was bad. "If a man plays with a woman who is not his wife," Jayme explained, "he is scolded and punished by his captains."[42] An unconverted Indian told Jayme, "although we did not know that God would punish us in Hell, [we] considered [adultery] to be very bad, and we did not do it, and even less now that we know that God will punish us if we do so." When the missionary heard this, he "burst into tears to see how these gentiles were setting an example for us Christians."

Jayme's version of the Kumeyaay statement seems to confuse rape and adultery, a problem that may have stemmed from linguistic and cultural misunderstanding. In any case, Jayme described two rapes and their consequences. In one instance, three soldiers had raped an unmarried woman who became pregnant. She was ashamed of her condition and ultimately killed the newborn infant, an act that horrified and saddened Father Jayme. The second incident occurred when four soldiers and a sailor went to a ranchería and dragged off two women. The sailor refused to take part and left the four to complete the assault. Afterward, the soldiers tried to convert the act from rape to prostitution by paying the women with some ribbon and a few tortillas. They also paid a neophyte man who had witnessed the assault and warned him not to divulge the incident. Insulted and angry, the Indians were not overawed by the rapists' threats and told Jayme. In retaliation, the soldiers locked the neophyte man in the stocks, an injustice that outraged Jayme who personally released him.[43]

The situation at San Diego was not unique. "There is not a single mission where all the gentiles have not been scandalized," Jayme wrote, "and even on the road, so I have been told."[44] Spaniards' sexual behavior did not escape the eye of Father Serra, who asserted that "a plague of immorality had broken out." He had heard the bitter complaints of the friars who wrote to him of disorders at all of the missions. Serra worried especially about the muleteers who traversed the vast distances between missions with their pack trains. Serra feared the consequences of allowing these unbridled characters among the Indians. There were so many Indian women along the road that Serra expected sexual transgressions, for "it would be a great miracle, yes, a whole series of miracles, if it did not provoke so many men of such low character to disorders which we have to lament in all our missions; they occur every day; . . ." Serra came perilously close to blaming the women for the sexual assaults that they suffered. Nevertheless, he believed rapes could imperil the entire mission enterprise by alienating the Indians who would "turn on us like tigers."[45]

Serra was right. In 1775, some eight hundred neophyte and non-Christian Kumeyaays, fed up with sexual assaults and chafing under missionary supervision, attacked Mission San Diego. They burned the mission and killed three Spaniards, including Father Jayme, beating his face beyond recognition.[46] Rapes were not the sole cause of the attack, but as Jayme and Serra had predicted, sexual abuse made California a perilous place. Still, the revolt did not dissuade some Spaniards from sexual involvement with Indian women. In 1779, Serra was still criticizing the government for "unconcern in the matter of shameful conduct between the soldiers and Indian women," a complaint that may have included mutual as well as rapacious liaisons.[47]

Serra's argument implied that without supervision some Spaniards acted without sexual restraints. Spaniards believed in a code of honor that rewarded sexual conquests, and soldiers may have asserted their ideas about honor and status by seducing California Indian women. There was no honor in rape. Honorable sexual conquest required a willing partner who was overcome by the man's sensuality, masculinity, and magnetism, not merely his brute ability to overpower her. Recall the San Diego rapists who tried to mitigate their actions by making a payment to their victims.[48] Serra argued that there were men of bad character who could not control their urges, but rape is a complex act that requires more than opportunity and a supposedly super-heightened state of sexual tension. Recent research shows that rape is an act of domination carried out by men who despise their victims because of their race or gender. Stress, anger, and fear also motivate some rapists.[49] It should not be forgotten that Spaniards were fearful of California Indians—outnumbered and surrounded by Indians who seemed capable of overwhelming them at any moment.[50] There were frequent minor skirmishes, livestock thefts, and occasional murders that reinforced the Spanish conception of the Indian enemy. As late as 1822 one missionary thought that it was impossible to know how many troops were necessary to defend the Mission San Buenaventura because there were so many un-Christianized Indians in the interior. "May God keep our neophytes peaceful and submissive," he wrote, "for they would not want for allies if they should rise against our Saint and our charity!"[51] It is not difficult to imagine that some men, sent to a dangerous frontier outpost, violently and subconsciously used Indian women as objects to ward off fear and dominate the numerous native population that the Spanish crown and Catholic Church sought to subdue, colonize, and convert.

Sexuality, unsanctioned and perversely construed as a way to control native people, actually threatened Spain's weak hold on California by angering the Indians and insulting their ideas about sexuality, rectitude, and justice. It is impossible to know how many rapes occurred in Spanish California, but sexual assaults affected Indian society beyond their absolute numbers. Moreover, Indian rape victims likely displayed some of the somatic and emotional symptoms of rape-trauma syndrome, including physical wounds, tension, sleeplessness, gastrointestinal irritations, and genitourinary disturbances. In our own time raped women are often stricken with fear, guilt, anger, and humiliation, and some raped women develop a fear of normal sexual activity.[52] There is no reason to believe that Indian women did not react to rape in similar ways. Fear of assault may have affected many women who were not themselves victims as they tried to help friends and relatives cope with the consequences of rape. Sexual assaults echoed in the Indian social world even as they frightened friars who feared the consequences of an outraged Indian population.

It is impossible to know how many free-will assignations occurred in California during the mission period, but it is safe to assume that such cross-cultural trysts were fraught with misunderstanding. Indian women, accustomed to looking outside of their communities for husbands, likely

viewed Spaniards as potential mates who could bring them and their families increased power, wealth, and status. Some women may have hoped that
sex would lead to marriage, but it seldom did.[53]

Indians responded to Spanish sexual importunities in several ways. Physical resistance to missions, as at San Diego in 1775 and on the Colorado
River in 1781, was one way to deal with rapists and other unwanted in-
truders. Marriage to a Spaniard was another strategy that could protect
women, but evidently only a few dozen Indians were able to use this tactic.
Other Indians, like the transvestites mentioned above, withdrew from
Spanish-controlled areas to avoid any infringement on their social life and
values. On the other hand, some women might have entered the missions
for protection that the mission setting provided from sexual abuse by Spanish soldiers. There is also reason to believe that Indians altered their sexual
practices as a result of meeting the Spanish. Prostitution, which had formerly been rare among the Indians, became common. In 1780 Father Serra
complained about Nicolas, a neophyte who procured women for the soldiers at San Gabriel.[54] A few years later a Spanish naturalist observed that
the Chumash men had "become pimps, even for their own wives, for any
miserable profit."[55]

Nicolas and other Indians had several reasons to resort to prostitution.
Spanish men seduced and raped the Indians' female kinfolk but did not
marry them. Perhaps Indians were recovering lost bride prices through
prostitution. Since there were Hispanic men who were willing to pay for
sex, prostitution might have seemed a logical way to enhance the economic
value of wives and daughters who were expected to be productive. How
women felt about being so used is not known, but the missions would have
been one avenue of escape for those who were unhappy with these new
conditions. In the early years of colonization, Indian women outnumbered
male neophytes, indicating that females found the mission especially attractive in a rapidly changing world.[56]

Another California Indian reaction to a new sexual world was physiologi-
cal: they contracted syphilis and other venereal diseases, maladies to which
they had not previously been exposed. So rapidly did syphilis spread among
Indians that, in 1792, a Spanish naturalist traveling in California believed
the disease was endemic among the Chumash.[57] Twenty years later the
friars recorded it as the most prevalent and destructive disease in the missions.[58] Syphilis was particularly deadly among the Indians because its
weakened victims became easy prey for epidemic diseases that periodically
swept the missions. In addition, stillbirths increased and infected women

died more frequently in childbirth. If they bore live children the infants were likely to have congenital syphilis.[59]

Despite the intentions of Serra and other friars, mission life did not necessarily provide neophytes with a respite from sexual activity. Friars declared almost unanimously that mission Indians committed a variety of sexual sins. Between 1813 and 1815 missionaries recorded that the neophytes were guilty of "impurity," "unchastity," "fornication," "lust," "immorality," "incontinence," and so forth, indicating that the mission experience had not fully inculcated Catholic sexual values in the neophytes.[60]

How could the fathers have known about the intimate lives of mission Indians? The Indians confessed their sins at least once a year, and suspicious priests questioned the neophytes closely about their sexual behavior. Franciscan *confesionarios* with lists of questions in California Indian languages provide some idea of the level of priests' interest in neophyte sex. Have you ever sinned with a woman, a man, an animal? Do you have carnal dreams? Did you think about the dream later? What is your relationship with the people with whom you sin? Have you given your wife or husband to someone else? Do you become aroused when you watch them or when you see animals having intercourse? What did you think? Do you play with yourself? Have you tried to prevent pregnancy? Have you ever *not* had sex with your wife when she wanted to? So the questions continued for many pages.[61] The investigation of Indians' sexual lives was thorough and relentless. And so missionaries knew that men and women fell short of ideal sexual behavior. The friars' frank words about Indian sexuality betray disappointment born of the unspoken realization that their best missionary efforts had not reformed Indian sexuality.

The combination of virulent endemic syphilis and sexual promiscuity created a fatal environment that killed thousands of mission Indians and inhibited the ability of survivors to recover population losses through reproduction. Franciscans — and some of their critics — believed that the carnal disintegration of the California missions occurred because the Indians simply continued to observe the sexual customs of native society.[62] The Indians were unrestrained libertines who had learned nothing of Catholic moral behavior in the missions, and were incapable of realizing that syphilis was killing them. This view is incomplete because it assumes that sexuality was unregulated in native society and that Indian sexual behavior was unchanged during sixty-five years of mission experience.

Perhaps mission Indian sexuality was a response to new conditions. Who would have understood desperate demographic conditions at the missions

3. CONFESSIONAL, MISSION SAN JUAN CAPISTRANO.

Mission Indians made this baroque confessional out of native sycamore wood, under the direction of Franciscan missionaries around 1776. The priest sat inside (probably behind a drawn curtain) to hear Indians confess sexual and other sins as they knelt and spoke through a screen. Drawing by Randolph F. Miller.

Courtesy of the California State Library.

better than the neophytes themselves? Locked into a system that assured their ultimate destruction, dying rapidly from unheard-of diseases, perhaps neophytes chose procreation as a means of group survival. Sadly, they failed, but it was not for want of trying.

It should not be assumed that neophyte sexual behavior was monolithic. Rather, it was influenced by both ethnic and gender considerations. By the end of the mission period missionaries had recruited substantial numbers of interior Indians to replace the neophytes who were rapidly dying. Many of the new converts were Indians from the interior, who formerly had fought against the coastal Indians.[63] In the missions, long-standing animosities could have released interethnic sexual aggression that was meant to assert dominance in this new setting. Priests reported that mission women who became pregnant resorted to abortion and infanticide, and these acts may have been based in Indian customs, especially in the case of the Chumash, who believed that unless the first child died the mother would not conceive again. But women had other reasons, too. Unwed mothers would be subjected to close questioning and punishment by priests. What if the father were a soldier who did not want his identity revealed, what then? Thus, Indian women who attempted to apply old norms to assure fertility contributed to the destruction of the Indian population.[64]

Whatever the causes of mission sexuality, neophytes relied on old ways and new ones to solve difficult problems in a new setting. In the end, efficacious solutions eluded them, but it is not accurate to say that Indians were immoral, amoral, or incapable of assimilating the message that the missionaries brought them. The mission experience demonstrates that Indians were simultaneously resolute and unsure, conservative and radical, forward looking and bound to tradition. They exemplified, in other words, the human condition.

Ultimately, the history of California's missions is a sad one that elucidates a series of human misunderstandings, failures, and terrible, unintended consequences. That Spaniards and Indians were often incapable of comprehending each other should hardly be surprising, because they came from radically different cultures. As was so often the case in the history of the Western Hemisphere, Indians and newcomers talked past each other, not with each other. This was true even of their most personal contacts in California. Sacred and profane, intimate, carnal, spiritual, ecstatic, bringing life and death — Indian and Spanish sexuality embodied the paradox and identity of their all-too-human encounter.

T W O

Customs of the Country:

Mixed Marriage in Mexican California

My most highly esteemed sir:

For some time I have wished to speak with you regarding a matter so delicate that in the act of explaining it, words have failed me to express myself as I should in order to reveal the favor which only you have the power to grant and to be the author of my felicity.

Perhaps the attentions which I have shown to your very charming daughter, Doña Anita, have been observed, as also, no doubt, my desire always to attend the many gatherings which were graced by her presence.

Her attractions have persuaded me that without her I cannot live *or be happy in this world. Consequently, I am begging for her hand. My circumstances are well known, and it is not necessary to say that my principal object will be to grant* all her desires *and to* become worthy of her esteem.

I am with the greatest respect, Your obedient servant who kisses your hand.[1]

ALFRED ROBINSON, 1834

Alfred Robinson, twenty-seven-year-old native of Massachusetts, figuratively kissed the hand of his future father-in-law, Don José Antonio Julián de la Guerra y Noriega. Robinson was an agent for Bryant, Sturgis and Company, a Boston-based firm that dominated California's hide and tallow trade. Don José was a native of Spain, soldier, respected man of affairs, and the richest man in the Santa Barbara region. His principal business was in raising thousands of cattle that he slaughtered for their tallow and hides, which he sold to Bryant, Sturgis, and similar companies. Doña Anita, the object of Robinson's desire, was thirteen years old.

The betrothal of Doña Anita to Alfred Robinson was emblematic of California's changed state of affairs. In 1821 Mexico had achieved its independence from Spain and California became a part of the new American nation. Mexico reformed the antiquated trade laws of Spain that in most cases had restricted colonies to trading only with the mother country. Consequently, enterprising Mexicans and Americans began to carry goods along the Santa Fe Trail, and California ports became open to merchants who obtained the necessary license in Monterey, the provincial capital. But what did California have to trade? There were hundreds of thousands of horned cattle grazing on the yellow coastal hills, but before the days of refrigeration it was impossible to ship fresh meat over great distances and markets for salt and jerked beef were limited. In 1822 Hugh McCulloch and William Hartnell, agents from a British company, arranged to purchase hides and tallow from the cattle-rich missions for three years. In exchange, they would provide manufactured goods and supplies to the missions. The McCulloch-Hartnell monopoly was short-lived. Bryant, Sturgis soon sent an agent who gained a share of the market and eventually dominated the California hide and tallow business, although they had many competitors.[2]

Under Spain, missions had been the primary economic institution of California. Franciscan missionaries controlled most of the arable land, vast livestock herds, and a workforce of thousands of Indians who tended the herds and plowed mission fields. The Mexican government would secularize the missions — convert missions to small parish churches and convey the vast pastoral holdings of the church to private ownership. Theoretically, mission Indians would receive land grants from the missions where they had lived and worked, but this seldom happened. Because the missions were so important to the economic well-being of California, the governors at first appointed secular administrators, who administered the missions as they were being broken up. Administrators could compel the former neophytes to labor on mission lands even as they were granted status as citizens. Few Indians were willing to work for new masters at their old missions. Most of them went to work for Mexican rancheros and became peons in the process, or moved to the interior where they lived with independent Indian communities.[3] Secular administrators liquidated the mission property and arrogated mission revenue to themselves. Ultimately, the Mexican government gave more than five hundred grants of land to applicants, who got tens of thousands of acres after paying a small filing fee and meeting nominal government requirements. Most of these grants were made from former mission lands. This transfer of property created a private latifundio system and an elite that was land-and cattle-rich, but money-poor.[4] It also made the daughters of the de la Guerra, Carrillo, Bandini, Vallejo, and other California families exceedingly attractive marriage partners. By making favorable matches, landed californio families could consolidate holdings through marriage, and newcomers—such as Robinson—could become a part of the gentry.

The hide and tallow trade would dominate the Mexican California economy through the mid-1840s. Every year American and British traders bartered manufactured goods for thousands of hides destined to be made into harness, boots, shoes, and leather goods. Some of these finished products returned " 'round the horn" to California, and were bartered to Californians for more dry hides and bags of tallow—at a profit handsome enough to attract Yankee investors and competitors from the United States and England. One observer claimed that more than 100,000 hides were shipped from California each year. It was a bloody and stinking business. Every year *vaqueros* (cowboys) would round up herds and select cattle for the hide trade. On some ranchos they would slaughter one thousand or more animals at a time. A vaquero first roped an animal by the horns, then another vaquero roped the hind legs. Together, the riders stretched the ropes taut and pulled the cow to the ground. That ended the phase of the work that californios did, for they would only do work that could be accomplished from the back of a horse. An Indian would kill the cow with a knife and skin the carcass. Indian workers dried the hides and rendered the tallow, made a little jerked meat, and left the carcasses to rot in the sun. The stench of death and decay lingered for months.[5]

Virtually no cash changed hands in the hide trade. Cow hides were known as California banknotes and were worth about $1.50, although the value varied according to the market. Sea captains and the few permanent merchants who established stores advanced credit to Californians who guaranteed their debts with hides from future slaughters.[6] Thus the californios, seemingly so rich in land and cattle, were snared in a system of debt and credit and made dependent on an international trade in which they traded raw materials for manufactured goods. This was a relationship that historian David Weber has called "the new colonialism."[7] Mexicans had cast off their old political masters, but in their haste to enter the capitalist marketplace they failed to recognize that as providers of raw materials in exchange for manufactured goods they were in a disadvantageous position. They were accustomed to doing business on a small scale with people whom they knew and often to whom they were related either by blood or by *compadrazgo*—a system of godparentage that linked Californians in a fictive kin network. Children received *compadres* (godparents) at birth and other important life events. These authority figures provided advice, security, and sometimes became foster parents in the event of the birth parents' death.[8] This elaborate network of blood and fictive kin connected californio fam-

4. CALIFORNIA METHOD OF KILLING CATTLE.
First a vaquero roped the horns, then another roped the animal's hind feet. Once they pulled the cow to the ground, an Indian cut its throat and it bled to death. Californios killed hundreds of thousands of cattle for their hides and tallow in this manner. The hide-and-tallow trade was the basis for the Mexican California economy from 1821 to 1846. American and British companies were the californios' principal customers.

ilies in the Spanish and Mexican periods and beyond. These extended biological and fictive families gave Mexican Californians identity and security. Additional kinship ties with Yankee and Anglo traders seemed to assure mutuality in trade and a degree of continuity with familiar traditions. It was logical that the de la Guerra family added William Hartnell, the first hide and tallow trader in California, as a son-in-law.[9] Many another californio family would follow the de la Guerra's example.

While the hide and tallow trade embodied a colonial relationship between frontier Mexico and the industrializing United States, marriages like Robinson's evoked another old institution — patriarchy. When Robinson begged for the hand of Don José's daughter, he was not merely observing a formality that had lost its literal meaning. Truly, Don José held the key to Robinson's happiness, "in this world," as the suitor said. The father could have prevented the marriage of Alfred and Doña Anita had he so desired, for in California the father's permission was required before a woman could marry. In theory a woman was not required to marry against her will, but law and traditions that spanned the Spanish and Mexican eras supported fathers' control over their daughters' marital future. Moreover, elite families often arranged the marriages of their children so that a good match would be assured rather than leaving this important matter to the whims of mere youthful passion. Betrothals of girls who had yet to reach menarche — which may have been the case with thirteen-year-old Doña Anita — were not unknown.[10] In theory, Mexican Californians could have married Indian women, and some of them did. Most californios were in fact from mixed or entirely non-Spanish stock, but elite families that claimed to have pure Spanish blood were deeply concerned about maintaining the supposed racial purity of their line. In this respect Anglo Americans could be helpful. Even though they were not Spanish they were white, and on that account were eligible to marry in the best families.[11]

Studies of the marriage record show that only a small fraction of Spanish and Mexican colonists married Indians during the Spanish period. In three northern California missions where there are good records (San Carlos Borromeo, Santa Clara, and San Juan Bautista), there were only forty marriages of Indians and non-Indians between 1770 and 1854 (see Table 2.1). This accounts for about 4.4 percent of all marriages, even though Indians vastly outnumbered the Spanish-Mexican population. On the other hand, Anglo Americans and Europeans comprised only a small fraction of the California population, but they accounted for one-eighth of the non-Indian marriage partners. The rate of intermarriage with Anglo Americans went up in the late Mexican and early American periods, but the pattern had been clearly established in the previous decade. The numbers are small, but their meaning is apparent: Indians were not attractive marriage partners; Anglo Americans were.

In colonial California, as in other frontier regions, there were far more men than women, a condition that drove male competition for eligible women and fostered early betrothal of some young girls. One extreme example serves to illustrate this principal. On September 2, 1776, Sergeant Ygnacio Vicente Ferrer Vallejo happened to visit his friends, the Lugo family, where he found that Señora Lugo was in labor. Evidently, she was having a difficult time of it and Sergeant Vallejo, who possessed some

Table 2.1 Interethnic Marriage at Three California Missions*

Period	MM	MC	CC	Sub-total	AM or AC	Percentage of Marriages w/A Partners	MN	AN	AA	Percentage of Marriages w/N Partners	Total
1770–1784	15			15			10			40.0	25
1785–1794	21	8		29			2			6.5	31
1795–1804	31	15	8	54			4			6.9	58
1805–1814	16	11	31	58			0			0.0	58
1815–1824	10	20	63	93	2		3			3.0	99
1825–1834	22	36	73	131	19	2.1	2		1	1.3	152
1835–1844	29	15	87	131	24	12.7	9			5.5	164
1845–1854	82	18	148	248	63	15.1	9	1	4	3.1	325
Totals	226	123	410	759	108	12.5	39	1	5	4.4	912

*Adapted from Sherburne F. Cook and Woodrow Borah, *Essays in Population History*, vol. 3, *Mexico and California* (Berkeley: University of California Press, 1979), 305.
  M=Mexican or Spanish born
  C=California born
  N=Indian
  A=U.S. or Northern European born

rudimentary medical knowledge by virtue of briefly having studied for the priesthood, was asked to attend the birth. Whatever assistance he rendered, a girl child was born, baptized María Antonia Isabela Lugo. Sergeant Vallejo was entitled to a fee on account of his successful midwifery, and (perhaps feeling that this was his lucky day) asked to marry the infant that he had helped to deliver. The parents agreed. Vallejo was a man of pure Spanish blood, or so he was able to document to Spanish authorities; therefore, it was important to him to marry a woman with similar bloodlines, even if he had to become engaged to an infant to do it. María Antonia, of course, had nothing to say about her marriage, which was consummated when she reached menarche, aged fourteen and one-half years, and her husband was forty.[12] Thus founded, the Vallejos became one of California's leading families. Such unions and the custom of compadrazgo linked the elite families of California in a kinship network that affected all phases of their lives.

Not all of the young women who were married by arrangement were complacent or content, but there was little that they could do about it.[13] Marriage, the production of legitimate children, and the protection of family honor were the common duties of most California women. Those who resisted faced the combined wrath of brothers, husbands, and fathers both temporal and spiritual. Even a governor's wife had to toe the mark. In 1785 Doña Eulalia Callis scandalously petitioned to divorce her husband, Governor Pedro Fages, claiming that he had sexually abused their eleven-year-old Indian servant girl. The governor denied it, but Doña Eulalia persisted in her public accusations of infidelity. She was arrested and held in a guarded room at the Mission San Carlos Boromeo while a priest in the pulpit condemned her actions and threatened to have her whipped. Thus she languished for two or three months until she agreed to reconcile with the governor, who claimed that she had made up the story of his infidelity to force him to resign the governorship and return to Mexico. Ultimately, Doña Eulalia may have had her way for Pedro resigned and the Fageses returned to Mexico in 1790. Historians have usually made light of this incident, with one even going so far as to claim that Doña Eulalia was a hysterical woman suffering from premenstrual syndrome.[14] Historian Antonia Castañeda, who has studied this issue more carefully than anyone, attributes Doña Eulalia's actions to her desire to save herself and her children from the unhealthy environment of California. Pregnant four times in six years, she had one miscarriage and lost an infant daughter eight days after her birth. Whatever her motives may have been, Doña Eulalia could not successfully challenge her husband in public. Neither he nor local church authorities would allow it. What chance did a woman of humble

5. DON ANTONIO F. CORONEL AND HIS WIFE IN A CALIFORNIA DANCE.
In his old age, Don Antonio demonstrates a few steps for a photographer in Los
Angeles, perhaps in the 1880s. He was born in 1817 and came to California with his
father in 1834. No doubt this is one of the dances that enlivened California fan-
dangos in the Mexican era. Even though Don Antonio fought against the Americans
during the Mexican–American War, he remained an influential man in Los Angeles
and held several elective office during the American period. Photograph by Randall.
Courtesy of the California State Library.

background have if this highborn Spanish lady could be imprisoned and
threatened with corporal punishment?[15]

Lack of power, however, did not keep all women from accusing men of
sexual crimes or of violating sexual mores themselves. Castañeda has shown
that californianas denounced seducers, and accused rapists. The record also
shows that women had their share of illicit affairs. In one case, Juan Francisco Bernal threatened to beat his mother after learning that she was
having carnal relations with Marcelo Pinto, a notorious soldier. There were
accusations and counteraccusations of adultery, corruption of minors, and
dishonor. Priests recorded the births of illegitimate babies in the mission

registers and were accused of fathering some of them. Sexual competition for females and women's desire to control their sexual lives made it impossible to uphold the absolute standards that Spanish-Mexican patriarchy demanded.[16]

This was the society that foreigners entered in the nineteenth century. For New Englanders like Robinson, the California world was quite different from their homeland in several respects. Of course, Bostonians had their own forms of patriarchy, and Anglo-Protestant men and women were as capable of rape, fornication, and adultery as were Hispanic Catholics. The formal rules of Anglo sexual behavior and marriage were in some ways similar to those that pertained in Hispanic California. Men and women were both supposed to be virgins when they married; extramarital sex was forbidden; divorce was very difficult to obtain.[17] In 1821 women's rights were as strictly limited in Boston as they were in Monterey. Women were legal appendages of their husbands, who usually retained custody of children in the rare event of divorce. In one respect, Anglo American women were even less free than their California counterparts because they lost control of their property when they married; californianas did not.[18]

In the early nineteenth century Anglo American beliefs about female sexuality differed markedly from Hispanic ideas. Until the mid-1700s Anglos believed that women enjoyed sex, although ideally sex was for procreation and not merely for pleasure. In the nineteenth century medical men and moralists began to propose a new notion — that women were naturally frail, nervous creatures who lacked much interest in sex except as a means to have babies. These theories emerged as women began to challenge patriarchal authority and the United States was experiencing the upheavals and uncertainties that accompanied industrialization. In such an unsettling time many men preferred women who did not challenge authority in or out of the marriage bed.[19] The "cult of true womanhood" was the prevailing ideology that governed women's behavior. Women were supposed to be pure, pious, and domestic. They aspired — or so it was thought — to nothing more than raising children, keeping house, and making the home an undisturbing sanctuary for the husband/father when he returned from his worldly struggle to gain a living for his wife and family.[20] Perhaps because men believed that women neither wanted nor desired sex, married as well as single men resorted to brothels to satisfy their sexual longings. As every young man at the time knew, the cities and towns of the eastern United States harbored houses of prostitution where supposedly perverse women catered to men's carnal needs.[21]

On the other hand, Spanish-Mexican men believed that women were naturally lustful creatures who were apt to meekly submit to the sexual demands of a would-be seducer. That is why families chaperoned young couples, even when they were engaged. It was important to maintain family honor and the unquestioned virginity of daughters. If a young woman was rumored to have had sex, her value on the marriage market was diminished — at least as far as making a good match with an elite family was concerned. Here was another reason to betroth very young girls and to marry them as soon after menarche as possible.[22] Of course, neither Anglo nor Hispanic women necessarily lived according to the sexual ideologies that prevailed in the nineteenth century.[23] But the ideals of their respective societies conditioned expectations about sexuality of Anglo and Mexican men and women alike.

The Anglo American hide traders who went to California in the Mexican era knew that they would have to remain for an extended time, perhaps for many years. Those who wished to marry during their sojourn would almost certainly have to marry a californiana, a match that would, it was hoped, secure domestic happiness as well as property and an advantage in trade. Hide traders would have to adjust to California marriage customs to marry a daughter from one of the elite families. Among other things, they would have to become Catholics. Church and state required that Protestants convert to Catholicism before a marriage took place and foreigners had to apply to the governor for permission to marry.[24] Naturalization was not required to marry, but for Mexican citizens there was land to be had for the asking. Religious and national qualms seldom deterred Robinson and his colleagues from marrying or acquiring land. Many a Boston man renounced his U.S. citizenship in order to gain the landed wealth that was so enticingly available. Thomas O. Larkin, although he did not marry a californiana, may have spoken for many of his fellow sojourners when he explained his willingness to marry a local woman if "I had any (say a little) love for the Lady, and the Lady had loot enough for me."[25] Of course, financial advantage was not the only reason that Anglos married daughters of the country. One Anglo expatriate explained to his friend Faxon Dean Atherton, a California trader from New England, that he wanted only "a nice little wife to my belly and one real friend at my back" for true happiness.[26] Atherton and his friend, whose business interests were in Chile, married Chilean sisters, thus providing for both of their bellies and backs. Whatever their motives for marriage may have been, the trade and the lure of land attracted scores of foreigners who converted to the Catholic religion, became Mexican citizens, and married California women.[27]

Robinson worked hard in the hide business, sailing up and down the coast trading with the ranchers and learning the ropes. He became a Catholic, but evidently did not become a Mexican citizen.[28] With the approval of Doña Anita's father, Robinson's citizenship proved to be no bar to marriage, although they waited until she was fifteen before marrying (perhaps delaying until she was sexually mature). The people of Santa Barbara celebrated the alliance between the Bryant, Sturgis agent and the de la Guerra family as if it were a state affair. So did the commander and crew of the Bryant, Sturgis vessel, *Pilgrim*, which lay in the harbor in front of the town. The *Pilgrim*'s crew prepared the ship's guns and flags to salute the new bride and groom when the captain on shore gave them a signal. They watched as Doña Anita went to the confessional in the Mission Santa Barbara church, dressed in black. They waited. Finally, the church doors opened and she emerged in a white gown with her groom alongside and a large wedding party behind. Richard Henry Dana, a sailor on board the *Pilgrim*, recorded the scene:

> Just as she stepped from the church door, a small white cloud issued from the bows of our ship, which was in full sight, the loud report echoed among the surrounding hills and over the bay, and instantly the ship was dressed in flags and pennants from stem to stern. Twenty-three guns followed in regular succession, . . . and our ship lay dressed in her colors all day.[29]

The commercial implications of the Robinson–de la Guerra marriage seemed clear enough, but the celebrants did not know that Bryant, Sturgis had just reduced the groom's trade-commission fees. Perhaps, from Robinson's perspective, this made the marriage even more desirable. A year later, Robinson was weary of "trudging the coast in search of hides," and he and Doña Anita moved to Massachusetts.[30] They evidently thought that this was a temporary move, for they left their infant daughter in the care of the de la Guerras. But Robinson did not abandon the hide trade while he lived in Massachusetts. He merely involved himself at a higher level by investing in two Bryant, Sturgis vessels bound for California. In 1839 he returned to California as Bryant, Sturgis's representative, but arrived in time to learn that the firm was dissolved, so back east he went. As the gold rush exploded in 1849, Robinson returned to California with his family and made it his permanent home.[31]

While Robinson's financial interests in California and the de la Guerras were obvious, it is also evident that he had more than a pecuniary association with his in-laws. He affectionately corresponded with them about family matters, even after Doña Anita died in 1853. He seemed to take great pleasure in discussing political matters with his father- and brother-in-law, and

6. A CALIFORNIA WEDDING PARTY.

This undated engraving depicts a Californio wedding party. The bride is in the front
(smoking a cigarette?) dressed in dark clothes. Perhaps they are on their way to the
church, where the bride and groom will confess their sins before she dons a white
wedding dress.

Courtesy of the California State Library.

took special delight in satirizing the Democratic party.[32] He also assured
the de la Guerras that he was a practicing Catholic while in "the land of the
Yankees!" as he put it. Surely, Robinson married for more than money.

Anglo-californio marriages were not always easily arranged, even when
the groom was willing to compromise — at least nominally — his religious
and national principles and the bride's father was agreeable to the match.
The marriage of Henry Delano Fitch, a Yankee sea captain and merchant,
to Josefa Carrillo, daughter of a prominent San Diego family, show how
complicated these affairs could be. Captain Fitch was about twenty-eight
when he proposed to seventeen-year-old Josefa. Her father agreed to the
marriage, and Fitch became a Catholic, but he was still a foreigner, although he had announced his intention to become a Mexican citizen. Un-

fortunately for the engaged couple, one of Josefa's former suitors happened to be governor of California, José María Echeandía. Perhaps because of the governor's interest in Josefa, Franciscan priests were unwilling to marry them. Echeandía had authority to secularize the Franciscan missions and there was no point in antagonizing him.[33] Finally, Fitch found a Dominican priest who agreed to perform the rite. When the ceremony was under way, one of the witnesses stopped it in the governor's name. Without the required witnesses, the priest would not perform the marriage.[34]

"Why don't you carry me off, Don Enrique?" Josefa suggested.[35] So Fitch and Josefa decided to secretly elope to Chile, where the laws were more liberal, but they neglected to consult Josefa's parents about this scandalous decision. In the best romantic tradition, Josefa's cousin Pio Pico (who would be governor himself one day) spirited her away to the *Vulture*, the unfortunately named ship where Captain Fitch waited to take her away. The pair wed in Valparaiso and remained for about one year before returning to California with their infant child. While they were away, rumors swept California that Captain Fitch had forcibly abducted Josefa, a rumor that the Carrillos may have concocted to protect family honor. Padre José Bernardo Sánchez, ecclesiastical judge for the bishop of Sonora, summoned Fitch to explain his actions. He merely sent his marriage certificate, but this mollified no one. Sánchez ordered Fitch's arrest and trial at Mission San Gabriel, near Los Angeles, and sent his wife to Monterey, where she was sequestered. In San Gabriel religious authorities examined the marriage certificate and questioned Fitch. Captain Fitch defended his marriage, complained that his business was being ruined, and fumed that if his marriage were declared invalid his son would be made a bastard.[36]

Far to the north, Josefa implored Governor Echeandía to permit her to go to San Gabriel to be near her husband. After three months the governor permitted her to go, but this belated act of mercy caused one priest to accuse the governor of infringing on ecclesiastical authority and to suggest that Echeandía be arrested and tried by the tribunal that was examining the Fitches! Cooler heads prevailed and the governor was not arraigned for his transgression. At San Gabriel the ecclesiastical court interrogated Josefa repeatedly. While this was going on, Fitch accused Josefa's parents of abusing her.[37]

After four months of accusation, incarceration, investigation, and interrogation, the religious tribunal decided that the Fitch-Carrillo marriage, though irregular, was valid. The Fitches were set free and allowed to reunite, but they had to perform penance at church and receive the sacraments that should have preceded their marriage ceremony. "Yet consider-

ing the great scandal which Don Enrique has caused this province," Padre
Sánchez declared, "I condemn him to give as pennance and reparation a
bell of at least fifty pounds in weight for the Church at Los Angeles, which
barely has a borrowed one."[38] Captain Fitch, who was undoubtedly tired of
defending himself, prayed and paid accordingly. With the example of the
Fitches before them, few Anglo men in California would think seriously of
eloping with a high-caste woman before getting parental, civil, and ecclesiastical permission.

The problem of legitimacy even plagued one of the few American traders
who married an Anglo woman in California — Thomas O. Larkin, the man
who was willing to marry a California woman if she had "loot" enough.
Larkin, who was to become perhaps the wealthiest and most respected
American in California before the gold rush, was born in Massachusetts in
1802 and as a young man went to North Carolina to find his fortune in
business. This proved disappointing, for he went bankrupt. He was successful in other areas of life, however. He claimed to be known as a "Ladies
man" because he possessed "more tongue, more flattery, more confidence
... more brass & perseverance" than others.[39] His biographers suggest that
he may have had some sexual conquests in North Carolina. Certainly, he
was interested in women and was not shy about flirting with them, but he
found no suitable marriage partners, in part because he could not find an
eligible woman with enough "loot." So he turned his attention to California, where his older half-brother, John B. R. Cooper, had settled, had
married one of the Vallejo daughters, and had thereby rapidly gained in
property. Now, Larkin thought, that was the ticket! When dreaming of
California love and loot, he rationalized that if he could get "a little of the
former and much of the latter [then] I'm a married man."[40]

So, in 1831, Larkin sailed to Monterey where he would begin a new life
in California as his brother's clerk. One of the passengers was Rachel Hob-
son Holmes, the twenty-four-year-old wife of merchant–sea captain John
A. C. Holmes. Captain Holmes sailed and traded along the Pacific Coast,
and Rachel was going to join him. In the meantime, perhaps even aboard
ship, she and Larkin had an affair, and in April 1832 Rachel became pregnant. This turn of events put both of the Americans in a difficult position.
As her belly swelled, Rachel waited for her husband in Santa Barbara with
American Daniel Hill and his californiana wife (who happened to be residing in the old Carrillo residence). We can only speculate about the scenes
she conjured about meeting Captain Holmes again. The lovers also had to
worry about whether the California authorities might charge them with
adultery or deport them. Well they might worry. William Heath Davis,

who married one of the Estudillo daughters, reported that californios sometimes dealt harshly with adulterers and fornicators. "The man who offended was imprisoned for two or three years," and, he added, "the woman was disgraced by cutting off the hair close to the head."[41] Instead of disgrace and punishment, a stroke of good luck came the adulterers' way. A letter reached Rachel's hand in October, when she was seven months pregnant. Her unwitting husband had died en route from Acapulco to South America.[42]

Now Larkin was free to marry Rachel, but would he? She carried his child, but did she have enough personal wealth to satisfy his desire to marry a wealthy woman? As it turned out, Rachel inherited three or four thousand dollars from Holmes, so she would bring some capital to the marriage, if not a princely fortune in land. But *who* would marry them? They were both Protestants, so the Catholic priests would not perform a ceremony. Larkin probably would have converted to the Catholic faith without qualms — he was a religious skeptic. Rachel may have had religious scruples that kept her from embracing the Catholic religion, but they were not strong enough to keep her from having her child baptized at Mission Santa Barbara. Isabel Ana was born on January 31, 1833, and baptized a few days later. The first child of American parents born in California was ignominiously recorded as the "illegitimate daughter of Rogers Laken and Rachel married to Guillermo [William] Holmes."[43] The name of the father may have been a corruption of Thomas Larkin, but it may be that Rachel tried to protect Larkin while still giving her child a fictitious father with a name that was phonetically similar to her true father's.

Larkin finally decided to marry Rachel, and solved the religious problem by having the American consul, John C. Jones, perform a civil ceremony on an American ship when Jones happened to sail to California from Hawaii. Jones performed the ceremony on board the *Volunteer* in front of Santa Barbara on June 10, 1833. Whatever the fears that the Larkins may have had regarding their adulterous affair, the *barbarenos* generously celebrated their marriage. The "wedding festival . . . was attended by the élite of Santa Barbara — beautiful ladies, mothers and daughters, with their husbands and sons, all of Castilian extraction," imagined William Heath Davis who witnessed the event as an eleven-year-old boy.[44] "There was music with dancing. . . . Native California wine and imported sparkling champagne were freely used, and all had a very enjoyable time."

The Larkins had to face a family tragedy almost immediately. Their daughter, Isabel Ana, died one month after their marriage. The Santa Barbara burial record listed her as the "infant daughter of Raquel Laquen

[Rachel Larkin] and Guillermo Cuper, both foreigners." Naming Guillermo Cuper (Cooper?) as Isabel Ana's putative father was a puzzling act. If
the birth record, which was also kept at Mission Santa Barbara, was meant
to name Larkin as the father, then why muddy the record after the baby's
death? If Rachel tried to shield Larkin with a pseudonym when the child
was born, why didn't she keep her story straight when the baby died? It is
evident, however, that Larkin was not willing to claim paternity of the child
when she died, perhaps feeling that it would cast a shadow on his reputation
as an honest trader and the legitimacy of his richly celebrated recent marriage. Any concerns that he may have had about his baby and the validity of
his marriage were misplaced. When Larkin himself became consul, he
learned that his predecessor Jones had no authority to marry him. In one of
the ironies of the Larkins' long and evidently happy and devoted relationship, the couple converted to Catholicism and remarried when Rachel was
very ill, and it was feared that she might die. Without Catholic baptism, she
could not be buried in a Catholic cemetery. If the Larkins were not legally
married, their children might be deemed illegitimate and denied their
rightful inheritance.

The experiences of the Larkins were unique, but they illustrate some of
the possible complications of courtship and marriage on the Mexican frontier. Even when California's daughters were not involved, the laws of Mexico and the customs of the country might be enforced. The Fitch elope-
ment proved that neither American citizenship nor a foreign marriage
certificate would provide substantial protection if a family's honor had been
sullied (and if the governor was a rejected suitor). But these were extreme
cases, and it is more likely that most Americans, like Alfred Robinson,
blended less abrasively into California society and the familial embrace of
their in-laws.

The precise number of marriages between californianas and Americans is
not known, but nineteenth-century historian Hubert Howe Bancroft compiled brief biographies of all of the prominent California pioneers, including marriage data. While his list is incomplete, it provides a reliable source
of information on the best-known mixed marriages. He recorded eighty
such unions between 1817 and 1848 (see Table 2.2).[45] Half of the men were
from the United States and nearly one-third were from the northeastern
states — mostly from Massachusetts. Forty percent of the grooms came
from the British Isles (nearly one-quarter were English). The men who
married into California's elite families truly were Anglo American.

Mixed marriages began as soon as foreigners began to arrive and continued throughout the Mexican period (see Table 2.3). The frequency of

Table 2.2 Origin of Foreign Husbands Married to Californianas

	No.	Percentage
United States		
Northeast	26	32.5
Southeast	3	3.8
Old Northwest	1	1.3
Old Southwest	7	8.8
Unknown	3	3.8
Total U.S.	*40*	*50.0*
British Isles		
England	18	22.5
Ireland	8	10.0
Scotland	6	7.5
Total British Isles	*32*	*40.0*
Canada	1	1.3
German States	1	1.3
Other	6	7.5
Total	*80*	*100.0*

Based on Hubert Howe Bancroft, "Pioneer Register," *History of California*, vols. 2–5 (San Francisco: The History Company, 1886).

marriages was fairly stable from the mid-1820s through 1845, but seemed to drop during the Mexican-American War (1846–1848). The smallness of the sample, however, may be responsible for the apparent pattern. The ages of husbands (when they could be determined) show that most were between twenty-six and thirty-five when they married (see Table 2.4). Bancroft did not provide enough data about the brides' ages to make any statistical judgments. Perhaps more revealing than the grooms' ages was the length of time they spent in California before marrying (see Table 2.5). Five to six years was the median period that grooms spent in California before marrying, although part of that time may have been spent on voyages back to Massachusetts, or waiting through a long engagement. Nevertheless, it is clear that most foreigners did not jump into marriages with californianas. This may have been due to the californios' strict rules of propriety as well as circumspection on the part of the prospective husbands. Bancroft's "Pioneer Register" is a limited source of data for mixed marriage, but it suggests that grooms and prospective in-laws considered marriage a very serious undertaking that should not be rushed into. Marriage was meant to be a permanent arrangement that would benefit the family for as long as it lasted.

Table 2.3 Date of Marriage

1816–1820	1
1821–1825	6
1826–1830	12
1831–1835	9
1836–1840	15
1841–1845	10
1846–1848	5

Based on Hubert Howe Bancroft, "Pioneer Register," *History of California*, vols. 2–5 (San Francisco: The History Company, 1886).

Table 2.4 Age of Husband at Marriage

20–25	4
26–30	21
31–35	9
36–40	7
41–45	6
46 and over	1

Based on Hubert Howe Bancroft, "Pioneer Register," *History of California*, vols. 2–5 (San Francisco: The History Company, 1886).

The "Pioneer Register" reveals one striking geographic trend about mixed marriages that speaks to the changing patterns of immigration that began in earnest in the 1840s. Bancroft recorded no mixed marriages between californios and Americans who lived in the interior. While maritime merchants married into Mexican families on the coast, a new group of Europeans and Americans began to filter into the great central valley of California. In 1827, Jedediah Smith led a party of trappers into the interior in search of beaver pelts. He found some, and he also found another potentially valuable export commodity—horses. Smith purchased horses from the ranchos on the coast and drove them north to Oregon, hoping that he could eventually sell them at a profit. Umpqua Indians foiled his scheme, took the horses, killed most of Smith's men, and barely missed putting an end to Smith. Nevertheless, scores of American trappers followed Smith into California by the southwestern route, and the British Hudson's Bay Company sent expeditions from Oregon as well. Some trappers emulated Smith's horse-trading venture, but not all of them relied on legal purchases

Table 2.5 Years in California Before
Marriage

0–2	6
3–4	18
5–6	10
7–8	10
9–10	8
11–12	3
13–14	0
15 or more	5

Based on Hubert Howe Bancroft, "Pioneer Register," *History of California*, vols. 2–5 (San Francisco: The History Company, 1886).

to acquire stock. Instead, they teamed up with Indians who lived in the interior — Yokuts, Miwoks, and ex-mission Indians — and who raided the coastal herds. Thus engaged in horse rustling, these newcomers cared nothing about maintaining good relations with elite Mexican families. Nor did they live permanently in the interior, preferring instead to make an annual journey to California and drive their stolen stock back to the Missouri frontier. While all this was going on, Mexican rancheros and soldiers periodically raided Indian communities in the central valley.[46]

Even though the California interior was an isolated region, between 1827 and 1839 it became an international frontier where Indians, agents from the Hudson's Bay Company, American trappers, horse thieves, Mexican soldiers, and rancheros converged. They struggled to control California's horse herds, a critical resource in an economy based on wild, long-horned cattle. Until 1839, however, Indians did not have to worry about any of these newcomers settling in the interior. Spanish and Mexican officials had deemed new mission projects too expensive and risky, so they left the venture to private parties who, they hoped, would take up land grants east of coastal settlements. Mexican rancheros were not quick to move into a region where they had been fighting with Indians for decades, so the government relied on foreigners to occupy this disputed district. In 1837, John Marsh, a former U.S. Indian agent who claimed to be a physician, made his home on a grant that he purchased on the western edge of the San Joaquin Valley.[47] Two years later, John A. Sutter convinced Governor Juan Alvarado that he was a man of great military experience who would be useful in suppressing Indian livestock raiding. Alvarado permitted Sutter to colonize the Sacramento Valley where the American River flowed into the Sacramento.

Marsh and Sutter not only made permanent settlements for themselves, they inspired other Americans to make the overland journey and settle in the California interior. Sutter's Fort, near the confluence of the American and Sacramento rivers, was the military heart of the Swiss-American's New Helvetia agricultural business and became the destination for overland immigrants to California. Sutter employed scores of American immigrants and hundreds of Indian laborers who kept his enterprise humming. To obtain Indian labor, Sutter relied on diplomacy, trade, and blunt force. He established an Indian army that intimidated surrounding tribes and protected his herds and those of his neighbors.[48]

While imposing his military and economic will on the Indian communities of the Sacramento and San Joaquin valleys, Sutter altered native traditions of courtship and marriage. Formerly Central California Indians forged alliances through marriage. Usually the prospective husband asked permission of the parents of his intended spouse. If they were agreeable, the young man brought meat from the hunt and other goods to the home of his in-laws. Then the couple could marry. Some powerful and rich men had two or more wives, but most had only one. As usual, marriages were meant to link families in a kinship network that assured friendship, prosperity, and allies in troubled times.[49]

Sutter, the self-proclaimed patriarch of New Helvetia, took it upon himself to intervene in the Indians' long-established marriage customs. Years later, he reminisced that "polygamy obtained among the Indians and I determined to stop it" because "the chiefs had so many wives that the young men . . . could have none."[50] Claiming that he had the interests of young Indian men at heart, Sutter put all of the marriageable men and women in rows facing each other. "Then I told the women one after another to come forward and select the man they wanted." Sutter denied "the chiefs more than one or two wives each," but he did not mention that white men were also competing for Indian women, including the lord of New Helvetia himself. Taking Indian helpmeets—at least temporarily—was a time-honored practice among fur trappers and traders, although fur men often abandoned their Indian wives when they left Indian country or when racially suitable wives became available.[51]

While Sutter subverted Indian marriage customs, he arrogated the authority of the Catholic Church and Mexican state in matrimonial matters as well. He evidently believed that he had civil authority to marry people because he was the New Helvetia *alcalde*. In 1844, he therefore married several American couples, including Cyrus Alexander (an American) and Rufina Lucero, who was from New Mexico. "Oh yesh," Sutter reputedly assured Alexander, "I ish der law, I cans perform der serremony, und all ish den right."[52] Alexander accepted Sutter's bland assurances and allowed the captain to marry him at the fort. Some time later a priest from the Mission Santa Clara informed the Alexanders and other couples whom Sutter had joined that they were not legally married, and that their wives must return to their parents until they were married in the church. Alexander was outraged because he believed that the priests were merely trying to extort money from him, and because his young son was now illegitimate. Three other couples who had married under Sutter received similar notification, but only two of them and the Alexanders dutifully — and angrily — went to Santa Clara to be married again. The disobedient man later teased the couples because the war with Mexico soon limited the priests' authority over civil marriages and asserted that by obeying the priests Alexander had admitted that his marriage under Sutter was illegal. Alexander retaliated by saying that his tormentor and his wife simply had no shoes and didn't want to get married barefoot. Such were the airs of propriety among Americans in the 1840s.[53]

The custom of taking an Indian wife may have been time honored, but it was not universally respected or admired in Anglo American society. "Squaw man" and "half-breed" were racial slurs that condemned interracial sex and the progeny that came from it. Once the frontier era had passed, male pioneers and their biographers often extolled their heroic exploits while politely forgetting to mention the Indian women who baked their bread and bore their children. Yet they often sneeringly divulged the sexual adventures of other fellows who crossed the color line. Captain Sutter was especially vulnerable to rumormongers. He had abandoned his wife and children in Switzerland to escape debtors' prison. In the Sandwich Islands Sutter picked up a Hawaiian mistress, Manaiki, who was his favorite consort at New Helvetia, but she had to share him with Indian women. Heinrich Lienhard, who was critical of everyone's behavior but his own, charged that there was a special room for young Indian women adjoining Sutter's apartment in the fort. Worse, he accused Sutter of having sexual relations with Indian girls as young as ten.[54] Lienhard may have embellished his accusations, but Sutter's own correspondence explicitly reveals a trade in boys and girls that hints at a sexual dimension.[55] Sutter captured these children during his attacks on Indian communities and sold or leased them to other ranchers. John Chamberlain, Sutter's blacksmith, said that "it was customary for Capt Sutter to buy and sell Indian boys & girls."[56] Accusations that Sutter was a pedophile are not proven, but charges of child abuse are conclusive.[57]

Just as Chamberlain exposed Sutter's transgressions, John Yates pointed to Chamberlain's sexual habits. The blacksmith was "given to gazing on the native females," Yates reported, and Chamberlain did more than look at Indian women. "I learnt that he had been married nineteen times to native women & to my own certain knowledge he was when I last saw him newly married to an American girl of thirteen."[58] Neither was Yates altogether blameless in this regard, for Yates kept two Indian mistresses. Eventually he married a sixteen-year-old immigrant, but the marriage foundered because the Indians refused to give up their white husband.[59] And so it went. Up and down the valleys, Americans and Europeans mated with Indian women in the 1840s, then the esteemed pioneers snickered and pointed their fingers at others a quarter-century later.[60]

For most whites, these unions were doubtless alliances of convenience that were necessary when frontier conditions prevailed and Indians were a large majority in the region. In addition to the domestic and sexual services of their Indian wives, whites gained friends, laborers, and allies through Indian kinship ties. Once equipped with a local Indian wife, these men were no longer mere interlopers but members of an Indian community. This status, reinforced with Sutter's military presence, enabled a small group of whites to live among Indians in relative security and to benefit from Indian labor. After the discovery of gold and the ensuing rush of new people to California, the need for native workers and soldiers subsided, so white men usually abandoned their Indian wives for new mates. The Indians—wives and kin alike—who joined in these unions gained temporary access to trade goods and a modicum of security in rapidly changing times. When times changed and the connubial arrangements with whites dissolved, they had to find new ways to satisfy these needs. In the end, they were left to rely on their own resources for survival during the extravagant upheavals of the gold rush and its aftermath.[61]

Intermarriages in the interior and on the coast occurred according to the needs of the people who lived in their respective regions. On the coast californios were clearly in political control, so Americans and others seldom violated the prevailing marriage laws and customs. Rancheros may have been in a disadvantageous position in a colonial trade network, but they were unquestioned patriarchs at home. Yankees like Alfred Robinson therefore kissed the hands of their fathers-in-law, joined the Catholic Church, and ofttimes became citizens of Mexico. More than that, Yankee husbands often displayed more than perfunctory attention to their religious

7. CALIFORNIA VAQUEROS RETURNED FROM THE CHASE.

This engraving ostensibly depicts men who have returned from their work of "chasing" cattle, or perhaps hunting. The men are dark, evidently of mixed parentage, heavily draped in serapes. In contrast, the women are lightly dressed with breasts exposed or clearly defined beneath a thin, revealing, low-cut blouse. In this Anglo artist's vision Mexican men were dark, mysterious, and probably dangerous. The women were open and available. Engraving by H. Eastman, 1854.

Courtesy of the Bancroft Library.

and marital obligations after the change in national sovereignty in 1848. To be sure, they had material reasons for keeping up appearances. Most of them had acquired substantial landholdings and might inherit even more when their fathers-in-law passed on. They also had children of their own to provide for. In American and californio minds alike, there was no racial problem in the marriages to elite California families. Californios insisted that they were white, that they were of unmixed blood, and they often claimed to be descended from Spain's noble lines. Whatever the facts may have been, Americans happily accepted this bleached version of California family history. It was a good thing for an American to be married into a California family.

A connection to an Indian woman, whether solemnized with Sutter's supposed authority or more casually effected, had little lasting value for the white men involved. American society scorned "squaws," "squaw men," and their "half-breed" children. Indians were not part of a landed gentry, but a despised racial minority whose fate, as far as most Americans were concerned, was to be dispossessed and obliterated. Once the country was settled, an Indian family could only hinder the social advancement of pioneers. Thus, the custom of mixed marriage in Mexican California proceeded along two paths. One was seemingly a highway to material wealth and social status; the other was a dead end to be abandoned at first opportunity. Both were well-traveled roads.

THREE

Crossing the Borders:

Sex, Gender, and the Journey to California

Ladies & Gentlemen.

I appear before you at this time, not as a public lecturer but as a narrator of events. Events connected with my own personal experience & observation. Neither the position of public speaking nor the facts that I am to relate are in harmony with my own feelings, for my nature intuitively shrinks from both. But I yeald to what I conceive to be the opening of providence & the sterne voice of duty. Truth is said to be "stranger than fiction." The facts connected with the history of my Fathers *family & my Captivity among the Indians passes all the material of a thrilling romance.*

For instance, upon the page are contrasted in vivid antithesis all the passions of the human breast, the most varied scenes in nature & the greatest extremes in social and moral development. The record contains exhibitions of warmest affection, the occasions of the greatest fear *& the display of the most reckless & cruel* fate. *It leads the anxious enquirer through the wooliest & wildest reagions of the "great west" & brings into view the rudest barbarism & highest civilization. With these preliminaries I ask the suspension of all criticism while I give you a recital of my wrongs.*[1]

OLIVE OATMAN, C. 1860

Olive Oatman was at first shy and hesitant when she stepped to the podium to describe her harrowing time as a captive among the Yavapai and Mohave Indians. Her reticence bespoke the modesty that American society expected of young women. The same society condemned women who spoke publicly on political matters such as abolition and women's rights, so she claimed to be a "narrator of events," a mere cipher for an all-wise Providence. But Olive warmed to the occasion as she uttered superlatives that were meant to convince the audience that they should buy her book after

45

they heard her lecture. Her book, which was actually written by Methodist minister Royal Stratton, would lead readers through the wild and wooly West where they would witness scenes of heroism and depravity. Who among the audience doubted her as they gazed on the young woman with the Mohave tattoo on her chin?

Like Olive Oatman, California immigrants were border crossers. Many immigrants passed through Mexico or other Latin American countries on their ways to California, and overlanders who technically never left U.S. soil necessarily passed through Indian country and the nations that inhabited them. When they crossed borders immigrants often paused, took stock, and confirmed their identity. The crossings of borders, and continents, and great waters tell us who these people thought they were and who they were not.

The journey to California involved crossing environmental, psychological, racial, and cultural borders as well as national boundaries. This was no less true after the United States acquired the Mexican cession as a result of the Mexican-American War. American travelers who bothered to write about such matters noticed these border crossings and often remarked on them in letters and diaries. Most writers were satisfied that their encounters with new people and places were convincing evidence of the superiority of the Anglo American way of life. Some of them considered the sexual and racial implications of their encounters. Under the best of circumstances the trip to California was challenging. Sometimes dramatic circumstances put huge new pressures on formerly reliable people and gendered institutions — family, religion, patriarchal authority, and the cult of true womanhood. Most people and their institutions survived the trip to California intact. Nevertheless, whether by land or by sea, the journey presented challenges to the cultural fabric that Americans took for granted.

Travelers who went by sea left behind the familiar anchors of terrain and terrestrial routine and faced the perils of sea. Buffeted by storms and afflicted with sea sickness, these poor souls sailed along until they abruptly arrived at a foreign port in the Caribbean or in Latin America, where they encountered new people and cultures. Their letters reveal not only their dismay with novel people and cultures, but their satisfaction with their cultural norms and prejudices.

John H. Beeckman, bound for gold-rush California by way of Cape Horn, wrote long, emotional letters to his wife of one year, describing his feelings about the new things he encountered. Beeckman was a northerner, but in 1848 he married the sister-in-law of ex-president John Tyler, who

8. FAIR WEATHER ON THE DECK OF A CLIPPER SHIP CARRYING GOLD SEEKERS TO CALIFORNIA IN 1849.

Although this engraving was completed more than forty years after the gold rush, this picture gives a fair idea of crowded shipboard conditions under the best of circumstances. Comfortable places for passengers to sit or lounge were in short supply. There would have been plenty of time to write to loved ones at home, and few opportunities to find privacy. Engraving by Bury 1894.

Courtesy of the California State Library.

gave away the bride at Tyler's Virginia home, Sherwood Forest.[2] Like thousands of other forty-niners, Beeckman hoped to make a quick fortune in California, but his disappointments began with his shipboard experiences. He hated the long voyage and pined for his wife and baby son. While his ship stood off the coast of Brazil, somewhere east of Recife, Beeckman sat upon the heaving deck and wrote to his wife, while a homeward-bound ship approached. He had lived through howling storms on the Atlantic and had expected to die at any moment. In his imagination, he explained to his wife, he called his loved ones around him and bade them farewell. Beeckman daily comforted himself with imaginary conversations with his wife until she seemed so near and his mental images so real "that unconsciously I address you aloud."[3] Beeckman was a quiet man who often abstained from conversation with friends and relatives at home as well as his fellow passengers. Yet a kinsman, who shared a cabin with Beeckman, recalled that he frequently expressed great love for his family. "Often in our lonely stateroom at night and on deck after all others had sunk in sleep," his relative reported, "have we conversed about the absent and dear ones thousands of miles away and at such times the bonds of affection as well as blood united us more closely to each other."[4]

Beeckman's morose personality bubbled to life when he arrived in Rio de Janeiro. First of all, he was delighted to be again on land. Second, there was much to see and describe to his wife. While there were scenes of beauty in Brazil, the people left much to be desired. The Brazilians were "puny" and did not compare favorably with the thousand or so Americans like himself who were en route to California and temporarily stranded in Rio. There were rumors of an insurrection and he hoped it would occur while he was there so he could see "how these poor miserable Portugese and Brazilian soldiers, most of whom are blacks, will fight." Beeckman left little doubt that such soldiers would not fare well. The force of American Argonauts alone could beat the whole Brazilian army who viewed "with surprise and astonishment" the class of men that "the United States sends out as pioneers and scouts to a new and unsettled country." According to Beeckman, Brazilians contemplated the crowd of singing, drinking Americans in their city with a mixture of awe and admiration. "They exclaim 'no wonder she stands so high among the nations of the earth and no wonder the armies of Mexico could not stand before her volunteers.'"[5]

Beeckman's contempt for Brazilians was rooted in religion as well as race. Out of curiosity, he attended a mass and visited a monastery which served only to confirm his low opinion of Roman Catholicism. The monks were "a jolly and unusual race" who treated him with cordial hospitality. Nonetheless, he viewed their richly decorated chapel with the eye of a bridled buccaneer. The "heavy silver lamps and chandeliers" and figures of saints and the Virgin Mary "covered with precious stones" were merely "gifts from age to age from the superstitious and bigoted." "The sacking of one such chapel," the otherwise quiet Beeckman thought, "would render one independent for life."[6] Perhaps for a fleeting moment the president's brother-in-law fantasized that he could cut short his lonely journey to the gold fields by looting a few chapels of the "superstitious and bigoted" and return home laden with precious booty for his beloved. But he quickly turned his attention back to his emotional geography: "Amid all these novelties I feel myself a stranger in a strange land."

In Beeckman's mind, race and gender relations were among Brazil's strangest and most disconcerting conditions. When he looked at sixteen- or seventeen-year-old young women, they appeared to him "to have reached the meridian of life, not one less than thirty-five, with faces sallow and wrinkled, forbidden and repulsive."[7] Why did Beeckman react so strongly against Brazilian women? Beeckman was an abolitionist who condemned the vicious treatment of slaves that he saw in Rio, but miscegenation disturbed him.[8] It was "disgusting and repugnant in the extreme to an American . . . to see the free blending together of all colors, negroes of the deepest dyes, mulattos and whites . . . all upon equality."[9] It was especially disturbing to observe "a white lady in her brilliant court pass smiling upon and receiving the attentions and addresses of a score of Ethiopians as black as midnight with as much apparent gusto and delight as though they were of the same material as herself." "Well I am a married man dearest so I shall not quarrel with their taste," Beeckman declared, thus hinting that if he were single he might challenge the colored suitors who courted women of different "material" than themselves.

Beeckman's first encounter with a Latino culture repulsed him. Racial mixing—especially white women with men of color—was abhorrent to him. Brazilian men seemed to him cowardly and ineffective, the women unrefined and sickly. He thought Catholics were backward and superstitious. Beeckman's ethnocentric pride, religious bigotry, and racial prejudice made it impossible for him to sympathetically observe the people of Rio. Indeed, when one considers his descriptions of the young women, one wonders if he could see them at all. Like many another American, Beeckman would carry these biases to California.

Beeckman would not have enough time to experience whatever transforming power California possessed. He landed in San Francisco, but found that he could not profitably sell the goods he had brought with him.[10]

9. COALING UP, KINGSTON, JAMAICA.

This 1852 scene must have reflected Americans' ideas about gender while it substantiated ideas about race and servility. Black women go up the gangplank carrying buckets of coal on their heads as white passengers look on. On deck, a white man appears to be whipping a small boy. John M. Lells, *California Illustrated: Including a Description of the Panama and Nicaragua Routes* (New York: William Holdredge Publisher, 1852).

Courtesy of the California State Library.

Then he went to Sacramento where he set up a small store, but in the winter of 1850 there was a flood that ruined his stock.[11] In April Beeckman steamed up the Sacramento River to the village of Fremont, about thirty miles above the city of Sacramento. While going ashore on a rowboat with a hunting party, the hammer of Beeckman's shotgun caught on his seat, snapped, and fired a load of buckshot into his breast. "My God I am shot," he yelled, and died in about twenty minutes. They buried him in a small cemetery at Fremont with a Presbyterian minister in attendance. Among the small band of mourners were several women from the town and an Indian who said "Adios, hombre," as the coffin descended and Beeckman was buried, a stranger in a strange land.[12]

Beeckman's reactions to Latin society were by no means unique. California-bound passengers who went by way of Panama also complained about experiences that insulted their sense of race and gender propriety. Henry B. Sheldon, a twenty-three-year-old Methodist missionary from Ohio, had a finely honed moral sense that came from his mother's spiritual teaching and his father's lifelong ministry in the Ohio conference. Sheldon had a "powerful physique" and a fine voice that aided him in preaching and singing the Lord's praise. Still, Sheldon's Methodist biographer reported, he was "playful because full of life, for which reason he was sometimes misjudged for actions performed with no thought of wrong."[13]

In the spring of 1852, young Sheldon took it upon himself to join a band of eight Methodist missionaries, "4 of us who are bachelors — and 4 who are married," who set off to San Francisco.[14] Unlike Beeckman, Sheldon enjoyed the voyage. Passengers entertained themselves by shooting the leaping dolphins who were lured to the ship with garbage. Human mortality was evident, too. Off Cape Hatteras, North Carolina, one of the passengers gave birth to a girl "called — 'squally Hatteras' — as it was quite stormy." "Squally Hatteras" did not live long. "Last night the poor babe was baptized by one of our number and in the night it died & was buried in the deep blue sea. It was christened 'Mary Lynch.'"[15]

On the voyage he took under his charge two women, a Mrs. Novett and her daughter. This act of Christian charity was all the more magnanimous because of their religious beliefs. "They are Catholics," he noted, "but very intelligent." Brother Sheldon's open-mindedness did not extend beyond the two Washingtonians, however. When they arrived in Panama, he found the place full of Catholic churches and was distressed to discover that Panamanian Catholics did not preserve the Sabbath on Sunday. "Mass was said in its 20 churches — in the morning the rest of the day was given to gaming Cock fighting Etc. —"[16]

Sheldon did not find the Panamanian people much to his liking, either. The women wore "a purple spotted lower gaudy — with flowers & frills in abundance," and nothing else. Like the women, the Panamanian men were seminude. American travelers hired local men to ferry them up the Chagres River in dugout canoes. "From 4 to 6 natives pole each boat," Sheldon reported. "They wear nothing but pants drawers or shirts tied on their waists."[17] Jessie Benton Frémont, wife of explorer John Charles Frémont, succinctly described these boatmen as "naked, screaming, barbarous negroes and Indians."[18] In one short phrase, Frémont expressed the mental connection that she and other Americans made between nudity, race, and culture. To be naked (which meant to be indecently dressed as well as

10. CROSSING THE ISTHMUS OF PANAMA IN 'FORTY-NINE.

Two women ride mules side-saddle over the difficult Isthmus of Panama trail. Two scantily clad men carry a third woman in a sling. These women no doubt responded to the trials of the Panama crossing in different ways. An accomplished rider who enjoyed the outdoors would have relished the experience, while an inexperienced equestrienne might have gripped the pommel for dear life. Perhaps the most fearful women preferred to be carried like a sack of grain. *The Wild West* (April 1857), 2.

Courtesy of the California State Library.

complete nudity) was to be uncivilized — a condition best represented by "negroes and Indians." Sarah Brooks, a married woman who crossed the isthmus with her daughter in 1852, reported that when her "boatmen discarded their small amount of clothing the female portion of our company sought the seclusion of their umbrellas, whereupon the gentlemen commanded the boatmen to resume their garments."[19] The closest encounter between Brooks and men of color was yet to come. Once on the Pacific side, she puzzled over how she and other passengers were to be transported to the ship that waited for them offshore, for there was no dock at Panama City. Then "without a word of warning, I was grabbed from behind. One black arm was around my waist, another under my knees, and I was lifted up and carried straight out into the water. I wanted to scream."[20] Some women did scream when confronted with Black men who wanted to help them. Jane Cleveland Burnett reported that when a young Black man tried to assist a white woman she cried out and a white man attacked the would-be helper with a knife.[21]

Physical contact between Black men and white women violated the common American racial and sexual taboos of the day. However misguided and racist her ideas about Black men may have been, we should not minimize the sense of violation that Brooks experienced when the Black porter swept her into his arms. Black men were not supposed to touch white women, much less carry them about. Beginning in colonial times, whites developed ideas about the supposed sexual abandon of Africans and African Americans, slave and free. Historian Winthrop Jordan has pointed out that these ideas were an inversion of the reality of slave life, a projection upon the slave of the master's promiscuous sexual behavior among Black women in the slave quarters. Throughout the colonies, and especially in the southern colonies, where slavery was most prevalent, white men bedded Black slave women who had little say in the matter. Whites justified their interracial sexual unions with tales of Black women's amazing sexual passion and amorality. How could they resist such temptresses? At the same time, whites believed that Black men had extraordinarily large penises that they employed with great skill and endurance. White men expended a great deal of psychic energy imagining that white women had to be protected from bestial Negroes when in reality Black women needed shelter from white men. In this sexually charged atmosphere, white women could not afford to be too forward with any man because sexuality was associated with blackness and slavery. A Black man who looked at a white woman risked his life, or at least the hide on his back. Despite these strictures, some white women and Black men braved the dangers of interracial sex, although such unions were rare.[22]

I I. THE BLACK MAN'S BURDEN.

The caption for this *Wide West* (April 1857) illustration reads, "Accommodation for transportation on the Isthmus routes, not shown in the handbills and advertisements" (2). The editor implied that prospective passengers would have objected to being carried by African-American men. The artist, however, depicts a woman who seems to enjoy being carried by a huge, Black man while the white males behind her seem far less comfortable with their portage. Only the extraordinary circumstances of the Panama crossing made it tolerable for a Black man to have such an intimate encounter with a white woman.

Courtesy of the California State Library.

The boundaries and possibilities of race relations were most evident in the South, but as Jordan suggests, the South and North were more alike than different in this respect. Comparisons with Caribbean life, where the sheer numbers of Africans ensured that whites forever would be a tiny minority, make his point more clear. English planters in the islands might dominate the slave population for a time, but in the long run English civilization would not prevail where space was so limited and Englishmen were so far outnumbered by their Black subjects. But on the North American continent there was seemingly limitless space for the white people and English culture to expand. Insofar as Black slaves and freedmen were a part of the future, they could be kept separate from white society. "It was geography rather than culture," argues Jordan, "which in the last analysis placed South Carolina closer to Massachusetts than to the islands."[23] Even among abolitionists (like Beeckman), it would have been a rare New Englander who countenanced miscegenation.[24]

Daily life in Latin American ports starkly portrayed the differences between American and Latin sexual and racial mores. Women like Mrs. Brooks received a palpable demonstration, much to their surprise. The white men who looked on while Black men casually exposed themselves in the noonday sun, or carried Brooks and her white sisters to waiting ships, had to quietly suppress whatever sexual anxieties these sights may have aroused.[25] They were strangers in a strange land, who could no longer impose their rules on nonwhites.

The experiences of seafarers and overlanders were as different as the geography that they traversed. Seaborne travelers adapted to a new regime of shipboard life and periodically confronted strange new lands and people in their voyages to California. Overlanders suffered a less abrupt change as they packed their wagons and left their homes. During the gold rush single men and husbands who left their wives and families dominated the stream of immigrants who crossed the Missouri River bound for the gold fields, but women formed a minority segment of the moving population in the wagon trains, as they did on ships. Often they traveled in family groups with husbands, children, and other relatives.[26]

The decision for a family to go to California was almost always the husband's, and the wife felt bound to go along. The tone of resignation is clear in Margaret Hereford Wilson's letter to her mother. "Dr. Wilson has determined to go California. I am going with him as there is no other alternative."[27] Historian Lillian Schlissel has compared the diaries of men and women on the overland trail and concluded that they viewed the experience very differently. Men thought of the adventure and the pot of gold at the end of the rainbow — whether land or precious metal — but women were concerned with the familial and emotional ties that they were breaking.[28]

No doubt there were some strong-willed and persuasive wives who convinced their husbands to remain at home, but we can only guess how many of them there were. Once the family was on the road, it was nearly impossible and unthinkable for a woman to leave her husband and return to friends, kinfolk, and familiar surroundings. A rare exception to this general rule reveals how difficult and wrenching such a decision could be. Lester and Olive Wellington Burnett moved to Michigan in the 1830s, but pioneer life proved hard and Olive missed her family. In 1838 she returned to Hampton, Connecticut, to be with her family and raise their son, Wellington. Lester remained in Michigan, but made periodic visits to Hampton and evidently gave the impression that he intended to return there permanently. In 1843, however, he informed his wife that he intended to stay in Michigan and that he wanted her to come and live with him. Olive then had a hard decision to make. Apparently she could not manage to begin the letter in reply to her husband, so she got a woman friend, C. S. Hovey, to begin it for her. "Ardently attached to her friends, home, and its associations," Hovey explained, Olive "has nobly resolved to leave and cling to her husband, and his interests."[29] Once the letter was begun, Olive took over. She was not looking forward to returning to Michigan, but "O how much stronger than death must be a womans love for her husband." She was not certain that she could withstand the rigors of frontier life and wanted assurances from Lester that she would find the necessities of life in Michigan. "Where am I going to live? Is it in a village as you have promised me? Shall I have conveniences and comforts? Shall I have intellectual and refined society? Can I bring up my children without their getting all the vulgarity of a settlement like the one we left there?"[30] Olive did not mention fear of Indians, but her in-laws were a consideration. "More than everything else," she asked, "shall I ever have to see your brothers? I think I could not live and have them cross my path." For Olive, love of family was a one-sided affair.

Olive went to Michigan, but did not gain the security of a permanent residence. Lester proved to be fiddle-footed. In 1850 he rushed to California, where he mined, developed a water company, and farmed. His son Wellington, by now a veteran of the Mexican War and a New York lawyer, followed in 1852. In 1855 he married Jane Cromwell of New York, who, as we have seen, traveled to California via Panama in 1856. Olive, too, went to California, where she lived with her husband, son, daughter-in-law, and grandson.[31] Whether by luck, or by design, she was again within a family circle.

The maintenance of family structures was so important to women like Olive Burnett that they reluctantly uprooted themselves and crossed the continent. In addition to severing bonds of family and friendship, women paid a price in hard, physical toil while traveling with their families. Overlanders divided responsibilities among women and men according to their gender, so the living arrangements of families in motion were much like the family organization that prevailed at home. Women cooked, washed, cleaned, and cared for the children, but with the added difficulty that travel entailed. Women were up before their menfolk so that they could cook a hearty breakfast over an open fire, and they were up late at night preparing food for the next day's journey. They had little to say about routes of travel, destinations, or defense, but they were responsible for keeping everyone fed and clothed.

Men's trail work reflected the common responsibilities that males had in American rural life. They were the heads of households who held decision-making authority. They decided on the route, drove the wagons, hunted game, and provided protection from Indians. Men instituted a quasi-military organization, posted guards, chose a leader, called him captain, and followed his orders for as long as they had faith in him. The role of patriarchal protector placed a heavy burden on the men who were expected to live up to it. Indian attacks on wagon trains were not as common as the popular imagination supposed. Indian and white trail relations were often tense, but they were infrequently violent. Often Indians traded much-needed food to the overlanders. Nevertheless, fear of Indians was a part of the overland experience, and men who had been plowing and planting were now expected to fight off a fearsome enemy. It should come as no surprise that not all of these men measured up to the expectations of themselves or the women who accompanied them. Men who were expected to act courageously to fend off Indian attacks were prey to every groundless rumor of impending Indian attack. They fired their weapons at shadows and mistook every distant silhouette as a marauding Indian.[32]

Fears of Indians and sexual assault were overblown, yet women and men were prepared for the worst. Women were especially frightened of Indians, for they were reputed to rape white women and scalp them to boot. Their fears were reenforced by captivity narratives that described the horrifying experiences of women who had been taken captive and later released. Women's accounts — and those of their male narrators — usually went out of their way to explain that despite the supposed savagery of their captors, Indian men did not molest them. There was no doubt some truth in this claim, especially among the eastern tribes, where white women were often adopted in the tribe and married.[33] On the western plains, however, in some cases Indians raped white women who were taken in war.[34]

Oral traditions of Indian depredations augmented the published captivity narratives. Storytellers could embellish Indian horror stories for the edification of juvenile listeners, who absorbed the implicit lessons about Indian savagery and depravity, and the necessity of combating heathenish ways with Christian fortitude. In Springfield, Illinois, Virginia Reed heard such tales from her grandmother, whose aunt had been taken by Indians on the Virginia-Kentucky frontier. Five years later, she made her escape to tell her story to family and friends, who passed it on, doubtlessly adorned with new and even more horrific details than the original narrator had provided. Virginia loved to hear these stories and begged her aged grandmother to tell them again and again. At night in her grandma's room she sat with her back against the wall so that "no warrior could slip behind me with a tomahawk." She listened to these fearful stories until it seemed to her that "everything in the room, from the high old-fashioned bedposts down even to the shovel and tongs in the chimney corner, was transformed into the dusky tribe in paint and feathers, all ready for the war dance. So," she recalled many years later, "when I was told that we were going to California and would have to pass through a region peopled by Indians, you can imagine how I felt."[35]

In 1846 Virginia's father, James F. Reed, organized a band of immigrants that included his neighbors, the Donner family, namesake of the Donner Party—the "Martyr Pioneers," as Virginia later called them. Snowbound in the Sierra Nevada, little Virginia and her siblings would witness worse horrors than any she had conjured in her grandma's bedroom, and none of them would come at the hands of Indians.[36] The Donner Party started from Springfield in the spring of 1846, and moved at a leisurely pace across the plains while the war with Mexico exploded in the Southwest. Virginia's grandmother chose to ignore the dire warnings of her captivity tales and embarked on the overland journey. Although she was an invalid, she could not bear the thought of being separated from her only daughter, Margaret. The Reeds fitted out a special wagon for her, but she died and was buried on the trail.

When the emigrants got to Fort Bridger, they decided to take the so-called Hastings' cutoff that swung south of the established emigrant trail and was supposed to eliminate more than three hundred miles of travel by cutting south to the southern shore of the Great Salt Lake. This route, a promotion of Lansford W. Hastings, cost them much time because they had to cut a new road through the timber in the Wasatch Range. Then they had to cross the barren salt flats, another ordeal that slowed them. The Hastings' cutoff sealed their fate. It was getting late in the season and they would not reach the Humboldt River before October 1. By now the Donners, Reeds, and others who had joined the party along the trail knew that they were in trouble. Their oxen were failing and they might not get across the Sierras before the snow flew. So, in mid-September, they sent two men ahead to Sutter's Fort in the Sacramento Valley, hoping that the generous Captain Sutter would send them relief.

Things got worse and tempers grew short as the wagons moved drearily along the Humboldt River. The teamsters had to double the teams to get up a long, sandy hill near present-day Winnemucca. One of the bullwhackers, a popular young swain named John Snyder, cursed and beat his oxen. James Reed, Virginia's father, argued with Snyder, who threatened to give Reed a hiding. In quick order, Reed pulled a knife, Snyder bludgeoned Reed, Reed stabbed Snyder, Mrs. Reed stepped in, and the wounded Snyder struck her, too. Then Snyder staggered up a hill and died. Snyder had been popular, and many resented Reed because he had money and an arrogant way. Some in the train wanted to lynch Reed then and there, but instead they banished him. With no choice in the matter, the desperate Reed rode on ahead to California, leaving his family behind.

Finally they reached the sweet, refreshing waters of the Truckee River and began to climb up the eastern escarpment of the Sierra Nevada. It was mid-October. On the nineteenth, a relief party from Sutter's Fort arrived. Charles Stanton, one of the party who had gone ahead for help, and two Indians who worked for Sutter brought seven mules loaded with food for the suffering emigrants. From October 31 to November 3 they tried to cross the pass above Truckee (now Donner) Lake, but snow drove them back. In desperation, the party retreated to the lake, made camp, and settled in for the bitter winter.

The final chapter may be briefly told. The marooned pioneers ran out of provisions, ate their livestock and dogs, boiled hides into a foul, glutinous soup, and starved and starved. Twice some of them tried to walk out, but returned, dispirited. In mid-December, five women and twelve men, including Stanton and the two Indians, trudged over Donner Pass and out into the snow-choked canyons of the Sierras. In a few days they ran out of the scant rations they had brought with them, and hunger gnawed at their guts. A Mexican teamster was the first to die on the forlorn trek, and others soon succumbed from hunger in howling Sierra blizzards. Survivors carved up the stringy meat and roasted the hearts of the dead. Someone began to talk of killing and eating the Indians who had risked their lives to bring them supplies. One of the whites warned them and they slipped away, but no matter. The starving whites caught up with the starving Indians, killed them, and ate their remains. Finally two bloody, emaciated, and nearly naked men and five women made it to a ranch. Their ordeal in the snow was finally over.

The arrival of these pitiful survivors and the continuing efforts of James Reed stirred additional relief efforts. In February and March, three expeditions went out and brought back victims from Donner Lake, including Virginia Reed. Rescuers found that these starving overlanders had also resorted to cannibalism. Still, there were a few who remained at the lake, and a final rescue effort was made in mid-April. They found only one man alive, Lewis Keseberg, who was accused of murdering people so that he could eat their flesh. Throughout his life, Keseberg unfairly bore the guilty stain of cannibalism; he had eaten human flesh, but so had many others. In one of the grim ironies of this pitiful episode, for a brief time Keseberg operated a restaurant in Sacramento. Most of his life was a dark coda to the frozen season in the mountains. Sacramento children stoned him in the streets and called him names. Keseberg became a recluse living in squalor, with two demented children from his second marriage.

It was difficult to organize rescue parties because the winter was extraordinarily harsh, and most able-bodied men were engaged in the Mexican-American War. Californians were horrified at the condition of the Donner Party and the stories of cannibalism that were beginning to circulate. The stories inspired sincere pity and heroic efforts to help the living, but there were also some tasteless jokes. Sheriff George McKinstry and U.S. Army Lieutenant Edward Kern helped to organize the relief efforts at Sutter's Fort, but McKinstry also warned Kern about the man-eating Donner women, who preferred their meat in nine-inch pieces.[37] John Sutter peevishly recalled the incident for historian Hubert Howe Bancroft. He had sent a food-laden pack train with Indian drivers to the Donner Party, but "the provisions not satisfying the starving sufferers they killed and ate first the mules then the horses and finally they killed and ate all my good Indians."[38]

From the first, those who examined the Donner tragedy were curious about the differences in mortality between men and women.[39] Men died at about twice the rate of women (see Table 3.1).[40] In the fall of 1846 the whole group included fifty-three men and thirty-four women, but in the spring women outnumbered men by twenty-four to twenty-three. More than half the men died, but only 30 percent of the women failed to survive. The figures show that twenty of twenty-four children aged five to fourteen survived the

Table 3.1 Donner Party Survivors by Age and Sex

Age	Male Survived?			Female Survived?			Total	% Died
	Yes	No	% Died	Yes	No	% Died		
1–4	2	5	71.4	4	5	55.6	16	62.5
5–9	5	2	28.6	4	0	0.0	11	18.2
10–14	6	2	25.0	5	0	0.0	13	15.4
15–19	1	1	50.0	1	0	0.0	3	33.3
20–29	5	10	66.6	6	1	14.3	22	50.0
30–39	2	4	66.6	2	0	0.0	8	50.0
40–49	2	1	33.3	1	3	75.0	7	57.1
50–59	0	1	100.0	0	1	100.0	2	100.0
60–69	0	3	100.0				3	100.0
Unknown	0	1	100.0	1	0	0.0	2	50.0
Totals	23	30	56.6	24	10	29.4	87	45.0

Based on Donald K. Grayson, "Donner Party Deaths: A Demographic Assessment," *Journal of Anthropological Research* 46 (Fall 1990), 223–42, Table 6, 234.

ordeal. All of the children who perished were boys. Why was female mortality comparatively low among Donner Party women? Was there some truth to McKinstry's warning about man-eating Donner women, latter-day incarnations of the Amazon cannibals that Montalvo had concocted in the sixteenth century? Were women somehow tougher than men? Did the men expend more energy than women and thus collapse sooner?

The reason for the Donner Party women's comparatively high survival rate seems to be a combination of biology and social conditions. Studies have shown that women withstand famine and cold better than men. Differences in mortality could have been due solely to this cause, but a close analysis of Donner Party mortality suggests other reasons. Males and females alike stood a better chance of surviving if they belonged to a large family. Those who traveled alone — men — or with small kin groups were most likely to succumb. Conversely, members of large families and extended kin groups stood a better chance of living through the Sierra Nevada winter. These data, while debatable because of the small size of the sample, suggest that women who were reluctant to sever their family connections to go to California were not merely sentimental. For the Donner Party, kinship was a matter of life and death.

In addition to size of kin group, male leadership was another variable that influenced survivorship.[41] Fifty-five percent of male heads of nuclear families failed to see the spring of 1847, and the mortality was highest among patriarchs who belonged to the largest kin groups (see Table 3.2).[42] In

Table 3.2 Mortality for Male Family Heads

Name	Family Size	No. Family Survivors	Kin Group Size
Survivors			
Breen, Patrick	9	9	9
Eddy, William	4	1	4
Foster, William	3	2	13
Keseberg, Lewis	4	2	4
Non-Survivors			
Donner, George	14	7	16
Fosdick, Jay	2	1	12
Graves, Franklin	6	5	12
Pike, William	4	2	13
Williams, Baylis	2	1	2

Based on Donald K. Grayson, "Donner Party Deaths: A Demographic Assessment," *Journal of Anthropological Research* 46 (Fall 1990), 223–42.

addition to the vicissitudes of starvation and freezing, these men bore the responsibility for leading their families into harm's way. They had failed to make the trip in time to cross the mountains, and now they would watch their wives and babies starve. Twelve-year-old Virginia Reed famously summed up the errors of the Donner Party leaders in her May 16, 1847, letter from California. "Never take no cutoffs and hury along as fast as you can."[43] It was the men — most of them now dead — who were to blame for the circumstances that made cannibalism the only alternative to starvation. It is not unreasonable to see them as victims of depression as well as hunger and cold.

Californians heaped scorn on only one of these surviving patriarchs — Keseberg. Breen and Eddy were recognized as heroes because they had helped to save others in camp and on the winter trek out. Foster was the man who killed Sutter's Indians, but insofar as this was known his actions were attributed to insanity.[44] Besides, after a brief respite, Foster returned with a rescue party to save others. But Keseberg, unable to travel with the relief teams because of an injured foot, had to stay the whole winter with the few others who were too weak to go. Tamsen Donner, who was healthy enough to make the trek out, stayed with her dying husband and the other invalids. When the final rescuers arrived in April, only Keseberg was alive. His German immigrant status, rumors about his taste for human flesh, and suspicions that he had killed a member of the Donner Party in the Great Basin made him a scapegoat. In the minds of nineteenth-century Californians, Keseberg was flawed, Old World, depraved, and perverted—a perfect stand-in for the patriarchs whose decisions had led the Donner Party to disaster.

Some of the survivors were willing to point a finger at Keseberg. In 1855 twelve-year-old Frances Donner told her friend Caroline Bullard about the hardships in the mountains. Caroline, duly impressed with the horrors of 1847, passed the Donner's story along to one of her friends back east. "You know that they must have faird hard." They were so hungry that the

> childrin pulled the buck skinn strings out of thair shoas and ate them. . . . As her father was sick her mother stayed there with him and a man by the name of Cheasburg killed her Mother and ate them and he killed 3 of his one childrin and ate them. I must turn [away from] this subject.[45]

It was bad enough that Keseberg had eaten Frances's mother, but now Frances—or perhaps Caroline—made him devour his own children. Of course, it was not true that Kesesberg had killed his children. He had only two children and one of them died on the forced march across the mountains, while Keseberg was still at the lake. The other child, his one-year-old son, died at the lake in late January, but there is no evidence that he ate the tiny body. From a child's perspective, this was the greatest imaginable violation of parental trust, the most heinous exercise of patriarchal power. Perhaps placing blame on Keseberg eased some of the Donner childrens' unresolved anger toward their parents. Father had failed to protect them. Mother chose father over the children and stayed at the lake while they went to California. Now the Donner children were orphans. The parents were to blame, but Keseberg became the object of their anger.

The Donner Party disaster was a macabre prelude to the gold rush. Their travails were a ghastly reminder of the risks that overlanders took when they decided to move west. Because men were in charge, it was understood that men's folly led the Donners and Reeds to their sorry fate. The women and children went along and lived or died as a result. The vast majority of overlanders made it to their destination without extraordinary difficulties beyond the hazards posed by disease, the sometimes treacherous trail, and the usual risks of nineteenth-century life. In the 1850s the trail was better marked than the one that the Donners followed, and the length of travel thus shortened. From 1841 to 1849 the average length of time for the journey was 134.6 days. In the 1850s overlanders averaged 112.7 days on the trail to California.[46]

12. LEWIS KESEBERG.

Californians portrayed Keseberg as a monstrous cannibal who ate human flesh because he liked it. He was one of many Donner Party survivors who resorted to eating the remains of their dead companions, but he was the only one who contemporaries found blameworthy. His German immigrant background and his unpleasant personality made him a plausible scapegoat for a disaster that was not of his making. C. F. McGlashan, *History of the Donner Party: A Tragedy of the Sierra*, 2[d] ed. (San Francisco: A. L. Bancroft, 1880), 220.

Courtesy of the California State Library.

13. GEORGIA DONNER, MARY BRUNNER, AND ELIZA DONNER.

After they were rescued from the Sierra, Georgia, Eliza and Frances (not shown) wandered barefoot among the rooms and tents at Sutter's Fort, cadging food and sleeping wherever they could find shelter. "We are the children of Mr. and Mrs. George Donner," they said, "and our parents are dead." Mary Brunner gave them food and ultimately took in Georgia and Eliza. They called her grandma. Eliza Poor Donner Houghton, *The Expedition of the Donner Party and Its Tragic Fate* (Chicago: A. C. McClurg, 1911), 256.

Courtesy of the California State Library.

In the 1850s the sheer number of immigrants made it nearly impossible
to get lost. The trail was often choked with traffic. Livestock cut a wide and
barren swath as they grazed their way across the prairies and mountains. A
blind traveler with a cane could have followed the wagon ruts, and might
have done as well as the sighted wagoneers who were forced to wear gog-
gles to keep out the dust that rose from the steady tramp of men, women,
horses, mules, and oxen. The trail was littered with garbage and cast-off
articles that had become too burdensome. Iron stoves, furniture, books,
broken wagons, and the carcasses of draft animals were strewn along the
trail as immigrants discarded things that were not essential or no longer
useful. The western half of the trail that crossed mountains and cruel des-
erts took the greatest toll on material goods of the wagon trains.[47] It was
hard to get lost, but one could lose the things that had taken a lifetime to
accumulate, family treasures that had been passed from generation to generation. Loss was a common denominator for the overlanders.

Human loss from disease and accident was a part of the journey, too, and
this took an untold emotional toll on the men and women who made the
journey. Cholera, smallpox, dysentery, pneumonia, and infections struck
down the very young, the old, the unlucky, and those who were weakened
by the journey. Between 1840 and 1860 cholera alone killed some two
thousand immigrants, compared with fewer than four hundred who died in
conflicts with Indians.[48]

The dread of burying a loved one on the trail was one of the worst
anxieties. Some immigrants hauled dying kin for miles just to be able to
bury them in a secure place, as Benjamin Bullard explained in 1854. One of
his daughters, Luana, got sick about two hundred miles from Fort Laramie
and the Bullard family gave up hope that she would make it. They stopped
for a whole day waiting for her to die, but she clung to life so they pushed
on. "Our prayers was that she might live to get to Salt Lake Citty where we
could buerry her . . . so that she would not be dug out by the wolves. We
saw hundreds of graves that was dug open and robed of the dead by the
wolves."[49] Luana was tenacious. After twelve days in Salt Lake City, she
improved enough so that she could finish the trip to California. "When we
got to Sacramento she was the poorest person I ever saw," her father wrote.
But happily, "She is well now and as fat as a pig."

If the statistics on Indian and white violence are correct, Indians had
more to fear from immigrants than vice versa. According to one careful
account, from 1840 to 1860 Indians killed 362 whites on the overland
journey, but overlanders killed 426 Indians.[50] Nevertheless, just as with
Virginia Reed in 1846, children were raised on accounts of bloody Indian

warfare, death, torture, and wretched captivity. The lurid books that re-counted captives' ordeals hinted at sexual assaults, but left details to the readers' imaginations. The story of Olive Oatman, a fourteen-year-old girl taken by the Yavapai Indians near the Yuma crossing in 1851, illustrates this point and speaks to the cultural complications of sex and gender that were involved in the overland crossing. The Oatman family was from Illinois and consisted of Royce and Mary Ann Oatman and their eight children (one of whom was born on the westward journey). The Oatman immigration was inspired in part by religious motivations, for they joined the Brewsterites, a Mormon splinter group led by James Colin Brewster, heading for the mouth of the Colorado River where they hoped to establish a new commu-nity called Bashan.[51]

Fifty-two Brewsterites started down the Santa Fe Trail from Indepen-dence in August 1850. As with the Donner Party, dissension divided the Brewsterites. By the time they reached Council Grove they began to argue over religious matters, although the nature of these disputes is not clear. In northern New Mexico the party argued about what route to take. Royce Oatman emerged as the leader of a faction that wanted to take the Gila River road. The rest, including Brewster, the religious sect's leader, insisted on sticking with the old Santa Fe Trail. In the end, the Oatmans and their friends (about twenty in all) decided to take the Kearny-Cooke road to the Gila River. The rest of the Brewsterites eventually settled in Colonia, near Soccoro, New Mexico. The Oatman party, with Royce as leader, pushed south and west toward the Colorado River of the West.[52]

Royce Oatman's decision to take the Gila route proved to be disastrous. By the time they reached the Pima villages their oxen were poor and food was in short supply. It had been a bad year and the Pimas, who usually were a dependable source of food for weary travelers, could give them none. Here, Oatman made a fatal decision. He decided to push on to Fort Yuma instead of remaining among the Pimas. This ended Oatman's leader-ship of anyone but his own family. The other families who had followed him away from Brewster decided to stay in the Pima villages. So, in Feb-ruary 1851, the Oatman family and their jaded oxen left their friends among the Pimas and moved slowly along the Gila toward the American post some two hundred miles away. By now Oatman had abandoned all thoughts of building a religious community in the desert and was deter-mined to go on to California, where gold beckoned. Predictably, the condi-tion of his animals worsened on the harsh desert trail. Now desperate, Oatman sent a letter with John Lawrence Leconte, a traveler he encoun-tered on the road, begging the commander at Fort Yuma for assistance.

"There is my self, wife & seven children and without help sir I am confident we must perrish."[53]

Having abandoned his religious aims, Royce Oatman became a prophet. A party of Yavapai men found this pathetic band of sojourners in March and killed everyone in the party except Olive, her younger sister Mary Ann, and her brother Lorenzo, who was wounded but managed to escape.[54] The dead and orphaned Oatmans were victims not only of the Yavapais, but of their father's stubborn sense of leadership. Royce Oatman was the most dangerous of western traveling companions — a man of little experience, strong opinions, and some persuasive ability.

The Yavapais took Olive and Mary Ann and kept them until they traded them to the Mohaves. In the course of their captivity, Mary Ann died of starvation. Olive lived among the Mohaves until 1856, when she was ransomed and reunited with her brother. Her life with these Indians is clouded by imperfect sources and conscious mythmaking on the part of Royal B. Stratton, a Methodist preacher who wrote the narrative of her captivity. Nevertheless, once it is stripped of varnish, Stratton's account, Olive's statements, and Indian sources indicate that Espanesay, a Mohave headman, took Olive to live with his family. She lived much like other Mohave women, who gathered wild plant foods in the unforgiving desert and farmed along the Colorado River flood plain. The Mohaves tattooed her chin in their customary way, probably when she reached puberty. A famous photograph shows her in a long-sleeved, high-collared dress that may have hidden other tattoos on her arms and body.[55]

Oatman's status while in Mohave society is unclear. In 1856, she told a Los Angeles newspaper reporter that Espanesay treated Olive and her sister "in every respect as his own children." The article went on to relate that "food was divided with them, they were not obliged to labor, but did pretty much as they pleased." This should not be understood to mean that Olive and her sister loafed while the Mohaves toiled. "Lands were allotted to them and they were furnished with seeds, and raised their own corn, melons and beans as the Indians did." Despite this good treatment, the Mohaves may have considered her to be a slave throughout her captivity. After all, Espanesay paid two horses, two blankets, and some beads for the girls. When famine came to the Mohaves her sister wasted away and died. Olive probably would have died, too, but her stepmother made a saving gruel from her seed corn, "which even the dying groans of her own people could not make her bring out." The same woman cried for a day and a night, "as if she were losing her own child," when Olive left the Mohaves.[56]

In 1856 a Quechan Indian came to the Mohaves and told them that they

14. OLIVE OATMAN BEFORE THE INDIAN COUNCIL.
Olive's Mohave captors and family discuss what to do after they learn that whites have discovered Olive's whereabouts. This illustration and others showing Olive as a sexually mature adolescent appears in Royal B. Stratton's narrative *Captivity of the Oatman Girls* (New York: Carlton Porter, 1859), 256. Stratton, a Methodist missionary, and Oatman toured the Midwest and New York selling the book to support Methodist work.

Courtesy of the Bancroft Library.

should give up Olive to the white soldiers at Fort Yuma. Evidently it was a difficult decision to part with her. Espanesay was reluctant to give her up. In 1903 Tokwa-a, a Mohave who had known Olive, quoted him as saying, "Well, I would like to raise this girl. We traveled far to buy her. We like her." Tokwa-a said that all the Mohave women were sorry to lose Olive and told her, "I like you much." Eventually, Espanesay agreed to give her up in return for a horse, although he claimed that he had not kept her by force.[57]

The Olive Oatman who arrived at Fort Yuma in February 1856 could barely utter a few words of English to the officer who interrogated her. She was soon reunited with her brother and taken to the home of the Thompson family in El Monte, California. The Thompsons had traveled with the Oatmans and other Brewsterites until the party split up in 1851. There, Olive and her brother remained until their cousin, Harvey Oatman, came from Oregon to take charge of them in June. According to a newspaper account, Colonel Thompson suspected that "an attempt was being made to entrap his ward," and he briefly objected to Harvey's bid to take Olive away. He may have objected on religious grounds. The Oregon branch of the Oatman clan were staunch Methodists, and Thompson may have scented a plan to use Olive's harrowing experiences to benefit the Methodist cause, or perhaps to discredit Mormons. Indeed, the Oatmans soon introduced Olive to Royal B. Stratton, a Methodist missionary from Yreka, California. In 1857 Stratton published a narrative of Olive's experiences based on his interviews with her. The book, however, was more Stratton's than Olive's. The reverend Stratton emphasized the importance of Olive's Christian faith, but made no mention of Mormons or Brewsterites in the narrative that he wrote. His purpose was to write a pious account that would inspire people to give money to build Methodist churches, and he was successful. Stratton was amazed to see how quickly his first edition sold out and prepared a second edition, and then a third, which was announced as the "twenty-first thousand" in print.[58] The Methodist missionary learned that there was some money to be had in huckstering his book, so he took Olive back to his New York home, where she went on lecture tour to publicize the book. Her Mohave facial tattoos created a sensation at her lectures, and she may have sold personal photographs as well as books at these events. The precise financial arrangements between Olive and Lorenzo Oatman and Stratton are unknown, but they evidently shared the profits from the book and lectures. Olive lectured from 1859 to 1865, staying with the Stratton family in New York for at least part of that time. In 1865, she stepped from the podium to marry a Texas banker who took her to Fort Sherman, Texas. She bore no children, but adopted a daughter. The tattoos faded with age, and the banker's wife frequently obscured the remaining marks of her captivity with a veil.[59]

Stratton and Olive had turned her captivity to financial advantage and perhaps improved her chances for a favorable marriage. But this was a delicate matter. Even though he insisted that Olive had not been touched, Stratton hinted at the sexual dimensions of Olive's captivity. "The marriage relation among them," he asserted, was "scarcely observed."[60] Husbands could abandon wives at will, he revealed, but did not mention that Mohave wives were also free to leave their husbands if they desired.[61] "Rapine and lust prey upon them at home," he roundly hinted. "Much of that dreadful period [of Olive's captivity] is unwritten, and will remain forever unwritten."[62] Now this was the sort of suggestive stuff that sold books in the 1860s! But Olive's reputation had to be protected, so Stratton stopped short of saying that Olive had been raped, seduced, or married. To blunt the obvious sexual inferences of his text, Stratton offered this remarkable statement:

"Honor to whom honor is due." With all the degredation in which these untamed hordes are steeped, there are — strange as it may seem — some traits and phases in their conduct which, on comparison with those who call themselves civilized, ought to crimson their cheeks with a blush. While feuds have been kindled, and lives have been lost — innocent lives — by the intrusion of the white man upon the domestic relations of Indian families; while decency and chastity have been outraged, and the Indian female, in some instances, stolen from her spouse and husband that she really loved; let it be written, written if possible so as to be read when an inscrutable but unerring Providence shall exact "to the uttermost farthing" for every deed of cruelty and lust perpetrated by a superior race upon an inferior one; *written* to stand out before those whose duty and position it shall be, within a few years, in the American Council of State, to deliberate and legislate upon the best method to dispose of these fast waning tribes; that *one of our own race, in tender years, committed wholly to their power, passed a five years' captivity among these savages without falling under their baser propensities which rave, and rage, and consume, with the fury and fatality of a pestilence, among themselves.*[63]

White assaults on Indian women were common in the mining districts where Stratton had been a missionary. These attacks drew criticism from newspapers, Indian-office employees, and citizens who were afraid that such assaults would endanger the frontier and lead to war.[64] Thus, Stratton upheld the honor of the Mohaves and Olive's purity with a broadside against ungodly white rapists, whom, he hoped, God would hold accountable.

Nevertheless, Stratton made it clear all Indians were hindrances to civilization, who should be "civilized" or destroyed. "The march of American civilization," Stratton frankly averred, "will yet, and soon, break upon the barbarity of these numerous tribes, and either elevate them to the unappreciated blessings of a superior state, or wipe them into oblivion, and give their long-undeveloped territory to another."[65] Evidently, Stratton foresaw no earthly reward for the Mohaves who had guarded Olive's chastity.

The biases against all Indians in the Stratton narrative contrast with Olive's first statements to an army officer in 1856. She differentiated between the Yavapais, who killed most of her family and overworked and beat the Oatman girls, and the Mohaves, who treated them like family and gave them whatever food they had.[66] Still, Oatman's lecture notes did not substantially depart from the story told in Stratton's book that she was there to sell. As in the book, her narrative was one of unremitting faith and courage in the face of constant brutality and hardship, a tale that possessed "all the material of a thrilling romance."[67] Insofar as the Mohaves showed any mercy, it was because they were moved by the Christian virtue and bravery of their captives. Given the purpose of her lectures, none of Olive's statements about Indians are particularly surprising. However, some of her remarks about the Oatman family stand out. She spoke about "my father's family," rather than her family. By the time she was giving these lectures in the 1860s Olive had been passed through many families, and her birth family may have seemed as distant from her as the Mohave Desert was from New York. Stratton's volume asserted that the Indians had not sexually abused Olive, but one of Thompson's daughters claimed otherwise. When Olive lived with the Thompsons in El Monte, she pined ceaselessly for a Mohave husband and children whom she had left behind. According to this account, Olive tried to return to them at every opportunity and was a "grieving, unsatisfied woman, who shook one's belief in civilization."[68] The rumors of a Mohave marriage have never been substantiated, although there were reports of "a beautiful, light-haired, blue-eyed girl, supposed to have been a child of the unfortunate Olive Oatman."[69]

Perhaps Olive did not have children by an Indian father, but her sorrow over the loss of her adopted Mohave kin may have been real enough. Stratton, who constantly emphasized Olive's anguish for her white family, did not feel obliged to mention her grief over the loss of her Indian family. In an odd reversal of the sexual inferences in his narrative, Stratton used Olive's supposed chastity to criticize white men who assaulted Indian women and destroyed native families. Yet he did not draw the obvious and ironic conclusion that the redemption of Olive meant the disruption of the mixed-race frontier family to which she now belonged.

Stratton was careful about the words that conveyed sexual meaning, but he — or his publisher — boldly printed illustrations of nubile, bare-breasted Olive dressed only in a bark skirt. He reported that when she came near Fort Yuma, "Olive, with her characteristic modesty, was unwilling to appear in her bark attire," and waited until an officer's wife sent her a dress to wear.[70] When properly dressed, she was presented to a cheering throng. Perhaps, but Olive sold books on the lecture circuit with seminude representations of herself and Indian women. It is doubtful that Olive had any control over the artwork adorning the book that she hawked so assiduously.

It is safe to say, however, that these images sensationalized her account and graphically portrayed some of the sexual dimensions of Indian captivity that women most feared.

The "fate worse then death" implied a strong possibility of sexual assault at the hands of men of another race, and at the least, Indian captivity would result in a loss of feminine modesty. A lifelong facial tattoo marked Olive's losses and was emblematic of women's worst fears of disaster on the trail. Olive's case suggests that abduction also entailed more complicated possibilities, such as radically rearranged family relations, fundamental changes in gender roles and relations, and divided personal and cultural loyalties. Women who left the secure orbit of their families and friends in the East hoped someday to see them again, or at least to gravitate into a new, stable web of family and female relations in the West. But like Olive, they could be unmoored entirely, lost forever, or returned to a society where they were no longer accepted and where they could not be content. She was fortunate to eventually settle into a permanent marriage and family relations, but anyone who read her story or who heard her lectures knew how lucky this final outcome was for her.

By land or by sea, the journey to California presented a challenge to common American ideas about sex, race, and gender. As with the Donner Party, a crisis could break down the usual boundaries between acceptable and unthinkable behavior. Patriarchal leadership could lead families astray and destroy them. Encounters with new people and unfamiliar cultures held American values up to comparative scrutiny. In the minds of most Americans, such comparisons reflected favorably on the old, familiar ideas and usages that they believed were emblematic of their own self-satisfied sense of racial, cultural, and religious superiority. The trip to California did not broaden the outlook of the women and men who made the journey; it deepened their prejudice.

FOUR

His Own Will and Pleasure:

Miners, Morals, and the Crisis of the Marriage Market

Our population, selected from the choice young men of all the most active nations of the world, has not been thrown together into the vast alembic of society, without developing many qualities, whose existence was hitherto latent. We live faster than any other people. We think more promptly; a thousand times more freely than our fathers of the east and of Europe. Our passions are stronger; our intellects keener; our prejudices weaker. Guarded by no fond mother, whose pious heart would grieve at the infidelity of her children, we think for ourselves on religious subjects; dreading not the verdict of village scandal-mongers, we enjoy to the full our present opinions; glorying in the isolation of our social position and our comparative freedom from social formalities, each cares to conform his actions solely to his own will and pleasure.[1]

CASPER T. HOPKINS, 1854

California, like other faraway and exotic lands, posed a challenge to the bourgeois values that dominated middle-class thinking in the United States. Some new Californians believed that this confrontation with new ways and ideas was a good thing. In the paragraph quoted above, Casper T. Hopkins argued that California men abandoned the stuffy notions of their mothers and thought for themselves. Hopkins's essay supported California's liberal divorce law while upholding Americans' commonly held ideals about the family, virtue, and true womanhood. Nevertheless, he reenforced the myth that Californians were more open-minded than easterners.

Others — perhaps a majority and at least a vocal minority — believed otherwise. Indeed, Hopkins reported that some representatives of "fogydom" asserted that divorce would "loosen the domestic ties, . . . encourage female

75

Table 4.1 Sex Ratios, California White Population

Year	Males per Female
1850	12.2
1852	7.2
1860	2.4

Derived from "Table No. 3 — Population Cities, Towns, &c.," *Population of the United States in 1860*, comp. Joseph G. C. Kennedy (Washington, D.C.: Government Printing Office, 1864), 30.

depravity, and reduce our social condition to a position analogous to that of Turkey or of Utah."[2] Editorials condemned divorce and feared that it was a manifestation of "social leprosy" that would bring down California society.[3] Unlike Hopkins, conservative editors and ministers thought that the rendezvous with other people, religious traditions, and gold-rush disorder amounted to a battle for spiritual supremacy, moral rectitude, and secular order. Marriage, the family, and the control of sexuality were central to their concerns. Social conservatives and Protestant missionaries meant to supplant unorthodox Califorianisms — whether the result of undisciplined mining society, life among Indians, or Spanish, Mexican, and Roman Catholic traditions — with the familiar usages of the eastern United States. California had to be delivered from "a few scattered and degenerate sons of Spain, and a few enterprising adventurers, and a few tribes of wretchedly degraded Indians," as Protestant missionary James Woods put it.[4]

If the hope of men such as Woods was to turn California into a Pacific Coast New England, the transformation was not a complete success. Amid extraordinary historical circumstances California achieved a unique regional identity that reflected a bit of the Mexican past and a large dose of American cultural norms — an identity that was something less and something more than its antecedents.[5] During the gold rush, many California newcomers confronted social conditions that were without parallel in their personal experience. This was true of women and men alike, and although these circumstances sometimes presented new opportunities and choices to them, these novel prospects were not always to their liking.

The structure of the California population determined much about sex and gender in the golden state. The gold-rush populace was overwhelmingly young and male (see Table 4.1).[6] This demographic fact meant that any young man was going to have a hard time finding female company, whether he wanted casual conversation, sex, or marriage. Either he had to

Table 4.2 Sex Ratios for White Age Cohorts in
1860

Age	Males per Female
15–19	1.2
20–29	3.1
30–39	4.3

Derived from "Table No. 3 — Population Cities, Towns,
&c.," *Population of the United States in 1860*, comp. Joseph
G. C. Kennedy (Washington, D.C.: Government Printing
Office, 1864), 30.

compete for the few eligible females in California, consort with prostitutes, or look homeward for companionship. As the 1850s wore on more women came to California, so the sex ratio improved over time. Nevertheless, in 1860 there were still more than two men for every woman. For older males, the situation was worse (see Table 4.2). There was nearly an equal number of young women and men in their late teens, a statistic that probably reflects the migration of families to California. But men in their twenties found only one woman for every three men, and for each woman in her thirties there were more than four men. Thus, gold-rush men and women existed in a marriage market with sharply different opportunities for successful mating. Men confronted a highly competitive California marriage market, which meant that many of them would not be able to marry. Women had a seemingly endless supply of men to select from, but also faced increased demands for their sexual, economic, and companionate services in a highly gendered and male-dominated world. For some Californians, the problem was not that there were too few women, but too many men.

The Bawdy Frontier

Prostitution may not be the oldest profession, as the trite saying goes, but it has a history that can be traced to ancient Greece and Rome. Brothels in Catholic Europe and Protestant America served the erotic demands of men who ignored the religious and legal proscriptions on sexual behavior in their time and place. Bordellos were located primarily in cities where there was a young, male clientele who patronized them. Cities and towns also attracted women who left their families in search of work and potential

A BACHELOR IN A TIGHT PLACE.

MATRIMONIAL JOYS.

My marriage as an act was wise,
　Above all other acts in life,
For I can gaze in two fond eyes.
　And call their fair possessor wife.
I'm proud of little mouths to feed ;
　It does me good to see them fed ;
Long of a wife I stood in need,
　'Till now I've one who kneads my bread.

It makes me happy, I declare,
　To notice one soul-cheering sign—
My little girl has jet black hair,
　And nose the very shape of mine.
I never fear an angry word
　When I away to town have been,
Nor would I be afraid to board
　A dozen young and handsome men.

A man's but half a pair of shears
　Who lives along without a wife,
And though he lives a hundred years
　He never lives but half a life ;
He's always out of humor, health,
　And very often, I believe—
Though he may be a man of wealth—
　He's sadly out at knees and sleeve.

He plods along without a wife,
　'Till past the age of manhood, when
He muses on his wretched life
　And thinks of what he might have been ;
Then in the bowl he seeks relief—
　His last example is the best—
He dies, and like a punished thief,
　Becomes a warning to the rest.

Published by Hutchings & Rosenfield, 146 Montgomery Street, San Francisco.

15. "A BACHELOR IN A TIGHT PLACE" AND "MATRIMONIAL JOYS."

This poem and cartoon were published in San Francisco in the 1850s. In the poem a man sings the praises of marriage using some of the usual mid-nineteenth-century tropes. His wife kneads his bread, mends his clothes, and keeps the marriage bed exclusively for him. He, on the other hand, feeds his family. The cartoon, however, makes the man a harried soul indeed, with grasping, pursuing females clutching at his coat. He seems to be trying to escape from the nest, while the women try to make husbands, especially as industrialization and urbanization accelerated in early modern times. Some of these young women found neither lawful spouses nor dependable employment, but they did find dissembling swains and exploitative employers who impregnated and then abandoned them. One of the dynamics of modernization, then, was to create both a demand for and a supply of prostitutes.[7]

In cities prostitutes were "ostentatious ornaments of their notorious quarters," as historian Peter Gay has put it. The cities possessed "carnal vitality," Gay writes, and were "schools of erotic education."[8] Cities with their gaudy and well-known vice districts were the most obvious loci of prostitution, but rural America, especially in the West with its oversupply of men, also had its institutions of sexual service. Soldiers, cowboys, teamsters, and transient male laborers of all kinds were customers for squalid, rural dens of prostitution. In the second half of the nineteenth century these places were unflatteringly known as hog ranches, a sobriquet that signified their rurality and the low repute of the women who worked there.[9]

Who were the American prostitutes? As historian Anne Butler has shown, most prostitutes in the American West were poor and young and they were often women of color — Indians, Asians, and Latinas. These general patterns of prostitution reflected the stratification of American society by gender, race, and class. Far from being an independent band of female entrepreneurs, prostitutes were victims of physical abuse, economic exploitation, and the scorn of a society that regarded them as social outcasts. Some of them were women who had fallen from the ranks of the middle class because of an unexpected plunge into poverty or an unfortunate pregnancy. Most came from the ranks of the poor, and not a few were themselves the daughters of prostitutes.[10]

The social and demographic patterns that marked American prostitution prevailed in California as well. As a volatile mining frontier, California possessed the qualities of urban vitality and rural isolation, as miners devel-

---

him stay. In the background men seem to be driving women like sheep behind a wagon train. Perhaps they are on their way to California. The cartoon juxtaposed with the poem confounds male and female images — the contented husband and the unsettled bachelor, the loyal helpmeet and the clutching, desperate spinster. Given the shortage of women in California during the 1850s, most bachelors would have been delighted to be surrounded by eligible women, even if they were up a tree.

Courtesy of the Bancroft Library.

oped far-flung placers and fed the coffers of the young metropolis of San
Francisco and interior commercial towns like Stockton, Sacramento, and
Marysville. The rush to the gold fields included people from all over the
world, but especially Anglo Americans, Europeans, Latinos, and Chinese
who engulfed the preexisting californio and Indian populations. While
California did not invent prostitution, the gold-rush experience, with its
racially mixed population, surplus of young males, and rambunctious economy, foreshadowed developments on other mining frontiers that followed.

The shortage of women and the surplus of gold in California attracted
prostitutes from around the world. In December 1848, Rosario Améstica,
alias Rosita, Anacleta, Rosa Montalva, Pancha, and Juana, shipped out of
Valparaiso, Chile, aboard the *Stauelli*. The port officer attempted to keep
her from sailing, but in the end she convinced him that she was entitled
to embark. Vicente Pérez Rosales, a Chilean passenger, described her as
"buxom and portly," and revealed that she had formerly worked in Concepción, Talca, and Valparaiso. Many of the passengers had known her on
shore and were happy to help her defray the cost of her passage. Pérez
Rosales claimed to be disgusted with Améstica and the men who patronized
her between bouts with seasickness, yet he admitted that she had her
charms. On New Year's eve, she entertained the assembled passengers with
"marvelously bawdy" songs while accompanying herself on a guitar. By
mid-January she promenaded "on deck like a ship of war in a steady tail
wind." By the time she reached San Francisco, "everyone on board had . . .
dealings with her," Pérez Rosales recorded, "except us, that is."[11]

Améstica's shipboard experiences may have been replicated many times
over by the prostitutes who went to California by sea, but it is not possible
to know how many independent prostitutes journeyed to California. However, there were occasional reports of the importation of women who were
evidently intended for the flesh trade, as in the case of a notice in the *Alta*
that a Frenchman had brought twenty of his countrywomen to San Francisco " — all they say are beautiful!" The news of their arrival inspired
"flotillas of young men" to go out and meet the ship that carried them.[12] A
few months later, a report in the San Francisco papers that two ships from
France had arrived with over three hundred women inspired a miner to
comment, "Gads, what a rich cargo. They will be worth their weight in
gold. . . . the imports of California are richer than the exports."[13]

Overlanders were not entirely bereft of sexual opportunities. These sexual liaisons are poorly documented, but two examples suffice to demonstrate activities that were probably widely known but seldom recorded. In
1849 Howard Stansbury reported that "a company of unprincipalled emi-

grants" committed "a gross and unprincipalled outrage" on some Shoshone women and killed the Indians who attempted to rescue them.[14] Another recorded sexual incident happened three years later, after tens of thousands of overlanders had passed through Shoshone country and sharply depleted Indian food resources. Travelers heedlessly killed game and overfished the streams, and their draft animals overgrazed the range and fouled watercourses. By 1852 Shoshones near the trail were suffering. In July, John Hudson Wayman, an Indiana physician, passed through Shoshone territory, near the present-day Utah-Nevada border. Wayman, who was obviously unhappy to have Indians in his camp, recorded "some d——d Indians sneaking around beging." Meanwhile, two of his companions "were conjureing around the Squaws," evidently hoping for sexual favors. Eventually, the two men gave an Indian woman "some victuals" with "care & solicitude without receiving any thing in return in sight." The woman led the men away from the wagon train and returned later "without any explanation," a suggestive chain of events that met with Wayman's disapproval.[15]

The argonauts' encounters with prostitution on the high seas and on the overland trek paled when they confronted the booming California gold-rush economy. The robust prostitute population no doubt amazed and delighted many men, but others were appalled. In 1852, Henry B. Sheldon, the Protestant missionary who had escorted two Catholic women to California, arrived at his first religious post, San Francisco. "This is a great city for a 'yearling,'" he marveled in a letter to his family, "almost a 2nd New York."[16]

Young Sheldon was as much a yearling as the city, and such men were easily led astray. He lived on the *Bethel*, a ship tied up at the San Francisco docks.[17] The landlord and the chief Methodist missionary was William Taylor, who was San Francisco's best-known street preacher in the 1850s.[18] Taylor was famous for standing on whiskey barrels to preach the gospel before the open doors of the saloons, gambling halls, and assorted dens of vice in the city by the bay and mining towns. "The chariot! The chariot! Its wheels roll in fire," he would sing, and the gamblers rolled out of the doors to hear him preach, or so he claimed.[19] But not all young men were drawn away from the high life by the preachers' words. Three of Taylor's contemporaries encapsulated the youthful and voluptuary spirit of the time.

[Gold] Dust was plentier than pleasure, pleasure more enticing than virtue. Fortune was the horse, youth in the saddle, dissipation the track, and desire the spur. Let none wonder that the time was the best ever made.[20]

Few young men who were so far from home could resist the temptations that San Francisco offered, and Brother Sheldon would find it difficult to abstain, too.

The California mission conference appointed Sheldon to preach in a district that included the Mission Dolores and the nearby "Spanish settlement" south of San Francisco's commercial center. Brother Sheldon was to evangelize at the mission on Sundays, and may have imagined that his principal challenge would be to dilute the Catholic influence of the Franciscans who had preceded him.[21] Imagine the astonishment of the young man from rural Ohio when he first spent a Sabbath at the mission. The mission had lately been the site of bear and bull fights, although these brutal entertainments had been outlawed. However, on Sunday there were often horse races. And worse, "The horses are frequently ridden by courtesans of whom there are in this city alone, nearly *one thousand* and there are no villages of any size in the country where they are not to be found — They are the *aristocracy.*" Courtesans rode in "the most splendid *carriages*, and on the most showy studs." He reported that all of the saloons, "if you pass in the evening," had prostitutes lined up at the bar in plain view of innocent promenaders, such as himself. "Who can find a virtuous woman," Sheldon asked rhetorically, adding with unintended irony that if one could be found her price would be far above rubies. The ratio of harlots to honest women was so great that the latter class had to "conduct themselves with the strictest propriety or be cast from the pale of good society," such as it was. San Francisco was not unique. As Sheldon noted, there were "no villages of any size" without prostitutes.[22]

Sheldon was deeply troubled by California's moral climate, and he was especially concerned about its impact on the young men who went there alone, without the support of family. He was gratified by the arrival of women and families on each ship that sailed into San Francisco Bay, but recognized the effects of bad company on single men like himself. "My disposition is so social," he told his mother, "& I am inclined to suit myself to the company that I am in so much that it often proves a snare to me — Oh for grace!" Not only did he need divine grace, the bachelor preacher needed an "assistant missionary," a wife.[23] "I want nothing physically more than 'The other half,'" he confessed.[24] Sheldon wondered if he would regret coming to California without a spouse, a question that the open prostitution he observed may have made more urgent.

Despite Sheldon's description of the San Francisco high life, most prostitutes lived desperate lives that were shadowed by violence, disease, alcoholism, and crime.[25] Only the most favored women were able to maintain a

16. MISSION DOLORES.

Also known as the Mission San Francisco de Asis, the Mission Dolores was the scene of horse races, bear and bull fights that Methodist missionary Henry B. Sheldon complained about. He was more impressed with the gambling and other illicit activities near the mission than with its religious function and symbolism. Here, Sheldon reported, "prostitutes road in 'splendid carriages' and on 'showy studs.'" Courtesy of the Bancroft Library.

high status in the world of vice, liquor, and gambling that they inhabited, let alone in the larger society. As Brother Sheldon warned, genteel women had to conduct themselves with care, lest they be taken for prostitutes. Virtuous women as well as men longed for increased female immigration to California, and they were not willing to associate with harlots in the meantime. Sarah Royce, mother of philosopher-historian Josiah Royce, recalled a San Francisco incident in 1850. Women from the various Christian churches had organized an "entertainment" to benefit a benevolent society. The event was proceeding pleasantly when a prominent business man entered, "bearing upon his arm a splendidly dressed woman, well known in the city as the disreputable companion of her wealthy escort." The woman in question may have been the man's mistress rather than a common prostitute, but such fine distinctions would have meant little to the devout Sarah Royce, who approvingly reported that at the behest of "the lady managers," a "committee of gentleman" asked the offending couple to leave. "While Christian women would forego ease and endure much labor, in order to benefit any who suffered, they would not welcome into friendly association any who trampled upon institutions which lie at the foundation of morality and civilization."[26]

Women who lived in the mining districts were no less anxious to disassociate themselves from prostitutes than those who lived in San Francisco. Mrs. D. B. Bates, a New Englander who lived in Parks Bar, Marysville, and San Francisco in the 1850s, reported that she had been "the unwilling observer of transactions, which, had they been related to me, would have shaken my opinion somewhat respecting the veracity of the narrator." She asked her readers to imagine a California town "where the females numbered more than two hundred," but "the pure, high-minded, and virtuous" residents "with all those ennobling sentiments which shed such a halo of loveliness around fair woman's shrine" would not have counted more than three or four.[27] There can be little doubt that in the unnamed town Mrs. Bates and two or three of her friends had a difficult time illuminating fair woman's shrine among so many prostitutes, faro dealers, and dance-hall women. She documented her point with the story of a woman who brought her fifteen-year-old daughter, "Lillie," to the mines, where she was seduced by a gambler who had abandoned his wife in the East. One sad scene followed another until Lillie had become one of those gaudily dressed San Francisco courtesans whom Brother Sheldon had described. And Lillie's tragic descent into immorality was not a singular tale, Mrs. Bates related. Many a woman had gone west to escape poverty and was tempted into moral ruin by the fast life and ready flow of gold dust. California "was a dangerous country" for single women to go to, "unless their principles were as firm as the rocks of their native hills."[28] Too close an association with men and women of low character, Mrs. Bates inferred, could destroy the virtue of formerly righteous females, thus keeping women from their rightful role — the reformation of male character and California society.

The pious Sarah Royce described the ejection of a woman of low morals from a San Francisco social event as a triumph for good society, but such conflicts could have serious consequences. In 1855 U.S. Marshal William Richardson, his new wife, and a woman friend attended a pantomime at the

"THE GREEN DEVIL SALOON."—See page 29.

17. THE GREEN DEVIL SALOON.

One of Alonzo Delano's *Pen Knife Sketches,* or Chips off the Old Block (Sacramento: Union Office, 1853), shows the rugged society of mining camps that women had to fit into. Drunken men, quarreling dogs, and dancers compete for space on the floor as the musicians play in the background. One dancer, evidently Delano himself, finds himself prostrate while a dog gnaws on his leg.

Courtesy of the California State Library.

New American Theater.[29] During the performance the women complained that a man was lewdly staring at them from the orchestra pit. Marshal Richardson confronted the man, who explained that he was looking at the woman seated behind the Richardsons, Belle Cora — keeper of an expensive bawdy house and the mistress of gambler Charles Cora. The women with Richardson unsuccessfully demanded that the two be removed from the theater, and after the show the marshal renewed the argument with the gambler. Two days later, Charles Cora killed Richardson with a derringer pistol. This killing inflamed public opinion, led to another murder, and culminated in the formation of a vigilance committee that hanged four men — including Charles Cora — and banished many others for their alleged crimes.[30] Neither the Coras nor prostitution were the underlying causes of the rise of the 1856 vigilance committee. Given San Francisco's political climate in 1856, if Cora had not killed Richardson some other event likely would have precipitated the emergence of the vigilantes. Rather, these famous events show that there were practical reasons for separating bourgeois women and men from their fellows of ill-repute. In the mid-nineteenth century, men were expected to defend the honor of their wives, mothers, sisters, and consorts. In a community where men customarily carried weapons, this could lead to violent death.[31]

While the chaos of early gold-rush society threw together people of all classes and castes, the social conventions of Anglo America exerted a centrifugal effect that stratified the population along well-known lines. People with solid bourgeois pretensions separated themselves from gamblers, prostitutes, and drunks, and it was one of women's duties to reenforce that separation. In California sisterhood was a divided institution, and courtesans, prostitutes, and saloon women were not members in good standing. As California's urban centers matured, city governments increasingly confined prostitution to well-defined vice districts away from the view of respectable women and their children, but where single men could easily find it. In San Francisco and smaller towns, the red-light districts were often associated with Chinatowns and other ethnic and racial enclaves, thus reenforcing Anglo ideas about race and sexuality. For example, the Los Angeles Mexican barrio, Sonora Town, became the vice district. The Chinese ghetto that grew up within the boundaries of Sonora Town was known as "Nigger Alley," further reenforcing and complicating prostitution's racial associations.[32]

Within the ranks of disreputable society, stratification occurred along racial, ethnic, and class lines. Because they formed the largest class of women during the early 1850s, California Indians were among the first

18. A BALL IN THE MOUNTAIN VILLAGE.

This humorous scene, also from Delano's *Pen Knife Sketches*, shows men lining up to dance with one of the few women at this social occasion. The hapless read newspapers and drink tea (or perhaps something stronger) while they wait their turn. Delano may have exaggerated the manners, but accurately reflected the demographic conditions in the mines where men far outnumbered women.

Courtesy of the California State Library.

prostitutes in the mining districts. Like other women of color, they were regarded by most Anglo miners as racially inferior and acceptable only for transient sexual gratification. Prostitution was not a usual part of California Indian society, but native women took it up in the most desperate circumstances. Starvation, Indian wars, and sexual assaults shaped their sexual lives.[33] The low prices that Indians received for their sexual services certified their low racial and sexual status among California's prostitutes. Moreover, Indian prostitutes ran risks in their own communities, as an 1851 incident in southern Oregon shows. After a young, one-eyed Indian woman had intercourse with a miner for some food, her husband appeared and threatened her. The next day, another Indian came to the camp and begged the whites to leave the women alone. He added that among his people the penalty for adultery was the loss of an eye.[34]

According to white observers, some central California tribes permitted husbands to punish unfaithful wives. W. P. Crenshaw, a special agent for the Office of Indian Affairs, thought that this indicated that Indians respected the institution of marriage, which was a good thing as far as he was concerned. "Few barbarous tribes of mankind," Crenshaw reported in 1854, "approach so near Civilization on the subject of marriage" as the Indians he had seen. Death had been the punishment for marital infidelity among the Nisenan, Konkow, and Maidu tribes, but Crenshaw reported only one recent execution in Sierra County, where the aggrieved husband had killed his wife with arrows. Otherwise, "for the last year they have permitted this crime to go unpunished when committed with whites." Consequently, adultery was increasing in Indian communities, especially in the vicinity of Nevada City, Grass Valley, Auburn, and Yankee Jim, where "lewdness among the young squaws" was "becoming very common." These liaisons had caused the spread of venereal diseases among Indians near the mining camps.[35]

Crenshaw made no direct connection between the increasing "lewdness" of Indian women and the death and poverty that he recorded in the same letter. He reported that in the central mines "death has reduced" the Indian population by "more than half in the last 4 years." He attributed their mortality rate primarily to disease, especially smallpox, but poverty and starvation were contributing factors. "Driven by pinching hunger," the Indians had to live on the offal from slaughter pens and the rotting carcasses of the emigrants' dead oxen. Little wonder that women turned to prostitution to feed themselves and their children. In the flush times of the gold rush, the prospect of easy money may have motivated some white women to take up the flesh trade, but dire poverty drove Indian women to prostitute themselves. Under these circumstances, the Indians who lived in the central mines were wise to waive punishment of wives who slept with white men.

Brute force as well as "pinching hunger" influenced the sexual lives of Indian women during the gold rush. White men kidnapped and raped native women with little fear of retribution from legal authorities. Under California's state constitution, a white person could not be convicted solely on the basis of Indian testimony.[36] Consequently, rapes of Indian women were widespread in gold-rush California. Whites even invaded rancherías and kidnapped tribeswomen for temporary sexual gratification. Even on a federal Indian reservation, the agents responsible for the Indian inmates raped women "before the very eyes of their husbands and daughters," a newspaper reported, "and they dare not resent the insult, or even complain of the hideous outrage."[37] Some observers blamed sexual assaults for Indian warfare in northern California.[38]

According to modern scholars, white men who raped Indian women did so for more complicated reasons than for mere sexual gratification.[39] The act of rape asserts the rapist's power over the victim and confirms her low status in his eyes. According to one psychologist, rape is "an effort to discharge . . . anger, contempt, and hostility toward women," and to "counteract feelings of vulnerability and inadequacy . . . and assert . . . power to control and exploit." Assailants are often moved by a "progressive and overwhelming sense of failure" and stress.[40] Other researchers emphasize that rapists lack adequate family ties.[41] Furthermore, in the mind of the rapist, Indian women's racial classification made them legitimate objects for sexual assault — a perspective that neatly reenforced the conquest and colonization of California Indians.[42] In the uncertain and clamorous gold-rush era, Indian women became objects through which violent men could express deep anxieties inherent in the frontier experience, sexual fears, and fantasies that were a part of the normative value system of Victorian American culture as well as the unique circumstances of California life. For the Indian women who lived in this disordered and violent world, rape and prostitution were different sides of the same coin. At least the women who took up prostitution exerted a modicum of control over their sexual lives and could contribute their proceeds to the meager fund of survival strategies that remained to them.

Indians were outraged at attacks on their women and often retaliated against white men who had assaulted native women, as in the case of Big Tom, a miner who met his end after abducting a Nisenan woman in 1855.[43] But some infuriated Indian men inflicted violence on tribeswomen who were the victims of white assailants. In 1859, a man named Abbott attempted to kidnap a Honcut Indian woman, and her husband killed her to keep her from the kidnapper. Subsequently, Abbott wounded the husband with a pistol. Then the rest of the Indians severely beat Abbott, a fate that some whites believed was well deserved. The local newspaper expressed indignation that a "squaw man" like Abbott could endanger the countryside by inciting the Indians in this way.[44] There were many similar incidents in California in the 1850s.[45]

The gold rush was a deadly period for California Indians, male and female alike. During the 1850s their population declined from about 150,000 to 30,000, but Indian women evidently died at a more rapid rate

than men, a circumstance that limited the ability of Indian society to recover demographic losses.[46] The deficit of Indian women intensified competition for potential wives in some Indian communities. In the mid-1850s,
John Sutter reported that fights over women were a special source of tension among the Nisenans who lived at his farm near Marysville. Sutter, who
had lived among these Indians since 1839, reported that during drunken
brawls Nisenan men assaulted women. One suitor murdered a woman who
had resisted his importunities.[47] While perhaps not typical, these incidents
show the horrific possibilities in a society with a rapidly declining population and few women.

The gold-rush population included people from Asia and Polynesia. Several native Hawaiians, or "Kanakas" as they were derisively called, had
come to California as John Sutter's indentured servants. One of them had
been Sutter's mistress.[48] Even before the gold rush California attracted
many Hawaiians. William Tecumseh Sherman recalled that when he arrived in Yerba Buena (soon-to-be San Francisco) in July 1847, the whole
population of the fledgling village was "about four hundred, of whom Kanakas . . . formed the bulk."[49] Some of these women turned to prostitution,
and Warren Saddler reported that a few of them were doing a brisk business
in Gold Run. His brief sketch of a Sunday morning in the mines conveys
how bleak prostitution in the mining districts could be. "We got up early —
went to the pit — Then over to Gold-run, to look about, found nothing very
flattering. We passed by the Grave-Yard — saw some persons digging
graves — several at work digging gold and hundreds at work gambling — all
in sight — and a party holding a sort of funeral and so it goes — You can
imagine what else there is — a house just below where there are several
Kanackers or Sandwich Island girls — there 'aint much of a crowd down
there,'" he added wryly. Saddler portrayed the tedium of the mining districts, where men waited their turn to have sex with a Hawaiian woman.
The view from the bordello must have been just as monotonous. There is
little romance in this vision of gold-rush prostitution.[50]

Chinese prostitutes have received more attention from scholars than all
other women of color who participated in the flesh trade. In the early
1850s, substantial numbers of Chinese men began to arrive in California,
but there were very few women who accompanied them. The 1852 state
census shows that there were 2,954 men, and only 19 women in San Francisco's Chinese population. Among these few women was Ah Toy, the first
Chinese prostitute in California, who arrived in late 1848 or early 1849.
Beginning as an independent prostitute with a white clientele, Ah Toy

married a white man, and became the lover of a vigilance-committee leader. In the early days of the gold rush, miners from the interior were so anxious to see her that they ran from the docks to her shanty, lined up, and paid one ounce of gold for her services. White commentators regarded her alternately as an exotic beauty and a public nuisance. She invested her earnings and became the madame of a Chinese brothel. By 1854, racial prejudice had advanced so far that local authorities applied laws against keeping disorderly houses exclusively to the Chinese, and in 1857 Ah Toy returned to China. Two years later she reappeared in San Francisco, but was less prominent than she had been in the early years of the gold rush.[51]

Ah Toy's decline in the bordello business was caused partly by racial discrimination, and partly by competition from the highly organized fighting tongs, Chinese syndicates that controlled vice in Chinatowns throughout California. The fighting tongs — which should not be confused with Chinese benevolent associations that existed at the same time — began importing Chinese women in 1853 or 1854. By 1860 there were 681 Chinese women in San Francisco, of whom 583 were prostitutes. Most of them were slaves imported by wealthy merchants and sold to brothel owners at regular auctions, where they reportedly brought three hundred to three thousand dollars. In the 1850s, new arrivals were auctioned at the San Francisco docks in full view of the police and spectators who watched as the young women disrobed and submitted to inspection. Eventually, public criticism forced these degrading spectacles to be moved to more secluded sites. This trade was said to have continued until the 1890s, when Protestant missionaries finally broke it up. Chinese secret societies controlled prostitution in San Francisco and elsewhere in the West where Chinese working men were their principal clientele. White prostitutes did not ordinarily accept Chinese customers, although Chinese women took whites. Because they were nonwhite slaves, whites regarded the Chinese as the most debased prostitutes, and critics of Chinese prostitution frequently mentioned their unfree status, which did not fit in with American political and sexual ideology, but which reenforced racist ideas about Chinese inferiority. They were also believed to be the most diseased courtesans, an idea that encouraged the 1870 California legislature to pass a law prohibiting Asian immigrant women from entering the state unless they could prove they were not prostitutes. Like other ethnically distinct prostitutes, Chinese women received a very low price for their work, as little as twenty-five cents, most of which went to their owners, who required their women to take all comers. Many Chinese prostitutes fled from the vice districts and otherwise tried to

19. CHINESE SLAVE GIRLS' BUILDING.

Probably taken in the twentieth century, this photograph purportedly depicts a building where young Chinese women were sold at auction in the 1850s. San Francisco was the main port of entry, and many Chinese women were sold into prostitution there. This photograph's notation indicates that similar sales were held in mining towns such as Mokelumne Hill.

Courtesy of the California State Library.

control their own lives, but it was a difficult struggle since they were at the mercy of the men to whom they were indentured. American law offered little relief.[52]

The story of Ah Toy and Chinese prostitution shows how ideas about race, culture, gender, and sexuality intersected in gold-rush California. The largest segment of the state's population consisted of white males, but most prostitutes were women of color. A close look at Sacramento shows how true this was. In 1860, federal census takers counted the townspeople in this medium-sized inland city. Situated on the Sacramento River, the town was the state capital and an important commercial center for the rich agricul-

Table 4.3 Sacramento City Population in 1860 by Race and Sex

Race	No. Males	No. Females	Total
White	8,113	4,265	12,378
Asian	808	180	988
Free Colored	253	141	394
Indian	13	12	25
Total	*9,187*	*4,598*	*13,785*

Derived from "Table No. 1 — Population by Age and Sex," *Population of the United States in 1860*, comp. Joseph G. C. Kennedy (Washington, D.C.: Government Printing Office, 1864), 30.

tural valley and adjacent mining districts. According to the published census, there were nearly fourteen thousand people living there, about two-thirds of whom were men, and most of them were white (see Table 4.3). Asians — most of whom were probably Chinese — were the largest minority (about 7 percent), but the published census did not specifically identify Mexicans or other Latinos who might well have been people of color. Nor does it mention prostitution.[53]

The unpublished manuscript census gives specific details about race and prostitution (see Table 4.4). More than three-quarters of Sacramento's prostitutes were women of color. More than 56 percent of the town's prostitutes were Chinese who had likely come to the valley by way of San Francisco's slave mart. Mexicans and other Latinas accounted for about 15 percent more. A small number of Black women added to the aggregate of prostitutes of color in the capital city.

On the whole, Sacramento prostitutes were young, with a mean age of twenty-three. One out of five were younger than eighteen; seven girls aged twelve to fourteen were available to satisfy the market demands of Sacramento's flesh trade. Distinctive age patterns marked the racial and ethnic diversity of these women. Chinese prostitutes were the youngest, with a mean age of twenty. They accounted for nearly 90 percent of teenaged prostitutes, although a few underage prostitutes were scattered among the U.S. white and Latina women. The mean age for all others ranged from twenty-five (U.S.-born whites) to thirty-two (European-born whites). The youngest members among this outcast class of women should properly be characterized as abused children, and those who were a little older in 1860 may have begun brothel life as children.

Most Sacramento prostitutes were also poor. Only six of them reported any personal property, and seven owned some real estate. These few elite

Table 4.4 Sacramento City Prostitutes by Age and Ethnicity in 1860

Race Ethnic.	Age 12–14		Age 15–17		Age 18–20		Age 21–25		Age 26–30	
	No.	%	No.	%	No.	%	No.	%	No.	%
U.S. White	0	0	2	1.0	3	1.5	13	6.3	7	3.4
Euro White	1	.5	0	0	0	0	3	1.5	7	3.4
U.S. Black	0	0	0	0	0	0	0	0	5	2.4
Mexican	0	0	0	0	1	.5	2	1.0	9	4.4
Other Latin	0	0	2	1.0	0	0	4	2.0	4	2.0
China	6	2.9	30	14.6	33	16.1	22	10.7	9	4.4
Total	7	3.4	34	16.6	37	18.0	44	21.5	41	20.0

women were all white, and some of them had accumulated substantial assets. Nearly half of that meager wealth was concentrated in a bordello on Second Street, where eight prostitutes, a Black cook, and a Black porter served Sacramento men. Kentucky-born M. C. Martin, who claimed to have one thousand dollars in personal property and ten thousand dollars worth of real estate, may have been the owner of this house — a remarkable achievement for a twenty-six-year-old prostitute. She may have shared ownership with two other women who lived there. Michigander Mary Hughes (twenty-three years old) and Georgian Alice Stewart (twenty-two years old), respectively, declared that they owned five thousand and three thousand dollars in real estate. They had like amounts of personal property. The three women owned 55 percent of the value of all property that prostitutes held in Sacramento. It is reasonable to suppose that this was one of the more prosperous bordellos in Sacramento.

Aside from these few outstanding exceptions, there is little to envy in the material and social lives of Sacramento's prostitutes. More than 60 percent of the city's harlots were minors or — in the case of the Chinese — unfree. Most of the pioneer prostitutes of early Sacramento were not a class of frontier entrepreneurs, but a poor, dependent, despised minority that was often marked by color. These women obtained few of the benefits of the gold-rush economy.

Courtship and Marriage

Prostitution embodied the relations of power, gender, race, and ethnicity in the context of a market economy that was driven by a deficit of potential

Age 31–35		Age 36–40		Age 41 +		Age Unknown		Total	
No.	%	No.	%	No.	%	No.	%	No.	%
0	0	4	2.0	1	.5	0	0	30	14.6
4	2.0	5	2.4	1	.5	0	0	21	10.0
2	1.0	1	.5	0	0	0	0	8	3.9
1	.5	2	1.0	0	0	3	1.5	18	8.8
1	.5	2	1.0	0	0	0	0	13	6.3
4	2.0	4	2.0	7	3.4	0	0	115	56.1
12	5.92	18	8.8	9	4.4	3	1.5	205	100

female sexual partners. The demographic and social conditions that characterized California affected courtship and marriage just as surely as they influenced prostitution. The lack of women meant that men who wished to marry had three choices. They could leave California and seek potential mates elsewhere, send away for a wife, or marry one of the few women in the state. Eligible women, on the other hand, could take advantage of an advantageous marriage market.

The experiences of the Bullard family children illustrate the differential operation of the marriage market on men and women in the gold rush. Benjamin and Eleanor Bullard emigrated from Michigan to California with their three sons and five daughters in 1853. The family settled in Sacramento, where they operated boarding houses. The oldest son, William, worked in the mines in Timbuctoo, Yuba County. The daughters remained with their parents until they were married, except for one who died. Most of the siblings wrote to their cousins and friends in Michigan. Courtship and marriage were frequent topics in their correspondence, and no wonder. Marriage opportunities abounded for women, a fact that was not lost on the Bullard family. As brother William put it, "Girls are bound to get married in this country [and were in] no danger of living to be old mades here."[54] In 1854, sister Andis married a man who owned a hotel and trading post in Fiddletown and ran a stage to Sacramento.[55] Sister Cordelia married a Sacramento man in the draying business the next year.[56]

Caroline, one of the younger daughters, penned a series of engaging letters that chronicled her transformation from a naive child to a teenaged belle. Her first impressions of Sacramento were less than encouraging. "We dont have menney appels and peaches," she explained, "but a good menney bed bugs and flees."[57] Nevertheless, Caroline quickly caught on to some of the advantages of California life for women. Sacramento was "a grate place to receive presents," and went on to enumerate the gifts she had received and the *cost* of each. The women dressed stylishly and all wore "low neck dresses. The little girls and big ones to and shorte sleeves."[58] Cordelia also remarked on women's dress. "Oh Aunt this is the greatest place you was ever in. It is all dress and nothing else. The ladies think they cannot step out of doors unless they have a silk dress on."[59]

The Sacramento social scene included an exhausting round of dances, where Caroline was in great demand. Mary, another of Caroline's older sisters, explained that "California is a fast country and a girl gets to be a young lady at twelve." Caroline, who was evidently in her early teens, soon had to beat the boys off with a stick. "Caroline has got to be a regular heart smasher," Mary revealed. "If you could only see the beaux that she has, and their hearts are ready to break on her account. Oh you would pity them."[60] She seemed to go to every dance and seldom missed a set unless she turned one down. One of these affairs went on until four o'clock in the morning. "Dont you think that is doing pretty well," she asked? Caroline had the energy and vivacity of youth. "When I went home I sat up till half past ten [in the morning] and then I went to bed and never woke up again untill twenty minutes of five then I got up and washed and got redy to waite on the table."[61]

Caroline would not wait on tables in her parents' boarding house for long. She had always liked school and regretted that her parents could not afford to send her to school until 1855 when she hopefully reported that she would study "natcheral philosophy and Algebrey."[62] Thus embarked on an aggressive program of personal improvement, Caroline became one of Sacramento's star scholars. Two years after matriculation she received a silver medal for an essay that she read in competition. An inscription on the medal read, "Caroline Bullard first scholar in Sacramento School No.1."[63] Now she was thinking about going on to high school, but if she did it was not for long. In 1858 she married A. A. Wood, a man who had crossed the plains with the Bullards.[64] Caroline was probably about sixteen and her husband was prosperous. He kept a stable for Sacramento teamsters, rented horses, and ran his own drays.[65]

Mary was the only marriageable sister who was reluctant to find a mate. For a time she seemed interested in a Sacramento blacksmith, but nothing came of it.[66] Mary was a little worried because there were plenty of men in California, "but not of the right stamp. You know I am rather old maidish in my choice of . . . a mate."[67] Mary had good reasons to get married, for she hated working in her parents' boarding houses. "If ever I was tired of anything it is living in a [public] house. It makes a perfect slave of a woman, for you have to wait on every body, and everything."[68] Around the time that she wrote these words Mary contracted tuberculosis, perhaps from one of the boarders on whom she waited. In 1858 she visited her sister Andis's family in the mountains, hoping no doubt that the mountain air would do her good. By now brother William had a mine with hydraulic machinery and tunnels. During Mary's mountain visit, William's claim caved in and injured him severely, breaking his arm, three ribs, and shattering the bone in one leg. Mary rushed to his cabin to nurse him, but became exhausted. In her weakened condition, the tuberculosis became acute. She died in June 1858 and was buried in the New Helvetia cemetery.[69]

By the end of 1858 only the youngest of the Bullard daughters was single, and she would marry in a few years.[70] As he watched his sisters marry, William expressed serious doubts about his chances for success in the California marriage market, in letters to his young Michigan cousin, Julia. In California, "the Girls are not very plenty." In his town of Timbuctoo, there was "one Girle . . . & I should judge thare was about two hundred young men from the age of 20 to 30 years." The rest of the mining towns had similar conditions. "Now Julia you see that the chances are slim for me to get a wife in California (for Squaw time is about over in California) so I think I shall have to go back to Michigan to get a Wife." If Julia knew of a young woman who wanted a husband, "just tell her that I am the *chap.*"[71] Of course, William was telling Julia that he was "the *chap*" for her. This was the beginning of a serious three-year correspondence with his young cousin, which he hoped would entice her to come to California and marry him.

William's reference to "squaw time" told a great deal about his ideas concerning suitable mates. There had been a time when an Indian would have been acceptable, but in the late 1850s that time was quickly fading even in the mines. William wanted a white woman, and not just any white woman would do. When he announced that there would be a Fourth of July ball a few miles from his mine, he declared that "as I dont like the kind I shant go. (The *kind* are Irish)."[72] William was aiming for Julia, a cousin with the requisite racial, ethnic, and probably religious characteristics that he valued. He made his racial views even more clear when he objected to the Civil War because it was being fought "to free the nigger." He was a "Demmocrat to the back bone" and assailed Republicans who belonged to the "Abolition Party."[73] They exchanged daguerreotypes and William hoped much, but in the end he was disappointed. In the fall of 1863, Julia told him that she had married. William took it well and hoped that they would continue their correspondence. "I shall feel just as proud of writing to and receiving letters from Mrs Julia Phillips as I did from Miss Julia Bullard." Besides, the lode of marriageable Michigan women might not yet be exhausted. "If one of your Sisters would like to hitch teams with your California Cousin just tell her to say so."[74] None of them did, but the "honest miner," as he called himself, finally hit pay dirt in 1868. He married Mary Farrell, a native of Ireland.[75]

The Bullard family's experience show plainly how the California marriage market favored women and worked against men who wanted to marry. Not only were there too few women, there were fewer still of the right "kind," as William Bullard put it. If a man wished to marry a woman of a particular ethnic, religious, or racial background, his chances for success were measurably reduced. Even the choosy William finally married an Irish woman, but only after ten years of fruitless prospecting had failed to turn up a woman with ethnic characteristics that he preferred.

The good-natured reverend Sheldon likewise found it difficult to locate a suitable spouse in California. However, his Pacific Coast sojourn had given him an opportunity to reflect on a woman he had known in Ohio, Miss Priscilla Welsh. Evidently, his parents had disapproved of his relationship with her and they may have hoped that his mission to the golden state would put an end to it. However, absence had made Henry's heart grow fonder. His loneliness and chronic diarrhea dosed with heroic portions of calomel and morphine may have added a dreamy urgency to his affection.[76] Priscilla accepted Henry's proposal and agreed to sail to California in late 1853. They were married in February 1854, and seven months later a son was born "early," or so the reverend Sheldon explained to his parents.[77]

Sheldon's letters made it plain that he loved Priscilla deeply, but their marriage was also a good business arrangement for the penurious preacher. Mr. Sheldon got twelve to fifteen dollars per week for his preaching, but this was mere pin money compared to his wife's earning power. Priscilla collected sixty-six dollars for a Sunday School exhibition, and she started a select school for which she received one hundred twenty dollars per month. They were also boarding a little boy and three girls at thirty dollars per month, exclusive of washing. Priscilla also gave piano and guitar lessons, and Henry was considering the purchase of a piano, an acquisition that he no doubt regarded as a good investment.[78] While Henry gathered in a harvest for the Lord, Priscilla brought home the bacon.

The Sheldons and the Bullards lived in a world of choices, however narrowly they may have limited the scope of their selections. They were white and they were free—characteristics that were by no means universal in the 1850s. Race and gender circumscribed the world of courtship and marriage, and those who lived outside the magic circle of white, bourgeois respectability had an even more difficult time in attracting and keeping mates. The limits that were placed on people of color were breathtakingly simple. John Dart, resident of Sonora and native of Mississippi, spoke with southern frankness about the influence of race on marital relations in the mines. "Free negroes are seen about when there is any Yankees," Dart explained to a friend, "but when they come across a man from the Southern States they have to toe the mark."[79] Dart lived in what he called the French neighborhood — probably a euphemism for Sonora's bawdy district — and routinely gave accounts of fights among the French women and the Mexican, Chinese, and African American miners. Dart analyzed these incidents with a finely honed sensitivity to their racial nuances. The plight of an African American miner caught his attention in late 1853. This freeman had married a Central American woman, but after residing in California for a few months she ran off with a white man, leaving her Black husband "disconsolate." Dart discussed the situation with the unhappy man. "I told him a big black ugly nigger" could not hope to hold on to a woman with "so many white men about."[80]

Dart's racial analysis could not have given any solace to the grieving black miner, but even the deeply prejudiced Dart recognized that race was not the only condition in play. "The devil gets in the women here, or perhaps it comes out of them. I suspect the latter. Eight women in ten that comes leaves their husbands."[81] Here was another effect of the gold-rush marriage market. Women could leave their old husbands for new ones who were richer or who otherwise suited them better. "It is rather a dangerous thing to marry a woman here for fear that some hombre will prosecute you or her for bigamy," the Mississippian claimed.[82]

Divorce

Dart exaggerated the proportion of women who left their husbands, but he was not alone in remarking on the phenomenon. Young William Stewart, the future U.S. senator from Nevada, noticed how the shortage of women in Nevada County affected their fidelity in 1850. Women were so scarce at the Buckeye Hill diggings that the appearance of one caused a near riot. When Stewart unexpectedly discovered a lone wagon with a clothesline sporting a woman's dress, he sent up the cry, "Oh Joe!" which alerted the men all along Deer Creek that something unusual was afoot. In a scene that could have inspired "Paint Your Wagon," they gathered around the immigrant camp

and encouraged the woman to come out. Evidently, she was too frightened
of the crowd of two thousand young, boisterous, bearded men to leave the
comparative safety of the wagon. They took up a collection of dust and
appointed Stewart to convince her to show herself to the miners. Every time
she emerged from the wagon, a shout went up and scared her back inside.
"She repeated this performance several times, and I kept slowly moving back
so the boys could have a good view of her," Stewart recalled. "I suppose half
an hour was occupied with her running back and forth while the boys looked
on in admiration, when I finally gave her the bag with all the good wishes of
the camp. She grabbed it and ran into the tent like a rabbit."[83]

The anonymous woman had been in the mines for less than a day and already it seemed that the wealth of Ophir was being showered on her merely
because she was a woman. The miners' display of appreciation for her
femininity must have been astonishing after the toilsome journey across the
plains. Surely no one in the wagon train had given her the kind of attention
that these sexually alert young miners had lavished on her. Perhaps because
of this avalanche of affection, the young couple moved on the next day.
The husband may have thought better of settling among so many gold-
laden men who were starved for female companionship. Certainly Stewart
thought it was a good decision, "for in those days it was a very usual occur-
rence for the young wife coming to that country to be persuaded to forsake
her husband on their arrival in the new camp."[84] Why? The hardships of
overland travel made the immigrant "men look rather rough and scrubby,
and they were all miserably poor," Stewart observed. "The women were
young, and after they had an opportunity to wash their faces, looked more
attractive — particularly to the miners who had been deprived of female society for many months and had accumulated some money."[85] So the miners
bought some new clothes and began to court the wives of other men. In a
settled country such behavior would be at least scandalous and very likely
dangerous, but in California it was accepted even if it was not respected.

While some wives responded to the illicit mating cries of well-off miners,
others sought divorce because their mates had abandoned or abused them.
Hopkins, who relished a world where every man acted according to his
"own will and pleasure," was particularly concerned with the impact of
gold-rush conditions on marriage and the family. Husbands — Hopkins
called them California widowers — often abandoned their marriages when
they left their wives back east. Other men brought their spouses with them,
but became dissolute in the wide-open days of the gold rush. So, Hopkins
argued, why should women be punished for the sins of their husbands?

A LIVE WOMAN IN THE MINES.—See page 16.

20. A LIVE WOMAN IN THE MINES.

Alonzo Delano, a keen observer of gold-rush life, provided this sketch of a newly arrived woman in the mines in his *Pen Knife Sketches*. It is reminiscent of William Stewart's description of an immigrant woman near Nevada City in 1850. The miners are highly enthusiastic and show their appreciation by firing pistols, dancing, and waving their hats. The comely woman, perhaps the wife of the man who proudly presents her to mining-camp society, demurely drops her eyes while standing before a tent and cooking fire — symbols that represent a more elaborate home and hearth and fully developed forms of domesticity to come.

Courtesy of the California State Library.

Because "the gallantry of public sentiment sympathizes with an ill-married female," he continued, public opinion inadvertently excited "against her the jealousy and revenge of a bad husband."[86] Rather than condemn the wife to a lifetime of spousal abuse, let her divorce.

Hopkins wanted to retain California's liberal divorce law, which he be-

21. NEAR NEVADA CITY, 1852.

An unknown photographer made this daguerreotype showing the men and equip-
ment that created a typical mining landscape. It might have been near the spot
where William Stewart discovered the immigrant woman and called "Oh Joe!" to
gather men like these to join him.

Courtesy of the California State Library.

lieved protected women's rights. An 1851 statute permitted women and
men to sue for divorce on grounds of natural impotency, adultery, extreme
cruelty, willful desertion, neglect, fraud, and conviction of a felony. The
state legislature and courts progressively liberalized divorce law throughout the nineteenth century. Aggrieved wives and husbands alike took advantage of this law, but more women than men sued for divorce. A careful
study of divorce actions in the 1850s and 1860s, in San Mateo and Santa
Clara counties, reveals that about three times as many women as men
sought divorces. More than 70 percent of female plaintiffs won a divorce in

court in these years, a success rate that climbed in subsequent decades. Perhaps because of the relative ease of obtaining a divorce, Californians divorced at a much greater rate than other Americans, a difference that increased during the nineteenth century. By 1880 the ratio of married to divorced couples in California (239:1) was about half that of the United States as a whole (481:1).[87]

The cruelty provision in the California divorce statute proved to be popular with women who sought divorces. Stewart believed that it was little more than a ploy that gave a shadow of legality to divorce proceedings that he witnessed in the mines. In the fall of 1851, Stewart was foreman of a jury that decided ten divorce cases in one day. "The charge in each case was extreme cruelty, and the principal witness for each plaintiff — in all cases the wife — was her new friend who was engaged to marry her as soon as she could get the old love off."[88] The jury granted ten divorces, and there were ten weddings in the afternoon. In his later years Stewart still believed that granting the divorce was the best thing that the jury could have done. Had they not done so, the women might have done something worse. As it was, "Some of them made good citizens and raised families, and when they grew rich became very aristocratic."[89]

Not all Californians were as satisfied with the practical results of the California divorce law as Stewart. When the legislature considered the 1851 divorce bill, the *Alta* editors categorically denounced it and all divorce laws:

> They are all reprehensible, all opposed to good morals, all at variance with the principle of marriage, all tending to encourage immorality, dissatisfaction and alienation of feeling, all incompatible with the great source whence the civilized world draws its ideas of the sanctity of an oath and the sacredness of the marriage contract, all an insult to the Bible and the principles of Christianity.[90]

The editors went so far as to compliment the Roman Catholic Church for its stand against divorce. California society was already so loose that men took wives with as much "sang froid" as they might when purchasing a horse. If a man did not like the animal he had bought or the woman he had married, he could always discard them and obtain suitable replacements. Women "fish for partners with as much unconcern as ever Isaac Walton flung a fly upon the surface of a brook."[91]

The divorce law passed and the *Alta*'s editors settled into a consistent critique of the law and the ways in which it was administered. Divorce was

22. NEVADA CITY, 1852.

Nevada City was a prosperous mining town that outlasted the gold rush and became the seat of Nevada County government. Here, William Stewart was foreman of a jury that granted ten divorces in one day and saw the divorcées marry their new lovers that same evening.

Courtesy of the California State Library.

too easy to obtain, they claimed, and was granted on frivolous grounds. Worse, a jury did not hear the cases. Judges gave the divorce actions to a referee who privately examined them, and made recommendations that the judges usually accepted.[92] "California is becoming notorious for the rapid, steam-engine manner in which the family tie is severed," said the *Alta*, "and it has almost come to be considered that there is an alienating quality in our very air."[93]

Alienating qualities were not located in the air, but in the demographic imbalances of California's population. There were too many men competing for too few women. This basic fact was plain in the operation of the marriage market, where women had many opportunities to marry and men had few. The same forces that impelled the marriage market drove the divorce mill. Relatively lax divorce proceedings in the golden state certainly presented new opportunities and options to women, but dissolutions of marriage are best understood in economic rather than feminist terms. Whatever the legal and moral arguments for divorce may have been, divorce added women to the marriage market—if only briefly—where men could select them. The general effect of liberalized divorce was to redistribute scarce resources—women—in the competitive and inflated gold-rush economy. Of course, the marriage market did not operate according to strict laws of supply and demand, nor did buyers and sellers follow only their own best material interests. Emotional, social, religious, and other factors were also at work. Still, it is noteworthy that without prompting from women, a government of men enacted a law that made it easier for women to dissolve their marriages. This statute benefited some of California's horde of single men as well as the dissatisfied wives whom it liberated.

Dame Shirley's Courtship, Marriage, and Divorce

Among California's dissatisfied wives happened to be one of the most well-known women of the gold rush era, Louise Amelia Knapp Smith Clapp, or Dame Shirley as she is more popularly known. Clapp became famous for her descriptions of mining life in letters that she wrote to her sister in 1851 and 1852. In 1853, she began publishing the letters in *The Pioneer*, the same journal that printed Hopkins's article on divorce in 1854. Since then the letters have been republished in book form several times, and Dame Shirley has become one of the most quoted sources on life in the mining camps.[94]

Dame Shirley's prominence in gold-rush history invites attention to her formative years in New England, where she cultivated her ideas about sex, gender, marriage, and (presumably) divorce. Dame Shirley began life in 1819 as Louise Amelia Knapp Smith, the daughter of a relatively well-off family with roots in Amherst, Massachusetts. Smith's parents died in 1832, leaving her and six siblings in the care of adult relatives and guardians. She attended Amherst Academy, where she learned to appreciate the popular authors and poets of her day. There is some evidence that she briefly taught school in Amherst, but otherwise she did not work. Evidently, she relied on her small inheritance and lived with friends and relatives. Altogether, Miss Smith led an agreeable, middle-class, cultured, New England life.[95]

In her regional travels, she encountered a remarkable man who encouraged her literary aspirations, Alexander Hill Everett. Everett was the older brother of Edward Everett, the well-known orator, clergyman, and sometime president of Harvard University. Alexander was as accomplished as his younger brother. He held diplomatic posts in Russia, the Netherlands, Spain, Cuba, and China. Everett edited the *North American Review* (1830–35), and corresponded with the leading literary figures of his day. His publications included works of poetry, translation, criticism, and history, comprising a bibliography that fills ten printed pages.[96]

Well traveled, erudite, and politically well connected, forty-nine-year-old Everett must have greatly impressed twenty-year-old Louise Smith when they met while riding in a Vermont stagecoach in 1839. They struck up a conversation as they rode along in the moonlight, reciting lines from their favorite poets. Everett, though a married man, was smitten and initiated a correspondence with Smith, who evidently was flattered at the intellectual attention that the older man paid her. He intimated that she had literary talent and helped her publish an essay in a magazine.[97] But Everett was not interested in Louise's literary talents only. After two years of letters filled with talk of history and literature, Everett began a new phase in his correspondence with Louise, after she revealed that she reserved his letters for her eyes only. He wished to be her "confidant," he declared, and especially wanted her to tell him about her romantic experiences. He encouraged her to write freely by revealing some of his own "love experiences" with "three fair dames with whom I was . . . over head and ears in love,— Platonic of course." All three women, like Louise, were "blooming spinsters, but have since been all, to use your expression, 'resolved into the nothingness of matrimony.'"[98]

His "love experiences" were poems that praised the physical beauty and other charms of the three young women to whom they were dedicated. The poems were "Platonic" enough, to the point of being formulaic and pedestrian, yet the emotional shift that they signaled warned Louise that her relationship with Everett was on a new and dangerous footing. Her response was uncharacteristically late and not as forthcoming as Everett had hoped. She had never been in love, she said, but he did not believe her. "I cannot quite trust what you say about never having felt la belle passion, that being a subject upon which ladies have always claimed the privilege of saying no when they mean yes." Even if she was being truthful, he assured

Louise that her time to fall in love was still to come. "When it does you must not forget to make me your confidant."[99]

In the meantime, "as you kindly request it," he would reveal one more of his love adventures.[100] Without mentioning names, Everett recounted his first meeting with Louise on the stagecoach where they struck up a conversation. Their pleasant talk about his travels was interrupted by a stop, after which a new passenger took Louise's seat in the crowded coach so that they could not continue their discussion when their journey resumed. Everett was resigned to a silent trip when Louise asked to exchange seats with another passenger so that she could sit opposite Everett and continue their talk. Everett and Louise were "obliged . . . to dovetail themselves together . . . so as to bring themselves into the least possible compass." Thus Everett was "tied up in the same bundle with a young lady," in whom he felt "an interest." Now in physical contact with Louise, Everett recited the romantic verse of Byron and other poets. He believed that they had been in "complete sympathy" and "that we were enjoying some of the most agreeable emotions, of which our nature is capable, in expressing our mutual thoughts and feelings in the finest poetry." This intellectual and moral harmony was "Love, in the higher purer sense of the term. . . ." To seal his case, he quoted Sir Walter Scott:

> It is the secret Sympathy,
> The velvet cord, the silken tie,
> Which heart to heart, and mind to mind
> In body and in soul can bind.

"I was therefore, (Platonically, of course) in love with the young lady," Everett confessed, "and I flattered myself, at the time, that the feeling was reciprocal." Everett was disappointed in Louise's "insensibility." Perhaps the feeling had been one-sided, but he still hoped that Louise had "a little more feeling than she is willing to allow."

Evidently, Louise was unwilling to share her feelings and experiences with Everett, but he continued to press her to confide in him. After all, he explained, "it is a part of the charm of a really confidential friendship between persons who are fitted to appreciate each other . . . to commune or write about the tenderest and dearest affection of the heart without reserve."[101] Perhaps such revelations were less charming to Louise because there was nearly thirty years difference in their ages. Maybe there was nothing to reveal. Possibly she sensed that the vast disparity in their ages, marital status, social condition, experience, and power made an intimate relationship between them inappropriate, even if it remained "Platonic, of course." And perhaps Everett was right in supposing that there was a little more feeling than Louise was willing to allow.

Everett began to sign himself "father confessor" and to refer to Louise as his "penitent," even though she evidently continued to resist his demands for intimate information. Yet she continued to reply to his missives, evidently appreciating the window to a wider literary, social, and political world that his letters opened to her. In late 1844, Everett sent Louise a letter that was more graphic than any he had written before. He told her of a dream that seems to have been erotic and asks her if she has had a similar dream. "I embrace you anew in the spirit," he concluded.[102]

Everett's description of the dream disturbed Louise. She told him not to dream of her again and she (or someone else) destroyed the part of the letter that contained his description of the dream. Everett chose to misconstrue Louise's concerns about his dream of her, and continued to ask her about her reaction to his letter.[103] "It seems to me that the 'largest liberty' of communication between a Father Confessor and a Fair Penitent, who have as much reason as we have to repose confidence in each other, would be mutually and entirely advantageous, as well as agreeable." To support his case, he quoted a French poem in which a woman wore garlands to induce the world at large to dream of her.

> Content, — perforce, — at least at night
> To clasp in dreams the vision bright
> I worship all the day.[104]

Everett took a diplomatic post in Macao, China, but he continued to urge her to comment directly on his dream. She adamantly refused and demanded that he not dream about her, but he insisted. "You . . . will not permit me, though an acknowledged and favored lover, (Platonic of course) so much as to dream about you." But how could he control his dreams? "Suppose that my dreaming Pegasus should happen . . . to take the bit between his teeth and overleap the prescribed bounds; — I should like to Know . . . how your ladyship will enforce your decree or ever punish me for breaking it."[105] Despite her admonitions, Everett went on dreaming about Louise and she consistently berated him for it. He argued against the logic of her position. How could she criticize him for communicating with her in dreams while she continued to write to him on "two sheets of paper," the immaterial difference being that the sheets in his case were "of cotton or linen cloth." Her objections amounted to mere "prudery."[106]

Everett's sophistry thinly masked his anger with Louise, a rage that was kindled when she refused to join his discourse about his nocturnal fantasies and that blazed bright when she told him that she was to be married. Louise's decision to be "resolved into the nothingness of matrimony" surprised Everett, who wondered if he had driven her to it. Had "all her displeasure, anxiety, [and] perplexity at the presumption of the said *directeur* [Everett] in alluding to dreams about the Penitent eventuated in initiating his example, and plunging head foremost into the same gulf of impurity, corruption and atheism, in which he is already wallowed up?" Who was the lucky man and how did they meet? he sarcastically asked. What were the details of the romance and the wedding she was planning? Why had she not revealed this attraction to him before? How did Cupid insinuate his arrow into her heart? "Oh woman! — but I forbear: I will say, however, that I owe you another lecture still longer than the preceding one, for such sins of omission & commission." In the meantime, "I salute most respectfully the tips of your seraphic wings & I [re]main your friend & father confessor."[107]

This was Everett's last letter to Louise. He died in Macao in May 1847. In death Everett may have had an even stronger hold on Louise's psyche. He had shared with her a premonition that he would die in China. Perhaps in death their disembodied spirits would meet again. "We may then exchange assurances of mutual affection without the intervention of 'half the . . . world' between us, and in a more satisfactory shape, than the shadowy [embodiments?] of Dream-land." Everett would have his way with Louise yet.

The power of Everett's continuing spiritual presence in Louise's life should not be underestimated. He did not introduce the idea of spiritualism to her, but seized on her deep-seated spiritual beliefs. As early as 1840, one of her young women friends had asked Louise to "remember how many times we spoke of the pleasure we should receive from communion in spirit although absent in the flesh. May my spirit often be cheered by such communions! He! He!!"[108] In 1854, Louise (now under the nom de plume Shirley) published her views on the spirit in *The Pioneer.* She believed that people were in awe of the dead because they knew not where the spirit lived. Perhaps it "crouches lovingly upon the pulseless bosom of its old companion," or "it may be gazing at us with its solemn, spirit-eyes, trying to make us conscious of its presence, and of its glad, wild freedom."[109] Thus, there remained the possibility in Louise's mind that Everett was watching even as she rambled in the California mines and penned her memorable gold-rush letters.

Perhaps Everett was correct in assuming that his importuning letters had somehow impelled Louise into marriage, but she had other reasons to marry as well. She was nearly thirty and her small inheritance (two thousand dollars) could not have been adequate to support her. Without a steady income Louise had few options. She could marry, rely on charity, or perhaps work as a schoolteacher. She chose to marry Fayette Clapp in 1848 or 1849, the lucky man to whom she referred in her last letter to Everett. In 1849, Dr. Clapp caught gold fever and the couple sailed for California.[110]

Whatever her motivation to marry may have been, Louise's marriage apparently was not a happy one. If they corresponded, she did not preserve his letters, but she complained about him in her letters to her sister. She portrayed Fayette as a sickly, inept bungler who got lost on the trail, made poor business decisions, and did not prosper in California.[111] Louise was not one to suffer silently while her husband blundered. Moreover, she was prone to fits of nervousness and recurring headaches that came to her "at the most inconvenient seasons."[112] It may not have been helpful to their relationship that Shirley publicly aired Mrs. Clapp's occasional complaints about Mr. Clapp in *The Pioneer,* however humorously they may have been phrased.

Louise's complaints about Fayette may have been linked to a more general critique of marriage, which, she believed, resolved women into nothingness. In describing a woman who made one hundred dollars a week by washing and ironing for miners, she added that while not all women could be *"manglers; the majority of the sex must be satisfied with simply being mangled."*[113] The mangling profession, of course, was beneath Louise whose genteel, middle-class upbringing forbade such occupations, no matter how well they paid. She was happy to pay inflated gold-rush wages to someone else rather than do her own laundry, even though her husband's earnings were inconstant at best.

Louise was not an especially supportive helpmeet; neither was she a feminist. In her letters, she denounced Bloomers and the women who wore them. Women who demanded their "rights" were deluded. "How *can* they spoil their pretty mouths and ruin their beautiful complexions," she asked, "by demanding . . . in the presence, often, of a vulgar, irreverent mob, what the gentle creatures, are pleased to call their 'rights'?"[114] Under the name Shirley, she dilated at length on this subject in the pages of *The Pioneer* in 1854. She argued for separate but equal spheres in the tropes of the cult of true womanhood. Women had no place in public discourse with all of its coarsening effects. Men were worldly and intellectual, while women were intuitive and domestic. Man thought "with that unimpressionable head of his;" woman "with her pure, lofty and passionate heart." She concluded her essay with a stanza from Johann Christoph Friedrich von Schiller's "Worth of Woman":

> Woman, contented in silent repose,
> Enjoys in its beauty, life's flower as it blows;
> And waters, and tends it with innocent heart,
> Far richer than man with his treasures of art;
> And wiser by far in her circle confined,
> Than he with his science, and flights of the mind.[115]

Alexander Everett translated and published "Worth of Woman," and had recited it for Louise during the initial carriage ride in 1839.[116] Seven years after his death, something of Everett's spirit was still with Louise.

In late 1852, the Clapps left the mines and ventured to San Francisco. By then their marriage was beyond repair. He decamped for the Sandwich Islands and eventually returned to Massachusetts, leaving Louise in San Francisco. It is impossible to say what role her literary ambitions may have had in his decision to leave. Whether Fayette knew or approved of his wife's publications is unknown. Her letters began to appear in *The Pioneer* in January 1854, and her essay "The Equality of the Sexes" came out in February. In November she began teaching in the San Francisco public schools, an occupation that lasted until 1878. She added to her meager teacher's salary by offering night classes in art and literature.[117]

Louise filed for divorce from her absent husband in October 1856, and a San Francisco judge, acting on the recommendation of a referee, dissolved the marriage in April 1857.[118] She was thirty-eight years old. Fayette must have been in touch with her about this matter, for he remarried "around 1857," as the Clapp family genealogist put it.[119] Interestingly, Louise did not remarry. In the inflated marriage market of the 1850s, it is difficult to believe that she lacked opportunities. She was well known in San Francisco society for her weekly literary salon and other cultural entertainments that she produced for schools and her church. Those who knew her described her as small and finely made, though a bit frail and prone to nervousness. One of her students, Viola Tingley Lawrence, reported that there was at least one male admirer, Galen Clark, discoverer and manager of the Mariposa Redwood Grove, where Louise once vacationed.[120] That she remained single was likely a matter of personal choice. With no children of her own, Louise adopted her orphaned niece, who became an artist of some note.

By all accounts, Louise felt the strain of her myriad responsibilities, but weekly outings to the ocean reinvigorated her and provided a chance to educate and amuse the pupils who accompanied her. One of her students reminisced about these day trips and pictured Louise, "shoes and stockings off," wading into the surf and then resting on warm beds of sand.[121] Perhaps she wondered if her father confessor's spirit watched as she squeezed the wet sand between her toes and the salt water dried on her ankles. Did she count herself fortunate to have reemerged from the void of marriage? Did she resolve never to obliterate herself again? The record is silent on these matters. In 1878, Louise returned to the East, where she lived until 1906. She died at Overlook Farm, a home for elderly women in New Jersey.[122]

Neither Louise Amelia Knapp Smith Clapp of Amherst and San Francisco, nor Dame Shirley, the much-quoted chronicler of mining life, fit neatly with the stereotypes that were constructed for California women in their own time or in ours. If she was not quite the submissive, domestic wife and mother that middle-class Americans ostentatiously celebrated, neither was she one to conspicuously violate the conventions of her time. She made use of California's liberal divorce law, but unlike most California divorcees, she did not remarry. Nor did she use her literary talent to gain a living as an author, although there is some evidence that she may have tried to do so.[123] Instead, Louise used her freedom in very conventional ways. She became a schoolteacher, acting out the role of feminine civilizer and redeemer of the West that Catherine Beecher and other Christian reformers had decreed for women.[124] Even in California, where people thought "a thousand times more freely" than easterners, according to Caspar T. Hopkins, there were limited opportunities for women outside marriage. Louise embraced those limits even as she broke the marital bond and defiled the institution that men and women of her generation held most dear.

Dame Shirley was by no means typical of the women who ventured to California in the gold rush, but her life serves to make a point about the social life that emerged in those seemingly chaotic times. Like many other Californians, she relied on past experiences and widely accepted conventions in making a life for herself in California. California law made it possible for her to divorce, but otherwise she behaved little differently than if she had been widowed in Massachusetts. Dame Shirley was a transplanted New Englander, not a new-made woman inspired by the opportunities that California's isolation and singularity may have fostered. She regarded her time in the mines as a brief adventure, not as a life-altering experience when it came to intimate matters. The other middle-class women in California seemed to agree.

For their part, California men seemed to long for the kind of social life that they enjoyed "back in the states," where the conventions of courtship and marriage — and chances for success in the marriage market — were well known and predictable. For most men, the allure of the fast life and flush times in the Bonanza West were temporary substitutes for the solid comforts of family life and spousal companionship. Insofar as they could, they lived their lives according to preferences and prejudices that were embedded before they went to California. Their hope was to replicate the society and culture of the East, and it was woman's task to help them do it.

FIVE

Amelia's Body:

The Limits of Female Agency in Frontier California

The woman was very well formed, and there was ample room for the passage of the child from the body. The neck of the uterus was hanging in the vagina about an inch & half, and that was the portion ruptured. On the removal of the uterus and its appendages from the body, the rupture referred to was about an inch & half. The neck of the uterus had undergone very severe inflammation, and had commenced decomposition and should judge that it had commenced many hours ago. The body of the uterus was very much inflamed, and [showed] considerable difference in the thickness of its parts. The inflammation extended from the mouth of the uterus and through its fimbriated extremities, and thence proceeded and involved the omentum, it was highly congested and considerably inflamed. The inflammation found together with the rupture at the mouth of the uterus was sufficient to cause death. Should think that the child had been six months in the uterus. The violence has been done by mechanical means I should think. The inflamation was not over a week standing, and was very violent.

S. B. SEWALL, M.D., 1860

We find the deceased has been pregnant. We find on making the Post Mortem examination The Omentum highly congested. . . . I think the death was caused by peritonitis. I think violence has been used to produce premature delivery.[1]

HENRY D. BATES, M.D., 1860

Details are sparse and the records are few, but on March 14, 1860, something extraordinary happened in Shasta County. On that date a very private matter became a public event as a community bore witness to what it suspected about the sexual lives of two of its inhabitants. The central figure in this incident was the body of Amelia Kuschinsky, the fifteen- or sixteen-year-old servant of a local merchant. Amelia was dead, and many believed her to be the victim of her employer, August Stiller, a cruel seducer who tried to hide his crimes with an abortion that took the young woman's life, or so they thought. The county coroner held an inquest over Amelia's body in Stiller's house, where she had died. The jury heard seventeen pages of testimony from twelve witnesses and reached a verdict: "We the Jury of Inquest over the body of Amelia Kuschinsky, a young lady aged about sixteen years, after examining the body, and listening to testimony in her case, give it as our verdict, that the said Amelia Kuschinsky came to her death at August R. Stiller's house on Dry Creek, on Wednesday the 14th of March AD 1860, from premature child-birth wilfully produced by violence by the hands of Dr Gutmann of Horsetown, and August R. Stiller of Dry Creek both of Shasta County Cal."[2]

A mob soon gathered at the Stiller house and seized Gutmann. Stiller had already fled. The crowd might well have lynched Gutmann for his alleged crimes, but for the timely arrival of Sheriff Follonsbee, who arrested Gutmann and took him to jail (probably in Shasta), where he posted bail of two thousand dollars. The local newspaper editor urged everyone to be calm until all the facts were known.[3]

The community in which these events unfolded consisted of several mining camps in southwestern Shasta County, where Pierson B. Reading found gold on Clear Creek in 1848. The next year, three hundred or more miners had gathered there and called the place Clear Creek Diggings. A few miles to the southwest, Dry Creek attracted its share of miners, as did Piety Hill, which was about one mile west of Clear Creek. In 1851, so one story goes, a prospector with one horse arrived at Clear Creek Diggings and the place became known as One Horse Town. Another version of the tale has it that a favorite horse that grazed in the vicinity was the town's namesake. However it may have been named, the place appeared as One Horse Town on an 1851 map and in the state census of 1852. Later, in the 1850s, it was renamed Horse Town, then Horsetown, perhaps because townsmen wanted to escape the unflattering implications of the earlier name, although phonetic renderings of the new expression might add even larger insults to the townswomen's pride. In its heyday, Horsetown had a population of about one thousand, which made it one of the largest towns in the county. It boasted a hotel, newspaper, post office, one Catholic Church, and fourteen saloons.[4] That the town was the home of at least two physicians in 1860 was testimony to its size and prosperity.

What stirred this rough community to action when the Shasta County Coroner's jury assembled in the home of August Stiller to examine Amelia's corpse? The eight jurors—all men—called twelve witnesses—six neigh-

23. SHASTA.

The town of Shasta, the Shasta County seat, looked much like this in 1860, when Dr. Gutmann was tried for causing the death of Amelia Kuschinsky by performing an abortion. The placid scene in this illustration belies the conflicts that were inherent in the county's population structure. As in other goldrush era communities, men far outnumbered women. This demographic fact caused intense competition for the few available women.

Courtesy of the California State Library.

borhood women and six men, including two physicians. First, the physicians performed an autopsy and found that Amelia had been pregnant. There was an inch-and-one-half rupture at the mouth of the womb that had begun to decompose. Doctor Henry Bates believed that the young woman had died of peritonitis—a painful infection of the membranes of the abdominal cavity. Doctor S. B. Sewall described the uterus and associated structures, noted extensive inflammation, and concluded that the injury was sufficient to cause death. The implications seemed clear to the physicians. A bungled abortion had caused the death of Amelia Kuschinsky. The jury concurred and accused Stiller and Gutmann of causing her death.[5]

The coroner's inquest revealed much more than medical details of Amelia Kuschinsky's pregnancy and death. Testimony also pieced together the social context in which these events occurred and disclosed much about small-town life at the end of the gold-rush era, especially attitudes about illicit sex and abortion. We also learn something about the world of western women and the special perils some of them faced in the mid-nineteenth-century California.

Exactly when Amelia arrived in the small community of Horsetown, or when she took up residence in the Stiller household, is not known. She was probably born in eastern Europe, since according to a neighbor's testimony Stiller had considered sending her back to the "old country again."[6] Stiller was from Prussia, and it is possible that he brought her with his family as a household servant.[7] He was a thirty-two-year-old merchant who had prospered in the gold-rush economy. He was married to Louisa, a twenty-nine-year-old native of Württemberg. They had two daughters, aged two and three, and a one-year-old son, all of whom were born in California.[8]

There would have been plenty of work for Amelia in such a household, and Louisa would have been glad for the help. Food preparation, splitting kindling, getting water, gardening, and cooking on an iron stove were arduous and time-consuming tasks. Keeping a house neat and reasonably clean in the hot, dusty California summer was a constant challenge. Washday for three adults and three children — at least two of whom were still in diapers — would have been downright harrowing. To do the job right, the women would have collected rainwater when it was available. Then they boiled it and shaved cakes of soap into it. Clothes sorted into whites, colored, work clothes, and rags were scrubbed on a board, rinsed, and hung out to dry. Whites required starching with a flour preparation and blueing. One woman who described this work in South Dakota concluded her account of the routine with "brew a cup of tee, set and rest and rock a spell and count blessings."[9] Surely on washday Louisa counted Amelia as one of her blessings. At other times, she might not have been so sure.

Louisa's life must have been difficult, even with the help of a servant. She had her children in quick succession, scarcely recovering from one birth before becoming pregnant again.[10] Louisa was pregnant with her youngest child when neighbors began to suspect her husband of having "improper intercourse" with Amelia.[11] At the inquest, Louisa claimed that she had been "kept in perfect ignorance of the whole affair," but it is difficult to believe that she could have remained completely ignorant of Amelia's condition or an illicit relationship with her husband in such close quarters. If Amelia and her husband were sleeping together, Louisa's feelings about it are impossible to know. She may have been angry and jealous, or perhaps she was secretly relieved that August's erotic needs were being satisfied elsewhere. Even if he was entirely innocent, Louisa could not have been pleased with the prospect of a pregnant servant. Instead of a helper, Mrs. Stiller would have another burden to bear on the bleak, California frontier.

August Stiller was born in Prussia in 1828. He reported his occupation as "trader" to the census taker, and he had done pretty well at it. He claimed to have three thousand dollars in personal property, evidently enough to support his young family and keep a servant. Precisely when he had arrived in California is not known, but all of the Stiller children had been born there, so it was no later than 1857. It seems likely that he had a store in nearby Horsetown where he took in the miners' dust in exchange for goods. If he was like other gold-rush merchants, he advanced goods to independent miners for a season of prospecting and hoped for a good return on his investment.

Stiller's prosperity and social station may be better understood when he is compared with another merchant in similar circumstances. Franklin Buck established his trading house in Weaverville, about forty miles northwest of Horsetown. He was married in 1859, but had no children. Buck figured that it cost he and his wife about ten dollars a week to live. "I have," he reported, "$1400 of my old capital on hand, so I consider myself rich."[12] He was not "rich," of course, but he was comfortably middle class and well-off enough to consider sending to San Francisco for a "good girl" to help his wife. "What do you think they get here?" he asked his sister. "*Forty dollars* a month," ten or fifteen dollars more than they fetched in San Francisco.[13] To pay for this luxury, Buck was partitioning the ground floor of his house for boarders.

Buck's experience implies that Stiller was a prosperous man, and gives some hints about how Amelia may have come to the Stiller household. Perhaps Stiller had sent a request for a servant to San Francisco and Amelia had responded because she could get an extra fifty cents per day. If so, judging by the testimony at the coroner's inquest, she entered the Stillers' service no later than sometime in 1858. She would have been no older than thirteen or fourteen. How she came to San Francisco, whether with family, friends, or as a servant child in some stranger's household, we may never know.

Many of the uncertainties about Kuschinsky and the Stillers that all judicious historians must express in this case were not matters of concern for the Stillers' neighbors. They testified at the inquest with great certitude, indiscriminately mixing their direct observation with suspicions, rumors, and hearsay. The Tubush family lived about one-quarter mile from the Stillers, and Mr. Tubush "suspected the deceased of having improper intimacy with Mr Stiller for over a year." He had overheard his wife talking with a Mrs. Bosini and Mrs. Stiller, who said that "she was not regular in

Menstruation, and advised her to take tanzy tea, and exercise to make her turns come on."[14] This had occurred about eighteen months ago, when Amelia would have been about fourteen. Adding to his suspicions, Dr. Gutmann had been summoned to the Stiller house and had left packages for them at the Tubush place. Two weeks before Amelia died, Mr. Tubush had visited the Stillers and "became satisfied from her appearance that she was pregnant." He had heard others state that she was pregnant, too.

Mr. Tubush, who claimed to possess remarkably detailed knowledge of Amelia's menstrual routine, had no trouble making a stern judgment about the state of affairs in the Stiller home and the cause of Amelia's death. "I have every reason to believe that deceased came to her death by means used to produce premature child birth," he testified. He added that "Mr Stiller & deceased from their extreme intimacy appeared like man and wife." Mrs. Tubush also testified that she believed that Amelia was "in the family way," but did not mention knowledge of the menstrual irregularities that her husband had attributed to her. Perhaps the coroner thought it would be indelicate to ask her about this subject.

Other witnesses also reported their belief that Amelia had been about six months pregnant at the time of her death, and the autopsy would seem to leave no doubt about her condition. But who got her with child? Jacob Lacinsky deposed that he knew of no one who "kept company" with Amelia, and besides, "Mr Stiller did not allow any young people to visit Amelia." Lacinsky also thought that Stiller and Amelia had a sexual relationship and he must have had strong convictions about it because he confronted Stiller with his suspicion. Not surprisingly, and with some justification, Stiller told Lacinsky that it was none of his business. Nevertheless, he explained that he did not want young men "to interfere with her, that he wanted to send her to the old country again." Presumably, Stiller did not want to send her home "in the family way" after a casual encounter with one of the young swains in the neighborhood. Charles Cook also swore that he had never seen any man around Amelia except for Stiller, and he "thought from the extreme intimacy of Stiller & Amelia, that something was wrong."

Stiller's defense for secluding Amelia to protect her from the attentions of Shasta County men is not implausible. According to the 1860 census taken a few months after Amelia's death, there were eighty-three women and eighty-four men between the ages of fifteen and nineteen in the county's white population (see Table 5.1). However, a glance at the next older age cohort shows how misleading was this apparently balanced sex ratio. Between the ages of twenty and twenty-nine there were 871 men and only 224 women. The imbalance was even worse among thirty to thirty-nine-year-

Table 5.1 Shasta County Population, 15 to 39 Years of Age

Age Cohort	Men	Women
15–19	84	83
20–29	871	224
30–39	1,027	158
Total	*1,982*	*465*

Derived from "Table No. 1 — Population by Age and Sex," *Population of the United States in 1860*, comp. Joseph G. C. Kennedy (Washington, D.C.: Government Printing Office, 1864), 22–23.

old Shastans — 1,027 men to 158 women. Thus the sex ratio of men and women of childbearing age was 4.26 to 1. We may assume that in a marriage market so favorable for women that even among the youngest cohort of sexually mature females there were few single women. If all of the women over twenty were married to Shasta County men and all of the women under twenty were single — an unlikely assumption that no doubt exaggerates the problem — there would have been more than eighteen single men for every single woman. Whatever the true figure may have been, one thing is sure: the competition for single women must have been ferocious.

It does not strain credulity to suggest the possibility that some enterprising young man may have found a way to seduce Amelia, despite Stiller's stated desire to guard her virtue. Nor is it difficult to imagine that Amelia may have looked beyond the Stiller household for company to keep. It is even imaginable that she sold sex to add to her servant's wages. These obvious possibilities, however, did not occur to anyone who testified at the inquest, where August Stiller was the only suspect named.

The matter of abortion — who did it and by what means — is also a murky issue, although the denizens of Dry Creek were quick to have opinions. The physicians who examined Amelia's body agreed that violence had been used to produce an abortion, but they did not venture beyond that. Dr. Gutmann, the suspected abortionist, had prescribed various medicines for Amelia, although they were not precisely identified. He may have tried abortifacients before attempting a riskier mechanical abortion. Evidently, "tanzy tea" had worked before. Gutmann claimed that Amelia's death had resulted from scarlet fever, but the other physicians saw no signs of it. Nor was Dr. Gutmann able to convince the neighbors that Amelia had scarlet fever. They thought he just wanted them to stay away from the Stiller place so that he could prevent them from knowing her true condition. They went there anyway. Mrs. Hartshorn visited Amelia two days before she died. The young woman, who was by then very sick, told her that "it had come from her." Hartshorn "understood her to mean that a child had come from her." She also related that the Stillers kept Amelia's room very dark "to prevent observation." Hartshorn laid out Amelia's body while it was still warm, and noticed that her clothes had not been changed during her sickness. Hartshorn thought that Amelia had not been treated right, and darkly hinted that "measures had been taken that were not justifiable." While she prepared Amelia's body for burial, August Stiller wept.

Other witnesses testified to the use of unidentified medicines — perhaps abortifacients — which made Amelia sick. Mrs. Stiller told Mrs. Lowe that Amelia had been taking medicine "for a long time." Amelia told Lowe that the medicine Dr. Gutmann had prescribed had caused her to lose the use of her limbs. When Lowe again came to see Amelia, the Stillers urged her to leave, claiming that she could not stand any noise. All this convinced her that "the girl was receiving unfair treatment." Mrs. Bozan also visited Amelia, who told her that a "big lump had come from her." Bozan was not easily fooled and suspected that Amelia had given birth. Amelia told her that "Mr Stiller Knew all about it, but that Mrs Stiller knew nothing." According to Bozan, Gutmann denied knowing that Amelia was pregnant until shortly before she miscarried. Gutmann told Bozan that he did not want anything said about these matters — a naive hope in this small California community — because he and Stiller were countrymen. (Gutmann was from Hanover.) Whether from scarlet fever, peritonitis, stillbirth, or mechanical abortion, Amelia was in great pain. Bozan said that she "screamed two days and two nights very hard." Utterly exhausted on the morning of her death, she was barely able to speak.

Townsmen had become suspicious of Gutmann and suspected that he was trying to abort Amelia's pregnancy weeks before her death. Frederick Entz had conversations with Gutmann about Amelia's condition. Gutmann said that she had scarlet fever and that her condition was so bad that he was reluctant to handle her case alone and wanted to have a consultation of physicians. Stiller refused to bring in other doctors. Gutmann also complained to Entz about people who "made themselves very busy about this case, and supposed that something was the matter with the deceased besides scarlet fever." Gutmann's concerns about local busy bodies were well founded. More than one person believed that the scarlet-fever story was merely a ruse to cover the true intentions of Gutmann and Stiller, who "meant to kill the unborn child."

When D. J. Luckman and Gutmann met on the road, Luckman confronted Gutmann with his suspicion that Amelia did not have scarlet fever. The doctor weakly replied that she had "an awful fever." Luckman said that he knew what ailed the young woman, implying that she was pregnant. Gutmann acknowledged this, but went on to say that she now had a fever and that she might not recover. "I told Dr Gutmann that it was too bad to kill an innocent girl." Gutmann muttered a reply that Luckman could not understand and rode on.

Shastans' plainly expressed accusations about Amelia's pregnancy, supposed abortion, and cause of death were met with circumlocutions and evasions from Gutmann and the Stillers. They were wise to be cautious about this episode, even if they were merely the victims of rumors. Abortion was against the law in California. In 1850, the first state legislature outlawed the use of abortifacients or instruments to "procure miscarriage" except to save the life of the mother. The penalty for violating this law was two to five years in prison.[15] The legislature had also adopted common law as the basis for California statutes, but added some additional measures as well. Common law recognized quickening—the fetus's first perceptible movement—as the first sure sign of pregnancy. Before quickening, women, midwives, pharmacists, and physicians were free under common law to use medicines and other means to induce menstrual flow if a woman missed her period. At the time, there was no certain way except for quickening to distinguish between pregnancy and a period missed for some other medical reason. This meant that, in effect, abortion in the first trimester of pregnancy was legal, although not always safe for the mother. The California law made these common procedures illegal. Evidently, some of the California legislators had been reading the 1845 Massachusetts and New York statutes that outlawed abortion for the first time in the United States. Those state legislatures had been prompted to action by sensational abortion cases that resulted in two women's deaths. The legislators passed anti-abortion laws because they hoped that some women would be saved from death, and because they were concerned about a declining birthrate and the growth of public advertising of abortifacients. These laws were not effective. Between 1849 and 1857 in Massachusetts there were thirty-two trials, but not one conviction under the anti-abortion statute. Conclusive evidence was difficult to obtain, and the only witnesses were likely to be parties to the crime.[16]

The first California legislature worked quickly and may not have given much thought to the abortion measure. In 1858, the legislature strengthened the law by making it a crime to advertise, advise, or even "hint" about how and where one might obtain an abortion or abortifacients. A convicted abortion hinter could expect to go to prison for no less than three and no more than ten years.[17] No wonder Gutmann and Stiller were circumspect.

As it turned out, Gutmann and Stiller had more to fear from the enraged mob that might have lynched them than they did from the law. A week after Amelia's death the court released Gutmann, citing conflicting medical testimony and noting Gutmann's otherwise good character. The presiding judge found that "A good deal of this testimony goes to show that the injuries might have been produced by the unusual way of the delivery of the child, or death might have ensued from other causes."[18] Court testimony does not survive, but it is not difficult to imagine some of the possible defenses that Gutmann could have made. He might have said that Amelia spontaneously miscarried, that there were complications, and that he had to operate in order to save her life. He might even have claimed that Amelia tried to abort the fetus herself. Perhaps he attacked the other doctors' testimony as prejudiced. According to the census, Dr. Sewall had only two hundred dollars in personal property while Gutmann had twelve hundred dollars worth.[19] Dr. Sewall could have been portrayed as a jealous competitor who was not as successful as Gutmann.

Perhaps there were other reasons to be prejudiced against Gutmann and Stiller. In 1855, Dr. Henry Bates, the other physician at the inquest, had been elected state treasurer on the American Party, or Know Nothing, slate.[20] The Know Nothings were frankly anti-Catholic and anti-immigrant and sought to lengthen the period of residence required for naturalization to twenty years. According to one California Know Nothing writer, "poor foreigners and ignorant exiles" perverted the political process because they went to the "ballot boxes as 'the Irish vote', or the 'German vote', and not as Whigs or Democrats, or States' rights men, or nullifiers or abolitionists." They had "no individual opinions. They follow their ringleader, and as he jumps so precisely do they all jump."[21]

The Know Nothing party prevailed throughout California in 1855, partly because of its nativist sentiments and partly because it promised to clean up the corruption of Irish democrats like San Francisco's David Broderick. Judging by these sentiments, Bates must have been a better bigot than he was a reformer. During his two-year term as treasurer, Dr. Bates embarked on many interesting and illegal financial adventures that were evidently meant to enrich himself while he pillaged the state treasury. Ultimately, his stewardship of public funds cost the people of California more than one-quarter of a million dollars while he enriched himself by about fifteen thousand dollars. The historian Hubert Howe Bancroft characterized Bates as a corrupt professional politician and chronicled his financial adventures under the heading "Men Who Should Have Been Hanged."[22] One way or another—as a scalawag, a bigot, or both—Bates was an impeachable witness. One might well wonder what Bates may have been thinking while he carved and probed Amelia's immigrant body and contemplated the plausible immigrant villains of the crime.

In the meantime, Stiller, "the alleged seducer," surrendered on Cottonwood Creek and was being held on five thousand dollars bail to answer any charges that might have been made. The local paper reported that the district attorney was skeptical and did not think that Stiller could be held on charges of first-degree murder, which was evidently the crime that some thought he had committed.[23] If the cause of death was uncertain, then the crime and the criminals would be difficult to identify. Stiller went free, for three months later the census taker found him living with his wife and three children at Evan's Bar, in Trinity County. They had not retained another servant. Gutmann continued to practice in Horsetown, where he lived with his Hanoverian kinsman, L. Gutmann, a trader, and an Irish miner. Although only a short time had passed, few of the names from the coroner's inquest show up in the census. Perhaps most of the men went off to better gold diggings when the spring weather freshened.

All of which leaves us with Amelia's body and its silent accusations and questions. Was she the victim of a crime, or was she an active participant in her own fate? Was she seduced, or did she consent to sex out of lust, boredom, greed, or a vain hope to gain advantage in California's booming marriage market? Did unscrupulous men force her to have an abortion? Or, like so many other women of her time, place, and circumstances, did Amelia opt for an abortion, perhaps after consulting with older and wiser women who recommended "tanzy tea, and exercise to make her turns come on." Somehow it is more appealing to portray Amelia as a full participant in the events that took her life, though her death remains a tragedy all the same. Seen in this light, Amelia was one of the hopeful women who came west seeking opportunity and adventure rather than becoming a passive victim of unrelenting patriarchy and dangerous medical procedures.

Young as she was, Amelia may well have taken an active role in her destiny, but she was not the sole author of it. Amelia possessed a body that was her entire estate in the world, but which she did not fully control. Her most private acts were matters governed by laws of the state and adjudicated by tribunals. Nor was the state her worst enemy. The whole community presumed to know—presumed to have the authority to judge—what she did with her body and with whom she did it. Her body was the object of

desire, not only of her lover(s), but the many who were not. Her corpse
became the province of medical opinion, an exhibition gallery for scientific
authority and male expertise. When they had all done with her, there was
nothing left but parts to bury.

Long before Amelia came to her sorry end, Amelia's body was an object
under the scrutiny of the community. How did they see her? Women and
men alike called her a girl, a term that reflected the customs of the age and
her dependency, but which ignored her sexual maturity. Nobody ever described her physically or emotionally, except for the extreme pain that she
endured. Was she blond or brunette? Plump or svelte? Did she ever smile
and flirt with visitors? Did she have a winning personality? Was she dull-
witted? Perhaps the witnesses and jury all knew her too well to go into such
matters while Amelia's body lay before them.

The testimony revealed little of Amelia, but much about the witnesses.
The language of men who testified at the inquest was different from that of
the women. Men used the rhetoric of moral outrage and confronted Stiller
and Gutmann with their suspicions. They were the ones who spoke of the
unseemly intimacy of Amelia and Stiller. Only men directly discussed the
possibility of an abortion and Gutmann's complicity. And a man brought up
Amelia's missed periods and the use of tansy tea.

The women summoned the language of abuse when speaking about
Amelia. The Stillers — including Mrs. Stiller — were not giving her proper
treatment and tried to turn away women visitors. The women frankly stated
that Amelia was pregnant, but only Mrs. Tubush possibly hinted at abortion
when she said that there was some "foul play used with the girl." Like the
other women, Mrs. Tubush emphasized that the Stillers were not treating
Amelia as they should. Perhaps the women felt that the less said about
abortion and its causes the better. Neither did the women speak of intimacy
between Stiller and Amelia, nor about how Stiller kept the other men away
from her. The men, with so few women available to them, thought that there
was something wrong about monopolizing Amelia's affections, but this was
not an item on the women's agenda. Morality and monogamy did not come
up in their testimony, but the plain facts of Amelia's pregnancy and the
Stillers' unfairness to her did. They could all imagine what it would have
been like to be in Amelia's situation, and they passed up the opportunity to
make moral judgments about her. She was a girl in trouble. When the Stillers
refused to let Mrs. Lowe see Amelia, she protested that she was a mother
herself, thus invoking her own moral authority and implying that Amelia
needed a mother's care.

And how did Amelia see her body? Did she look in the mirror and see her only capital, something that she might hope to invest in California's marriage market and gain a profit? And why not? Was she to go on serving other women and their husbands and their children for the rest of her life? Perhaps she thought herself pretty, and perhaps she was. Or did she see in the glass a body that was as mysterious to her as it is to us? Was it merely a figure with functions and frailties not fully understood, something from which "it," a "lump," would come — as formless and ill understood as her own person was to her? How did you comprehend yourself, Amelia?

Here is what we may know for sure of your short, sad life. You were a poor servant whose work would now be classified as child labor. You were far from home with no family to depend on. A man — a lover or an assailant — made you pregnant. You died a terrible, painful death. A coroner's jury inspected your remains, suspected much, but proved nothing. The coroner folded his report in thirds, and filed it in a drawer where it lay forgotten for more than a century.

The bare facts of your life tell more about the world in which you lived than they reveal of you. They show that the lot of women in California was highly variable and included considerable risks even among white women. Ethnicity, class, age, circumstances, and the law defined the boundaries of their lives. True, the barriers were permeable — perhaps more so in California than in other places of the time — but the passage required extraordinary talent, imagination, perseverance, and courage. In a pinch, it was helpful to have luck on your side. For poor and young women like Amelia, the best chance for security lay in the marriage market rather than in the marketplace. Then as now, sexual attraction was a factor in the social calculus that resulted in marriage, but Amelia's experience demonstrated that sexuality was a risky attribute for young women. Whether they chose to use their bodies or men took advantage of them, they could not fully control the outcome. Customs, the law, and luck determined their fates — risky business in a place as riven with racial, ethnic, economic, and religious differences as gold-rush California.

Horsetown did not prosper after Amelia died. A drought came to California and turned the landscape to dust.[24] William Brewer passed through the place in 1862 and described the neighborhood as "dry hilly country, with high mountains along the north, the soil very dry and covered with scattered trees and bushes." By then mining had taken its toll. "The whole region is scarred by miners, who have skimmed over the surface and left the region more desolate than before."[25] In 1868, Horsetown burned, then gold dredging obliterated the town site as miners wrung the last bits of gold from the ravaged land. Today only a plaque serves as a physical reminder of the town's brief, clamorous existence.[26] The site of Amelia's grave is unknown. Gold dredges heaved up the only monuments for her, millions of skull-sized cobbles stacked in long, regularly shaped tailings piles that stretch for miles across the California countryside.

Intimate Frontiers

✠

The stories of Amelia Kuschinsky, Henry Sheldon, Eulalia Callis, Alfred Robinson, William Bullard, Louise Smith, Dame Shirley, and all the others limn the broad outlines of California's intimate frontiers. A strong current of social conservatism runs through these stories. California's multicultural character may have reenforced that tendency. Security lay in old habits, well-known customs, the comfortable conventions of the old country, whether it was Spain, Mexico, the United States, or someplace else. Californians meant for their respective societies to transform California, not vice versa. The novelist Montalvo understood this principle, and so did most of those who came long after he had penned his romance.

For a century and more, California had too many men.[1] This basic demographic fact meant that there was intense competition for women, some of whom benefited from a favorable marriage market. This condition encouraged families to betroth prepubescent californianas in the Spanish and Mexican eras, a custom that harked back to Iberian practice. These arranged marriages created unions that benefited families, buttressed patriarchal authority, burnished family honor, and reenforced the power of an oligarchy of elite landholders. The young women who formed interfamily links seldom had much to say about it; when they did speak up there was little chance that they would be taken seriously. If parents decided that a marriage was to take place, there was not much that a reluctant fiancé could do about it. In the meantime, chaperons closely watched them so that they did not breach patriarchal authority and sully family honor. Most Americans who married californianas seemed content to play by the rules that californio fathers had long since established.

24. "OPENING OF THE ENREQUITA MINE."
This painting by Alexander Edouart depicts the blessing of a new quicksilver mine in late 1859 or 1860. For Mexican Californians the opening of a new mine was a public event that the whole community celebrated because the mine would benefit the community. But there were risks. Here, the priest blesses the mine to protect the miners who will work underground. In the background, women and musicians participate in the ritual. The communal sense of risk and benefits contrasts sharply with Anglo ideas about individual speculation and enrichment. See "Blessing the Mine," *Scenes of Wonder and Curiosity from Hutchings' California Magazine, 1856–1861* (Berkeley, California: Howell-North, 1962).
Courtesy of the Bancroft Library.

During the gold rush, monstrously imbalanced sex ratios seemed to decree that any woman who wanted to marry could find a mate in California. Evidently, most marriageable women did just that. There were few palatable alternatives to marriage for women anywhere in the mid-nineteenth century, but by all accounts forty-niners were willing to pay women handsomely for domestic labor that befuddled most men — cooking, washing, sewing, keeping house.[2] Some women undertook such work on a commercial scale by opening restaurants, bakeries, washhouses, and boarding houses. They benefited from the economic opportunities that the gold rush afforded because the scarcity of women's labor made it more valuable, but all complained that it was hard work. Moreover, it is hard to see how women who worked could expect to gain more than a modest living. Like miners who complained bitterly and constantly about high gold-rush prices, women also had to pay inflated California prices for food, shelter, and the commodities they needed to work at their trades.

While women who were willing to labor outside the home gained financial advantage and a measure of independence, cooking, sewing, and taking in washing and boarders were emblematic of a decline in status elsewhere in America — a fate of poor widows who were to be pitied. Anne Crampton, an English immigrant living in Huron, Michigan, with her husband and large family, was such a woman. Her brother, Johnson Beal, went off to the gold rush, but her husband continued to farm in Huron. She teased Johnson about coming home to marry, "for it is a good farming country and [there are] plenty of rich farmers daughters. I have some comes hear to look at your likeness and you are . . . picked out and so you [k]now of quite a chance if you have not got a Calafornia lady in view."[3] Her brother did not come home, and eventually married an Irish woman. In the meantime, disaster struck his sister Anne. One morning, while shearing sheep her husband collapsed and was dead by eleven o'clock that night. "He did not re[a]lize any thing after they got him home," and "was not able to speak one word to me nor one look to [k]now me nor the poor children," she explained to Beal. His death was so sudden that it was "dreadfull to bear it. I am left alone in a strange land with 8 fartherless children one a infent 6 months olde."[4]

What could Anne do? Friends advised her to go to Ann Arbor, where her sons could "learn traids and me take in sewing and boarders."[5] Might she do better to run a boarding house in California? she asked. Johnson's reply was not preserved, but it was 1861 and the flush times were over. He evidently did not recommend California for a widow with eight children, so Anne went to Ann Arbor, where she took in university students. She asked Johnson to send her money. "It is good times enough here for men as they get good wages," she reported, "but womens wages is not near higher as their[s]" because there were "so many irish and niggars running and doing all sorts of work for a little of nothing so that we have to work very hard to live."[6] She addressed the letter to her brother and sister-in-law, née Mary Shannon, who may have questioned her husband about sending one hundred dollars to Anne with her frankly stated prejudices. How many nineteenth-century women would have willingly seized an opportunity to run a boarding house whatever the economic opportunities may have been? Mary Bullard, I suppose, spoke for most women when she complained that running a California boarding house made "a perfect slave of a woman, for you have to wait on every body, and everything."[7]

The gold rush did not produce a feminist movement or substantive advances in women's political and social condition. Minority status does not usually confer power on the powerless, and California was no exception to the rule, not that there was a great clamor for social change. Men said that they wanted more women to come to California, and women in California said that they wanted to replicate the domestic world that they had known. "What California wants is woman," Mrs. S. A. Downer explained in *The Pioneer*. "Woman in her highest and holiest nature; not only as she came from the hands of her Maker—pure, innocent, and loving—but with a higher consciousness, a greater inward development; in short, a woman as she should stand in the nineteenth century—the companion, the friend, the co-worker with man in the great cause of humanity; true-hearted, noble-minded, stern-principled, faithful and affectionate, as well as winning. . . . We are no advocate of Women's Rights," but for woman in her proper sphere, the home.[8]

Mrs. Downer spoke for middle-class white women and values that did not have much to do with lives of poor women like Amelia Kuschinsky, much less women of color and harlots. The young and the poor did not gain much in California except, perhaps, in the marriage market, and not everyone participated on an equal footing. Most Americans preferred to marry women of their own nationality, class, religion, and color. Others were suitable partners in bordellos, or worse, fitting objects for rapists. These outcast women—especially Indians and Chinese—bore the mark of color and exotic cultures. Men who extravagantly praised the supposed worth to California society of bourgeois white women and defended their virtue paid scant attention to the lot of a poor Indian woman.

The conditions that elevated the worth of some women in men's eyes proved to be a curse for men. Unmarried men had a hard time finding eligible women. They could go home for a wife or take their chances among the slim pickings in California. Married men feared that anxious and well-heeled competitors might alienate the affections of their spouses, a problem that easy divorce laws exacerbated. The young men who came to California and stayed, or who moved on to new mining frontiers in the West were most adversely affected by the numbers game. Here is the origin of a western stereotype: the solitary, grizzled old prospector looking for precious ore with only his burro for company. He had a better chance of striking a lode than finding a wife in the West.

Patriarchy had its burdens, too. In theory, a male head of family had much power over the women and children under his control, but he had responsibilities, too. In making decisions for the family, he was responsible for making the *right* choice in life or death situations, a not unlikely possibility on the overland trail. Not all men were up to the job that everyone expected them to do while crossing the continent. Most of them were farmers, merchants, and mechanics, without frontier experience. It is difficult to fault Donner and Reed for heeding what seemed like good advice and taking the Hastings cutoff, but their inexperience caused many other bad decisions that ate up time. In the end, the patriarchs would watch as the horrible results of their incompetence unfolded in the snow.

The Donners, Reeds, and Oatmans were unlucky, incompetent, and exceptional. Most men and women survived the trip to California, however harrowing it may have been. Once the immigrants reached their destination, they set about the great mission that had been assigned primarily to women in nineteenth-century America — the establishment of civilization and society that had spawned them, Spanish Franciscans and American Methodists alike. By so doing, they made California safe for the sex and gender orthodoxies that they revered. The virtue of this venture they never questioned. They seldom appreciated the value of the societies they overthrew or the people they displaced. Each newcomer transformed California the exotic into California the familiar, a long established pattern that yet continues.

Part of the transformation involved the domestication of the turbulent — often violent — recent past. The domestication of violence and disorder made past events into a progressive force, or at least tamed bad behavior and made it seem less dangerous, even good. California's Anglo men and women wanted California history — especially the gold rush — to reenforce the values of bourgeois society that they celebrated. The hard realities of early California history quickly blurred into a sentimental haze of romantic pioneer recollections and histories. Historians Theodore and John Hittell, and especially Hubert Howe Bancroft, celebrated the achievements of the forty-niner generation.[9] In his multivolume history of California, Bancroft emphasized commercial successes (such as his own) and chronicled the thrift, energy, and industry of Yankees while denigrating Mexican Californians as lazy. He believed that California had an energizing quality that called forth the ambition inherent in Anglo men. He even claimed that this tendency was so strong that he had no desire to engage in "boyish excesses" (such as sexual philandering) when he arrived in San Francisco as a single twenty-year-old in 1852. Instead of cavorting in the city's bordellos, he sold books and stationery, collected a library and manuscripts, and devoted himself to writing the history of California and the West.[10] Such was the effect on Bancroft of San Francisco's brisk moral climate and the powerful fascination of the state's history.

Bancroft's celebration of the establishment of Anglo American social and political customs on the California frontier was sometimes a challenging task in the face of the historical evidence that he had compiled. The prevalence of vigilance committees and lynching presented a difficult problem, for it seemed to contradict American concepts of law, order, and justice. Bancroft took a special interest in the many episodes of lynching and mob violence that occurred during the gold rush, characterizing them as "Popular Tribunals." Bancroft justified lynch-mob violence as "the right of the governed at all times to instant and arbitrary control of the government." Mob justice was subject to "the grossest abuse," Bancroft admitted, but there was a "latent sentiment" among "intelligent people" that such outbreaks, though "a regretted necessity," operated for "the welfare of society."[11] Thus Bancroft domesticated lynch mobs.

The lynching of the Mexican woman Juanita (also known as Josefa) was an especially challenging incident for Bancroft to chronicle. The story of Juanita is well known to everyone who has read about the gold rush for she was the only woman to die at the hands of a lynch mob. In 1851 she was living in Downieville with a Mexican gambler. On the Fourth of July townsmen and local miners celebrated the event with political speeches and general drunkenness. Details are unclear, but Joe Cannon, a popular young Englishman, evidently knocked in the Mexican couple's door during the general rowdiness that night. The next morning he went to the shack to apologize. Juanita, who may have thought Cannon was going to attack her lover, or who (according to some accounts) reacted to Cannon calling her a prostitute, killed Cannon with a Bowie knife. A mob gathered, called a jury, and sentenced Juanita to be hanged at four in the afternoon. All accounts agree that she went to her death with uncommon courage, ascending the makeshift scaffold without assistance and adjusting the noose so that it did not tangle her hair. On the gallows, she said that she would do the same thing again if her honor was similarly affronted. Then the mob hanged her.[12]

The event was immediately infamous in California, although some believed that the act was justified. The first newspapers to report the event were appalled that the denizens of Downieville had hanged a woman, no matter the provocation, and could hardly believe the first accounts that came to them.[13] Likewise, some eyewitnesses condemned the lynching of a

25. HANGING OF THE MEXICAN WOMAN.
Juanita, also known as Josefa, was the only woman known to have been lynched in the mines during the gold rush. Little is known of her except that she was Mexican. She killed a popular white man who burst into her room in Downieville. At the kangaroo court that judged her, she claimed that the man had violated her honor, but the drunken men who presided hanged her anyhow. The witnesses claimed that she went to her death in a brave and dignified manner that shamed her executioners.
Courtesy of the California State Library.

woman on principles of gender as well as due process.[14] The nineteenth-century philosopher-historian Josiah Royce was horrified that the mob had killed a woman, and modern historians — with justification — have averred that Juanita would not have been hanged if she had been an Anglo American woman.[15]

Oddly, Bancroft used the lynching as an occasion to praise Americans' reverence for women and to showcase their determination to protect the helpless members of their own race. Miners could "cut each other with knives . . . riddle enemy or friend with bullets and smile at it," Bancroft wrote. "They could strangle a sluice-box thief, snap the neck of a Chinaman by a twist of his pigtail, whet their appetite for breakfast by the butchery of a ranchería of natives," he continued, "but injure a child, ill-treat an old man, or do violence to woman, they could not."[16] It is clear that Bancroft's miners made distinctions between helpless whites and people of color. Yet women belonged to a special category. "She might be chaste and fair or wicked as Jezebel," still "she was . . . the expression of their innermost ideal of the beautiful and good."[17] So, according to Bancroft, "it was a rare thing in California, extremely rare, for rough men to lay their hands upon a woman."[18]

How could such men hang the comely, brave Juanita? Bancroft blew up Cannon's character so that he assumed mythical proportions. He was the best and strongest of men, the most entertaining, popular, handsome, and gentle miner in camp. In Bancroft's account, Cannon had "the arms of Hercules," yet "he would not harm a fly." He was English, but celebrated the Fourth as heartily as any good American. In short, Cannon was "the finest fellow that ever swung a pick or dislodged a bowlder."[19] To Bancroft's mind, Cannon was the archetype of the worthy forty-niner. Stalwart and brave, simple and good, hardworking miners like Cannon hewed a state out of the placers and quartz of the California frontier. It was Juanita's bad judgment to kill this godlike figure and thus bring down the popular wrath of the multitude of miners of whom he was emblematic. Bancroft stopped short of approving her lynching, but he commiserated with the men who committed the deed. Thus, he used this violent act against a woman to uphold the myth of the woman-revering, honest miner who seized power to effect justice, evidence to the contrary notwithstanding.

California's contentious history was rich with possibilities for journalists and fiction writers as well as historians. Bret Harte, Mark Twain, and Ambrose Bierce added their interpretations to the factual accounts, and they sometimes saw the implications of gender and race in their stories. Harte was the only one of the three who directly experienced gold-rush life. In 1854, he ventured to California when he was not quite eighteen. Harte briefly tried his hand at mining, but decided to become a writer, beginning as a printer's devil. His travels took him to Union (now Arcata), on Humboldt Bay, where he worked for the *Northern Californian* setting type, writing stories and editorials when the editor was out of town.[20]

In 1860 the young journalist confronted some of the vicious facts of California frontier life. One February night, several bands of white men mercilessly slaughtered about 150 Indians who lived peaceably around Humboldt Bay. At dawn, one contingent attacked a sleeping Indian community on a small island in front of Eureka, killing three men and fifty-seven women and children.[21] Tribesmen brought some of their murdered kin to Union, where Harte saw them. "Old women, wrinkled and decrepit, lay weltering in blood, their brains dashed out and dabbled with their long gray hair," he wrote in the *Northern Californian*. He saw "infants scarcely a span long, with their faces cloven with hatchets and their bodies ghastly with wounds." As these vulnerable people "huddled together for protection like sheep, they were struck down with hatchets."[22]

Harte's public outrage over the murder of Indians conflicted with the more philosophical views of his employer, Stephen G. Whipple, who had been away on business when the massacre occurred. He understood that Harte's outburst was offensive to many whites and might drive away advertisers. Whipple was a sometime special agent for the Office of Indian Affairs, and within a few months of the Indian Island killings he was whipping up support for a state-sponsored volunteer force to fight Indians. Whipple eventually commanded such a force and assumed the rank of colonel.[23] Clearly, Harte's views were in conflict with Whipple's and Harte had to go. Whipple offered a friendly, if droll, farewell to his young assistant in the *Northern Californian* when he departed for San Francisco. "We wish our friend the success to which his talents entitle him, and cordially commend him to the Big City."[24]

Harte flourished in the "Big City." He went to work for the *Golden Era*, a literary magazine, and eventually became editor of the *Overland Monthly*. Anton Roman, founder of the *Overland Monthly*, declared that California was "near the end of its frontier days . . . having passed from naïveté to satire, reached the stage in which its early days became romantic."[25] Harte's voice was perfect for the new era of romantic recollection. Gold-rush stories like "The Luck of Roaring Camp" and "Outcasts of Poker Flat" were best-sellers that brought Harte to the favorable attention of eastern critics as well as western readers.

Harte's work was rooted in actual experience and observation, but there was none of the graphic gore that marked his journalistic writing in Union. Still, his choice of subjects was shockingly realistic to some readers. "The Luck of Roaring Camp" opens with a prostitute giving birth to a baby boy who was probably sired by one her customers. The whore's name was Cherokee Sal, a pseudonym that revealed she had tainted blood to go along with her tainted life. Sal died soon after the babe was born, and the rough-hewn men of Roaring Camp collectively adopted the orphan. They called the boy "The Luck," and for a time the infant seemed to bring luck to the camp as the placers produced generous amounts of dust in "The Luck's" first summer. He likewise brought an increased level of propriety. The coarse miners improved their manners and cultivated a rude domesticity in the womanless Roaring Camp. (After the death of Cherokee Sal the Roaring Campers decided that they did not want another prostitute in their town.) They abandoned profanity when "The Luck" was near, especially the formerly popular curse, "Damn the luck!" Hard men developed a tender side for the "Ingin baby," dressed more neatly, decorated their cabins, and talked about attracting families to Roaring Camp—all for the sake of "The Luck." But it was not to be. A cruel winter storm flooded the camp and swept away the men who had given loving care to the infant. One of them, Kentuck, had protected the baby in his arms as they were washed downstream. Kentuck was found near death with the already dead baby cradled in his arms. When informed that he was dying, Kentuck said "Dying . . . he's taking me with him,—tell the boys I've got the Luck with me now," and he passed away.[26]

Harte's sentimental story about compassionate pioneers struck the right chord with his western readers. Indeed, he provided the fictional analog for Bancroft's gold-rush history. Their miners only *seemed* to flout the values and virtues of nineteenth-century America. At heart they were old softies who longed for the homely virtues that pervaded the cult of true womanhood. In all of Harte's gold-rush tales, social outcasts and unlikely rustics confirmed the validity of mid-nineteenth-century American bourgeois values. At the same time, prostitutes with hearts of gold, chivalrous gamblers, and their progeny seldom reaped rewards for their virtuous behavior. In Harte's stories the wages of sin was likely to be death, disaster, disappointment, and disability no matter how colorful, deserving, or well intended the characters may have been.

Harte could not tame real frontiersmen, but he domesticated their fictional representations. The imaginary men of Roaring Camp were very unlike the real ones who lived around Humboldt Bay and the mining camps that Harte had known. Roaring Camp miners loved and nurtured a lowborn Indian baby. Indeed, one of them gave his life for "The Luck." The real men of Humboldt Bay killed Indian babies and their mothers with axes. One might well wonder what the perpetrators of the Indian Island massacre thought when they read about "The Luck," and what other less than admirable pioneers thought of Harte's appreciative portrayal of California's rough frontier life.

Harte's literary popularity and power as an editor attracted the attention of other writers. Mark Twain, Ambrose Bierce, and Louise Clapp (Dame Shirley), among many others, wanted to publish in the journals that Harte edited.[27] Twain and Bierce apprenticed under Harte's tutelage, but he rejected Clapp's contributions. Some contemporaries believed that Harte plagiarized the *Shirley Letters* for his colorful gold-rush tales, but Louise defended Harte from these attacks and maintained a cordial relationship with his family. After retiring from teaching she returned to the East Coast, ending her years in a home for old women that Harte's nieces ran.[28]

Twain ventured west in 1861, when his brother was appointed territorial secretary of Nevada. After chronicling the news of Virginia City for the *Territorial Enterprise*, Twain moved to California where he continued his journalistic career.[29] His most famous contribution to gold-country literature, "The Celebrated Jumping Frog of Calaveras County," depicts deeply bored men who passed the time by wagering on the most trivial and random events — the length of a frog jump, which of two birds would fly first from their perch, how far and fast a bug would travel. Dog fights, cat fights, chicken fights all captured the sporting attention of men in Calaveras County. After hearing about how one inveterate gambler gulled another over a wager on a frog jump, Twain, the unwilling audience to an oral recounting of these mother-lode entertainments, could take no more of this nonsense and deserted the narrator. Of course, Twain told this tale with great hilarity, but he also made clear that life among such a crowd of bumpkins was unbearable.[30]

Twain had little to say about women in frontier California (and Nevada where he saw the flush times of the Comstock), and it was not especially flattering. He recognized that female scarcity improved their value as prospective companions, and mercilessly lampooned women who put on airs at a ball. Affecting a society-page style, Twain described the women's attire. One wore "an elegant *pâté de foie gras*, made expressly for her, and was greatly admired." Another was "superbly arrayed in [only?] white kid gloves. Her modest and engaging manner accorded well with the unpretending simplicity of her costume, and caused her to be regarded with absorbing interest by every one." No doubt. The "queenly Mrs. L. R. was attractively attired in her new and beautiful false teeth," and their effect "was heightened by her enchanting and well sustained smile." But woe to "Miss X," who had ceased to associate with Twain. "Every body knows she is old; every body knows she is repaired (you might almost say built) with artificial bones and hair and muscles and things, from the ground up." The pretensions of women and the men who sought them were among the commonplace matters of frontier life that furnished rich fodder for Twain's brilliant, mocking style.[31]

Twain's fun was a harmless parody of California life that westerners could enjoy (except for the unlucky women whom he parodied). The work of Ambrose Bierce operated on a deeper and darker level of Californians' consciousness. Bierce was the youngest of the three authors, and the last to come to California. After serving in the Union Army during the Civil War, Bierce worked as a treasury department agent in Alabama. Then he joined a U.S. expedition that inspected western roads and military posts that took him to San Francisco, where he joined the likes of Harte, Twain, and the rest of the city's literary crowd. Bierce was perceptive, witty, and sardonic. He honed his satirical skills in "The Town Crier," which appeared in *The News-Letter*, a weekly column that skewered everyone who came within Bierce's view.[32]

California's local color and the recent gold rush captured Bierce's attention just as it had seized Harte and Twain. But he caught a whiff of something else, too, something more sinister and deeply repressed, a story of interracial sex and murder. His short story "The Haunted Valley" was set somewhere in the rural hills. The story concerned a drunken misanthrope called Jo. Dunfer who had a special hatred for the Chinese. Dunfer told Bierce that he killed a Chinese laborer called Ah Wee because he could not trust him to work properly unless he was within sight. Later, Bierce happened on Ah Wee's grave and learned that Ah Wee was a woman, even though Dunfer referred to her as "he." Finally Dunfer died and one of his former employees — now gone mad — revealed that Dunfer had won Ah Wee in a San Francisco poker game and that she had been his lover. He was "ashamed to acknowledge 'er and treat 'er white!" the mad man ranted, so Dunfer concealed her sex by disguising her as a male laborer. Still, Dunfer was possessive and suspicious of Ah Wee. When he happened to see the insane informant (who also loved Ah Wee) snare a tarantula that had run up her sleeve, Dunfer mistook the act for a sign of intimacy between the two. He took up an axe and viciously struck Ah Wee in the side. When Dunfer discovered his mistake, he knelt beside Ah Wee who reached up and took his face in her hands and looked in his eyes until she died.[33]

Bierce's bitter story captured some of the icy truths that most Californians wanted to ignore. Interracial sex was incidental to the California scene, yet it was shameful, something to hide. Women of color were commodities to be wagered, bought, sold, and murdered at the whim of white men. Unlike Bret Harte's stories, there was nothing edifying about "The Haunted Valley" for Californians. Harte had seen real men use real axes on Indian women, but could not describe such scenes in his fiction. Bierce used a fictional axe to open an old California wound. Perhaps his tale rang true to the axe murderers of Humboldt Bay and the auctioneers who sold Chinese women to brothels in San Francisco and the mines.

Bierce was on to something, but his voice was distinctly unique in nineteenth-century California. Most preferred to recall California's past in the same way that Harte and Bancroft portrayed it—sentimental, progressive, and uplifting, or as a harmless, rollicking, Mark Twain tale. History, fiction, and pioneer recollection blended to create a meaningful memory for Anglo Californians, one that omitted or domesticated unsettling images of sex, gender, and culture that once had characterized California society. Their version of the past validated Anglo hegemony while glossing over details that did not fit the preferred pattern. But the details remained embedded in the stuff of history—old letters, diaries, records, fallible memories, and the very landscape. Bierce knew that California could not escape its past, knew that its valleys were haunted by painful memories of the many collisions of myriad races and cultures. He also understood some of the sexual, racial, and gendered dimensions of the state's multicultural frontier, and he knew the human costs.

In his old age Bierce went to Mexico, perhaps to report on the revolution, or perhaps to violently die there—a kind of respectable, soldierly suicide for a Civil War veteran who had spent his career making people look at unpleasant truths. In 1913 he disappeared there and the circumstances of his death remain unknown. More than sixty years after Bierce mysteriously disappeared, the Mexican writer Carlos Fuentes wondered in his novel *Old Gringo* what the California journalist had learned about crossing borders and frontiers. "Each of us has a secret frontier within him," Fuentes imagined Bierce saying. "That is the most difficult frontier to cross because each of us hopes to find himself alone there, but finds that he is more than ever in the company of others."[34] What the imaginary Bierce said about his mental frontier applied as well to the historical frontier. Whatever their heritage, all Californians found themselves in the company of others. However much they may have preferred to be alone, or exclusively among their own kind, they could not escape being among others. Spaniards could not escape Indians, Mexicans could not escape Anglos, Anglos could not escape all of the others who preceded and followed them to an intimate frontier of barely acquainted strangers. Californians' ideas about gender sometimes mediated and often exacerbated discordant social conditions and the tensions they entailed. In the end, the frontiers of the heart and mind reenforced California's frontiers of difference, no matter how strong ran the currents of passion, longing, and desire.

Notes

INTRODUCTION

1. Montalvo quoted in Dora Beale Polk, *The Island of California: A History of the Myth* (Lincoln: University of Nebraska Press, 1991), 125.

2. Jack D. Forbes, "Hispano-Mexican Pioneers of the San Francisco Bay Region: An Analysis of Racial Origins," *Aztlán* 14 (Spring 1983), 175–89; Adrian Bustamante, "'The Matter Was Never Resolved': The *Casta* System in Colonial New Mexico, 1693–1823," *New Mexico Historical Review* 66 (April 1991), 143–64.

3. Reginald Horsman, *Race and Manifest Destiny: The Origins of American Racial Anglo-Saxonism* (Cambridge, Mass.: Harvard University Press, 1981), 225–26.

4. John D'Emilio and Estelle Freedman, *Intimate Matters: A History of Sexuality in America* (New York: Harper and Row, 1988), 123–24. There is much suggestive (but inconclusive) evidence for homosexual liaisons in gold-rush California. See Susan Lee Johnson, "'The Gold She Gathered': Difference, Domination, and California's Southern Mines, 1848–1853" (Ph.D. diss., Yale University, 1993), 195, 266–75. As Johnson writes, "ambiguous records abound" (273).

5. Gerda Lerner, *The Creation of Patriarchy* (New York: Oxford University Press, 1986), 239.

6. Donna C. Schuele, "Community Property Law and the Politics of Married Women's Rights in Nineteenth-Century California," *Western Legal History* 7 (Summer/Fall 1994), 248–52; David J. Langum, *Law and Community on the Mexican California Frontier: Anglo-American Expatriates and the Clash of Legal Traditions, 1821–1846* (Norman: University of Oklahoma Press, 1987), 232–43; Janet Lecompte, "The Independent Women of Hispanic New Mexico, 1821–1846," *Western Historical Quarterly* 12 (January 1981), 19.

7. Joan Wallach Scott, *Gender and the Politics of History* (New York: Columbia University Press, 1988), 42.

8. On the construction of gender see Joan Wallach Scott, "Gender: A Useful Category of Analysis," in Scott, *Gender and the Politics of History*, 28–50; Carroll

Smith-Rosenberg, *Disorderly Conduct: Visions of Gender in Victorian America* (New York: Oxford University Press, 1985), 19; Susan Lee Johnson, "'A Memory Sweet to Soldiers': The Significance of Gender" (with commentary by Albert L. Hurtado and Deena J. González), in *A New Significance: Re-envisioning the History of the American West*, ed. Clyde A. Milner, II (New York: Oxford University Press, 1996), 255–88. On the history of sexuality, see Michel Foucault, *The History of Sexuality*, vol. 1, *An Introduction*, trans. Robert Hurley (New York: Pantheon, 1978); Peter Gay, *The Bourgeois Experience: Victoria to Freud*, vol. 1, *Education of the Senses* (New York: Oxford University Press, 1984); D'Emilio and Freedman, *Intimate Matters*; Jeffrey Weeks, *Sexuality* (New York: Ellis Horwood and Tavistock, 1986). On race and gender in the American West, see Antonia Castañeda, "Women of Color and the Rewriting of Western History: The Discourse, Politics, and Decolonization of History," *Pacific Historical Review* 61 (November 1992), 501–34; Peggy Pascoe, "Race, Gender and Intercultural Relations: The Case of Interracial Marriage," in *Writing the Range: Race, Class, and Culture in the Women's West*, ed. Elizabeth Jameson and Susan Armitage (Norman: University of Oklahoma Press, 1997), 69–80.

9. Foucault, *History of Sexuality*, 1:19.

10. Sade quoted in Foucault, *History of Sexuality*, 1:21.

11. Foucault, *History of Sexuality*, 1:33.

12. Ibid., 1:145.

13. Mary Shannon to Johnson Beal, Sept. 8, 1858, Johnson Beal Papers, California Room, State Library, Sacramento.

14. Ann Stevens quoted in Robert L. Griswold, *Family and Divorce in California, 1850–1890: Victorian Illusions and Everyday* (Albany: State University of New York Press, 1982), 89.

15. Polk, *Island of California*, 121–32; on California as an island, see also Edward Byerly, "The Illumination of Terra Incognita: A Cartographic History of California, 1541–1903," (Ph.D. diss., Arizona State University, 1997), chap. 2.

16. Albert L. Hurtado, *Indian Survival on the California Frontier* (New Haven: Yale University Press, 1988), 1, 52–53, 65–71, 169–92.

17. Robert F. Heizer and Albert B. Elsasser, *The Natural World of the California Indians* (Berkeley: University of California Press, 1980).

18. David J. Weber, *The Mexican Frontier, 1821–1846: The American Southwest under Mexico* (Albuquerque: University of New Mexico Press, 1982), 207–41; Douglas Monroy, *Thrown among Strangers: The Making of Mexican Culture in Frontier California* (Berkeley: University of California Press, 1990), 99–162, and passim.

19. Ramón A. Gutiérrez, *When Jesus Came the Corn Mothers Went Away: Marriage, Sexuality, and Power in New Mexico, 1500–1846* (Stanford: Stanford University Press, 1991); Patricia Nelson Limerick, *The Legacy of Conquest: The Unbroken Past of the American West* (New York: Norton, 1987); Richard White, *The Middle Ground: Indians, Empires, and Republics in the Great Lakes Region, 1600–1815* (New York: Cambridge University Press, 1991).

20. John Mack Faragher, "The Frontier Trail: Rethinking Turner and Reimagin-

ing the American West," *American Historical Review* 98 (February 1993), 106–17; Patricia Nelson Limerick, "Turnerians All: The Dream of a Helpful History in an Intelligible World," *American Historical Review* 100 (June 1995), 697–716. For a sampling of this writing, see Patricia Nelson Limerick, Clyde Milner, and Charles E. Rankin, eds., *Trails: Toward a New Western History* (Lawrence: University Press of Kansas, 1991); Donald Worster, *Under Western Skies: Nature and History in the American West* (New York: Oxford University Press, 1992); Clyde A. Milner, II, Carol A. O'Connor, and Martha A. Sandweiss, eds., *The Oxford History of the American West* (New York: Oxford University Press, 1994).

    21. David A. Weber, *"The Legacy of Conquest,* by Patricia Nelson Limerick: A Panel of Appraisal," *Western Historical Quarterly* 20 (1989), 317.

    22. Carlos Fuentes, *The Old Gringo* (New York: Farrar, Strauss, Giroux, 1985), 5.

CHAPTER I

    1. Maynard J. Geiger, O.F.M., *Letter of Luís Jayme, O.F.M. San Diego, October 17, 1772* (Los Angeles: Dawson's Book Shop, 1970), 38–39.

    2. Francisco Palóu, *Palou's Life of Fray Junípero Serra,* ed. and trans. Maynard J. Geiger (Washington, D.C.: Academy of American Franciscan History, 1955), 49.

    3. Alfred L. Kroeber, *Handbook of Indians of California* (1925; repr., Berkeley: California Book Co., 1953), 647, 748, 803; Lowell John Bean, "Social Organization in Native California," in *Native Californians: A Theoretical Retrospective,* ed. Lowell John Bean and Thomas C. Blackburn (Socorro, N.M.: Ballena Press, 1976), 105–12; Heizer and Elsasser, *Natural World of the California Indians,* 28–56.

    4. Bean, "Social Organization," 106–10; John Bushnell and Donna Bushnell, "Wealth, Work and World View in Native Northwest California: Sacred Significance and Psychoanalytic Symbolism," in *Flowers of the Wind: Papers on Ritual, Myth and Symbolism in California and the Southwest,* ed. Thomas C. Blackburn (Socorro, N.M.: Ballena Press, 1977), 133.

    5. Robert F. Heizer, "The California Indians: Archaeology, Varieties of Culture, and Arts of Life," *California Historical Society Quarterly* 41 (March 1962), 5–6, 10–12; Nona C. Willoughby, "Division of Labor among the Indians of California," in *California Indians,* Garland American Indian Ethnohistory Series, 6 vols. (New York, 1974), 2:60–68.

    6. Robert F. Heizer, ed., *Handbook of North American Indians,* vol. 8, *California* (Washington, D.C.: Smithsonian Institution, 1978), 498, 502, 511, 523, 544–45, 556, 566, 602, 684–85; Thomas Blackburn, ed., *December's Child: A Book of Chumash Oral Narratives* (Berkeley: University of California Press, 1975), 56–58, 137–38, 154–55.

    7. Several recent works examine the berdache tradition in North America. Cf. Walter L. Williams, *The Spirit and the Flesh: Sexual Diversity in American Indian Culture* (Boston: Beacon Press, 1986), 17–127; Will Roscoe, *The Zuni Man Woman* (Albuquerque: University of New Mexico Press, 1991), 123–46, and passim;

Gutiérrez, *When Jesus Came*, 33–35. For references to berdache in California, see Heizer, *Handbook, California*, 8:131, 134, 159, 466, 502, 512, 689; Kroeber, *Handbook*, 46, 180, 497, 500, 647, 748, 803.

8. Gutiérrez, *When Jesus Came*, 176–240; Rámon A. Gutiérrez, "Honor Ideology, Marriage Negotiation, and Class-Gender Domination in New Mexico, 1690–1846," *Latin American Perspectives* 12 (Winter 1985), 81–104; Ramón A. Gutiérrez, "From Honor to Love: Transformations of the Meaning of Sexuality in Colonial New Mexico," in *Kinship Ideology and Practice in Latin America*, ed. Raymond T. Smith (Chapel Hill: University of North Carolina Press, 1984), 237–63.

9. Vern L. Bullough, *Sexual Variance in Society and History* (Chicago: University of Chicago Press, 1980), 347–457; on sins against nature, see 378–89. An instructive essay on how actual behavior could vary from church teachings is Jean-Louis Flandrin, "Sex in Married Life in the Early Middle Ages: The Church's Teaching and Behavioural Reality," in *Western Sexuality: Practice and Precept in Past and Present Times*, ed. Philippe Aris and André Béjin, trans. Anthony Forster (Oxford: Basil Blackwell, 1985), 114–29.

10. See especially Ramón A. Gutiérrez, "Honor-Ideology and Sexual Inversion in Colonial New Mexico," paper presented at the Annual Meeting of the Western History Association, St. Paul, Minn., October 1983. No one has applied Gutiérrez's suggestive ideas to California. See also Lecompte, "Independent Women of Hispanic New Mexico," 17–36. On honor and seduction, see Verena Martínez-Alier, *Marriage, Class and Colour in Nineteenth-Century Cuba: A Study of Racial Attitudes and Sexual Values in a Slave Society* (London: Cambridge University Press, 1974), 109–12. For a sinister analysis of Mexican *machismo* and its role in sexual behavior, see Octavio Paz, *The Labyrinth of Solitude*, trans. Lysander Kemp, Yara Milos, and Rachel Phillips Belash (New York: Grove Press, 1985), 73–88. On women in other parts of Spanish America, see Guillermo Céspedes, *Latin America in the Early Years* (New York, 1974), 56–62; James Lockhart, *Spanish Colonial Peru, 1532–1560: A Colonial Society* (Madison: University of Wisconsin Press, 1968), 150–62.

11. Céspedes, *Latin America in the Early Years*, 56–62. For data on racial amalgamation on the northern frontier, see Henry F. Dobyns, *Spanish Colonial Tucson: A Demographic History* (Tucson: University of Arizona Press, 1976), 133–80; Alicia V. Tjarks, "Comparative Demographic Analysis of Texas, 1777–1793," in *New Spain's Far Northern Frontier: Essays in the American West, 1540–1821*, ed. David J. Weber (Albuquerque: University of New Mexico Press, 1979), 135–69.

12. Serra to Antonio María de Bucareli y Ursua, Aug. 24, 1775, in *Writings of Junípero Serra*, 4 vols., ed. Antonine Tibesar (Washington, D.C.: Academy of American Francisco History, 1955–66), 2:149.

13. Serra to Antonio María de Bucareli y Ursua, March 13, 1773, in Tibesar, *Writings of Junípero Serra*, 1:325.

14. Serra to Bucareli Aug. 24, 1775, in Tibesar, *Writings of Junípero Serra*, 2:149. While Serra approved of handsome subsidies for marriages of Catalán men and Indian women, he also made it clear that he did not want to apply such liberal

rewards to the mixed-blood leather jackets who manned the presidio. Evidently Serra, like many other Hispanos on the northern frontier, accepted as a matter of course the social superiority of *peninsulares* who should receive preferential treatment. On marriage, ethnicity, and race in California and the Southwest, see Gloria E. Miranda, "Gente de Razón Marriage Patterns in Spanish and Mexican California: A Case Study of Santa Barbara and Los Angeles," *Southern California Quarterly* 63 (Spring 1981), 1–21; Jack D. Forbes, "Hispano-Mexican Pioneers," 175–89; Gutiérrez, "Honor Ideology, Marriage Negotiation, and Class-Gender Domination," 81–104; Oakah L. Jones, *Los Paisanos: Spanish Settlers on the Northern Frontier of New Spain* (Norman: University of Oklahoma Press, 1979), 246.

15. Jones, *Los Paisanos,* 12–13, 252–53.

16. Pedro Fages, *A Historical, Political, and Natural Description of California by Pedro Fages,* trans. Herbert Ingram Priestly (1937; repr., Ramona, Calif.: Ballena Press, 1972), 48.

17. Ibid., 33.

18. Herbert E. Bolton, trans. and ed., *Font's Complete Diary: A Chronicle of the Founding of San Francisco* (Berkeley: University of California Press, 1931), 105.

19. Palóu, *Palóu's Life of Fray Junípero Serra,* 198.

20. Ibid., 199.

21. Ibid., 199.

22. Ibid.

23. Boscana, quoted in Alfred Robinson, *Life in California during a Residence of Several Years in that Territory,* (1846; New York: Da Capo Press, 1969), 334–35. Boscana also noted transvestism and homosexual marriage, which he regarded as a "horrible custom" (283–84).

24. Ibid., 282.

25. Sherburne F. Cook and Woodrow Borah produced a remarkable range of demographic data and analysis for eight northern California missions in *Essays in Population History,* vol. 3, *Mexico and California* (Berkeley: University of California Press, 1979), 177–311. For Catholic policy on remarriage, see 278–80.

26. Cook and Borah, "Table 3.9: Marriages of Converts Who Had Previously Been Married by Indian Custom," in *Essays in Population History,* 3:282.

27. Palóu, *Palou's Life of Fray Junípero Serra,* 194.

28. Cook and Borah, "Table 3.9," *Essays in Population History,* 3:282.

29. Serra to Felipe de Neve, Jan. 7, 1780, in Tibesar, *Writings of Junípero Serra,* 3:409–13; responses of the Indians Leopoldo, Senen, and Fernando Huililiaset to *interogatorio,* June 1, 1824, in S. F. Cook, ed., "Expeditions to the Interior of California: Central Valley, 1820–1840," *University of California Anthropological Records* 20, no. 5 (1962), 153–54.

30. Señán to José de la Guerra, June 19, 1816, in José Señán, *The Letters of José Señán, O.F.M.: Mission San Buenaventura, 1796–1823,* ed. Leslie Byrd Simpson, trans. Paul D. Nathan (San Francisco: John Howell-Books, 1962), 87.

31. Lasuén to Antonio Nogueyra, Nov. 28, 1795, in Fermin Francisco de Lasuén, *Writings of Fermin Francisco de Lasuén*, trans. and ed. Finbar Kenneally, 2 vols. (Washington, D.C.: Academy of American Franciscan History, 1965), 1:363.

32. Lasuén to Tomás Pangua, Feb. 3, 1794, in Lasuén, *Writings*, 1:363.

33. Francis F. Guest, O.F.M., *Fermín Francisco de Lasuén (1736–1803): A Biography* (Washington, D.C.: American Academy of Franciscan History, 1973), 207.

34. Lasuén, "Refutation of Charges," June 19, 1801, in Lasuén, *Writings*, 2:220.

35. Palóu, *Life of Fray Junípero Serra*, 66.

36. Lasuén, *Writings*, 2:206–07.

37. Guest, *Fermín Francisco de Lasuén*, 201.

38. Ibid; and Francis F. Guest, "Cultural Perspectives on California Mission Life," *Southern California Quarterly* 65 (Spring 1985), 6–22.

39. Heizer, *Handbook, California*, 8: 511, 544–45.

40. Daniel J. Garr, "Rare and Desolate Land: Population and Race in Hispanic California," *Western Historical Quarterly* 6 (April 1975), 135–37.

41. Jayme, in Geiger, *Letter of Luís Jayme*, 38, 39.

42. Ibid., 40, 41.

43. Ibid., 44–46.

44. Serra to Antonio María de Bucareli y Ursua, Apr. 22, 1773, in Tibesar, *Writings of Junípero Serra*, 1:341.

45. Ibid.

46. Hubert Howe Bancroft, *History of California*, 7 vols. (San Francisco: 1886–1890), 1:249–54. Franciscan historian Maynard J. Geiger attributes rape as a principal cause of the San Diego revolt in Geiger, *Letter of Luís Jayme*, xxx.

47. Serra to Rafael Verger, Aug. 8, 1779, in Tibesar, *Writings of Junípero Serra*, 3:349–51.

48. Gutiérrez, "Honor-Ideology and Sexual Inversion."

49. A. Nicholas Groth, *Men Who Rape: The Psychology of the Offender* (New York: Plenum Press, 1979), 60–61; Julia R. Schwendinger and Herman Schwendinger, *Rape and Inequality* (Beverly Hills: Sage Press, 1983), 202–4; P. Robert, et al. quoted in E. A. Fatah, "The Use of the Victim as an Agent of Self-Legitimization: Toward a Dynamic Explanation of Criminal Behavior," in *Victims and Society*, ed. E. C. Viano (Washington, D.C.: Visage Press, 1976), 108; Suzanne Ageton, *Sexual Assault among Adolescents* (Lexington, Mass.: Lexington Books, 1983), 111–12.

50. Bancroft, *History of California*, 1:362–64. Soldiers' fears of native people were no doubt augmented by the Diegueño attack on Mission San Diego and the Yuma destruction of the Colorado River missions in 1781.

51. José Señán to the Commissioner, Nov. 9, 1822, in Señán, *Letters*, 165.

52. Ann Wolbert Burgess and Lynda Lytle Holstrom, "Rape Trauma Syndrome," *American Journal of Psychiatry* 131 (September 1974), 981–86.

53. Lasuén, *Writings*, 2:212; Cook and Borah, *Essays in Population History* 3:267–78, 304–10. See also Garr, "Rare and Desolate Land," 134–37.

54. Serra to Felipe de Neve, Jan. 7, 1780, in Tibesar, *Writings of Junípero Serra,* 3:409–13.

55. José Longinos, *Journal of José Longinos Martínez: Notes and Observations of the Naturalist of the Botanical Expedition in Old and New California and the South Coast, 1791–1792,* ed. and trans. Lesley Byrd Simpson (San Francisco: J. Howell Books, 1961), 55.

56. Sherburne F. Cook, "Population Trends among the California Mission Indians," *Ibero-Americana* 17 (1940), 29–34.

57. Longinos, *Journal,* 44. While prehistoric Californians suffered from numerous health problems, like other Indians in the Western Hemisphere, they had not been exposed to the infectious crowd diseases, nor is there evidence for syphilis in precontact times. Phillip L. Walker, Patricia Lambert, and Michael J. DeNiro, "The Effects of European Contact on the Health of Alta California Indians," in *Columbian Consequences, Volume 1: Archaeological and Historical Perspectives on the Spanish Borderlands West,* ed. David Hurst Thomas (Washington, D.C., and London: Smithsonian Institution Press, 1989), 349–64. See also Brenda J. Baker and George J. Armelagos, "The Origin and Antiquity of Syphilis: Paleopathological Diagnosis and Interpretation," *Current Anthropology* 29 (December 1988), 703–737.

58. Maynard J. Geiger, O.F.M., trans. and ed., and Clement Meighan, ed., *As the Padres Saw Them: California Mission Life and Customs as Reported by the Franciscan Missionaries, 1813–1815* (Santa Barbara: Santa Barbara Mission Archives, 1976), 71–80.

59. Sherburne F. Cook, "The Indian versus the Spanish Mission," *Ibero-Americana* 21 (1943), 22–30.

60. Geiger and Meighan, *As the Padres Saw Them,* 105–6.

61. Madison S. Beeler, ed., *The Ventureño Confesionario of José Señan, O.F.M.,* University of California Publications in Linguistics, Vol. 47 (Berkeley: University of California Press, 1967), 37–63; Harry Kelsey, ed., *The Doctrina and Confesionario of Juan Cortés* (Altadena, Calif.: Howling Coyote Press, 1979), 113–16, 120–23.

62. Cook, "Indian Versus the Spanish Mission," 101–13.

63. Sherburne F. Cook, "The Physical and Demographic Reaction of the Nonmission Indians in Colonial and Provincial California," *Ibero-Americana* 22 (1943), 1–55.

64. Longinos, *Journal,* 56; Lasuén, "Refutation of Charges," May 28, 1801, in Lasuén, *Writings,* 210.

CHAPTER 2

1. Maynard Geiger, O.F.M., ed. and trans., *The Letters of Alfred Robinson to the De la Guerra Family of Santa Barbara, 1834–1873* (Los Angeles: The Zamorano Club, 1972), 3.

2. Weber, *Mexican Frontier,* 138.

3. Hurtado, *Indian Survival on the California Frontier,* 32–39.

4. Weber, *Mexican Frontier,* 15–42, 62–68, 180, 190, 196–97; Manuel P. Servín, "The Secularization of the California Missions: A Reappraisal," *Southern California Quarterly* 47 (1965), 133–49; C. Alan Hutchinson, "The Mexican Government and the Mission Indians of Upper California," *Americas* 21 (1964–65), 335–62; Daniel Garr, "Planning, Politics, and Plunder: The Missions and Indian Pueblos of Hispanic California," *Southern California Quarterly* 54 (1972), 291–312; W. W. Robinson, *Land in California* (Berkeley: University of California Press, 1948), 29–31, 61.

5. Robinson, *Life in California,* 85–86; Susanna Bryant Dakin, *The Lives of William Hartnell* (Stanford: Stanford University Press, 1949), 156–57; Hubert Howe Bancroft, *The Works of Hubert Howe Bancroft,* vol. 34, *California Pastoral* (San Francisco: The History Company, 1888), 344; Bancroft, *History of California,* 3:641.

6. Harlan Hague and David J. Langum, *Thomas O. Larkin: A Life of Patriotism and Profit in Old California* (Norman: University of Oklahoma Press, 1990), 56–61; Weber, *Mexican Frontier,* 122–46.

7. Weber, *Mexican Frontier,* 122–46.

8. Richard Griswold del Castillo, *La familia: Chicano Families in the Urban Southwest, 1848 to the Present* (Notre Dame, Ind.: University of Notre Dame Press, 1984), 42; Richard Griswold del Castillo, *The Los Angeles Barrio, 1850–1890: A Social History* (Berkeley: University of California Press, 1979), 97–98; Miranda, "Gente de Razón Marriage Patterns," 1–21.

9. Dakin, *Lives of William Hartnell,* 62–64.

10. Antonia I. Castañeda, "Presidarias y Pobladoras: Spanish-Mexican Women in Frontier Monterey, Alta California, 1770–1821" (Ph.D. diss., Stanford University, 1990), 238–84; Miranda, "Gente de Razón Marriage Patterns," 1–21.

11. Forbes, "Hispano-Mexican Pioneers," 175–89; Manuel Patricio Servín, "California's Hispanic Heritage: A View into the Spanish Myth," in Weber, *New Spain's Far Northern Frontier,* 117–33; Miranda, "Gente de Razón Marriage Patterns," 8.

12. Alan Rosenus, *General M. G. Vallejo, A Biography* (Albuquerque: University of New Mexico Press, 1995), 5; Castañeda, "Presidarias y Pobladoras," 238–39.

13. Genaro Padilla, " 'Yo Sola Aprendí': Mexican Women's Personal Narratives from Nineteenth-Century California," in Jameson and Armitage, *Writing the Range,* 188–201.

14. Bancroft, *History of California,* 1:390–93; Donald A. Nuttall, "The Gobernantes of Upper California: A Profile," *California Historical Society* 51 (Fall 1972), 253–80; and Donald A. Nuttall, "Remarks," The Spanish Beginnings in California, 1542–1822, A Symposium, University of California, Santa Barbara, July 15–19, 1991.

15. Castañeda, "Presidarias y Pobladores," 262–66.

16. Ibid., 266–71.

17. D'Emilio and Freedman, *Intimate Matters,* 19–20.

18. Weber, *Mexican Frontier,* 215; Lecompte, "Independent Women of Hispanic New Mexico," 18–19.

19. Carroll Smith-Rosenberg, "The Female Animal: Medical and Biological Views of Woman and Her Role in Nineteenth-Century America," *Journal of American History* 60 (September 1973), 332–56.

20. Barbara Welter, "The Cult of True Womanhood, 1820–1860," *American Quarterly* 18 (Summer 1966), 151–74.

21. D'Emilio and Freedman, *Intimate Matters*, 50–51, 130–38.

22. Ann Twinam, "Honor, Sexuality, and Illegitimacy in Colonial Spanish America," in *Sexuality and Marriage in Colonial Latin America*, ed. Asunción Lavrin (Lincoln: University of Nebraska Press, 1989), 118–55; Lecompte, "Independent Women of Hispanic New Mexico," 17–35; Gutiérrez, *When Jesus Came*, 176–240; Elizabeth Kuznesof and Robert Oppenheimer, "The Family and Society in Nineteenth-Century Latin America: An Historiographical Introduction," *Journal of Family History* 10 (Fall 1985), 215–34; Patricia Seed, "The Church and the Patriarchal Family: Marriage Conflicts in Sixteenth- and Seventeenth-Century New Spain," *Journal of Family History* 10 (Fall 1985), 284–93; Gutiérrez, "Honor Ideology, Marriage Negotiation, and Class-Gender Domination," 81–104; Gutiérrez, "From Honor to Love," 238–63.

23. On illicit sex in Anglo America, see D'Emilio and Friedman, *Intimate Matters*, 109–38.

24. Bancroft, *History of California*, 3:177–78.

25. Larkin quoted in Hague and Langum, *Thomas O. Larkin*, 40.

26. George Henry Bowen quoted in Doyce B. Nunis, Jr., ed. *The California Diary of Faxon Dean Atherton, 1836–1839* (San Francisco: California Historical Society, 1964), xvii.

27. See Bancroft, "Pioneer Register and Index," appended in his *History of California*, vols. 2–6.

28. Doyce B. Nunis, "Preface," in Robinson, *Life in California*, v–ix.

29. Richard Henry Dana, *Two Years before the Mast* (New York: New American Library, Signet Classics, 1969) 225–26.

30. Robinson quoted in Nunis, "Preface," vii.

31. Nunis, "Preface," vii–xii.

32. Geiger, *Letters of Alfred Robinson*, 39–41. Oddly, Robinson urged them to vote the American, or Know-Nothing, ticket in 1855.

33. The source that attributes Franciscans' unwillingness to marry Fitch is questionable. However, the claim is plausible. All sources agree that a Dominican priest agreed to marry the pair, and the great majority of priests in California were Franciscans. Mrs. Fremont Older, *Love Stories of Old California* (1940; repr., Freeport, N.Y.: Books for Libraries Press, 1971), 86.

34. Bancroft, *History of California*, 3:140–41.

35. Josefa Carrillo quoted in Bancroft, *History of California*, 3:141; Dictation of Mrs. Henry D. Fitch, Bancroft Library.

36. Bancroft, *History of California*, 3:142–43.

37. Ibid., 3:143, n. 64.

38. Sánchez quoted in Bancroft, *History of California*, 3:144.

39. Larkin quoted in Hague and Langum, *Thomas O. Larkin*, 31.

40. Ibid., 34.

41. William Heath Davis, *Seventy-five Years in California*, ed. Harold A. Small (San Francisco: John Howell Books, 1967), 160.

42. Unless otherwise noted, the circumstances of the Larkins's courtship and marriage are contained in Hague and Langum, *Thomas O. Larkin*, 39–44.

43. Baptismal entry quoted in Hague and Langum, *Thomas O. Larkin*, 40.

44. Davis, *Seventy-five Years in California*, 6.

45. Bancroft probably had less than 10 percent of the mixed marriages that occurred in California. In only three of twenty-one missions there were 109 such marriages between 1815 and 1854 (see Table 2.1). Bancroft noted only those people for whom there was a sufficient record to note some biographical information, so the poor and unknown did not make it into his "Pioneer Register." On the other hand, Bancroft's sources are reliable and he usually had data for the best-known families. He was especially interested in American pioneers.

46. Hurtado, *Indian Survival on the California Frontier*, 39–47.

47. George D. Lyman, *John Marsh, Pioneer: The Life Story of a Trail-blazer on Six Frontiers* (New York: Charles Scribner's Sons, 1930), 212–13.

48. Hurtado, *Indian Survival on the California Frontier*, 47–54.

49. Alfred L. Kroeber, *Handbook*, 401–2; Bean, "Social Organization," 106–8.

50. Sutter, "Reminiscences of John Augustus Sutter," MS, Bancroft Library, Berkeley, Calif.

51. William R. Swagerty, "Marriage and Settlement Patterns of the Rocky Mountain Trappers and Traders," *Western Historical Quarterly* 11 (April 1980), 159–80; Jennifer S. H. Brown, *Strangers in Blood: Fur Trade Company Families in Indian Country* (Vancouver, B.C.: University of British Columbia Press, 1980), 73–74, 111–30, 199–230; Sylvia Van Kirk, *Many Tender Ties: Women in Fur Trade Society, 1670–1870* (Norman: University of Oklahoma Press, 1980), 28–52, 231–42.

52. Sutter quoted in Charles Alexander, *The Life and Times of Cyrus Alexander*, ed. George Shochat (Los Angeles: Dawson's Bookshop, 1967), 70. The Sutter quote was evidently passed from Cyrus Alexander to his nephew Charles Alexander, who lived with him for many years.

53. Alexander, *Life and Times*, 52, 69–73.

54. Marguerite Eyer Wilbur, trans. and ed., *A Pioneer at Sutter's Fort, 1846–1850: The Adventures of Heinrich Lienhard* (Los Angeles: The Calafía Society, 1941), 76–78.

55. Sutter to William A. Leidesdorff, MS 122, Apr. 17, 1846, and MS 129, May 11, 1846, William A. Leidesdorff Collection, Henry E. Huntington Library, San Marino, Calif.

56. John Chamberlain, "Memoirs of California since 1840," MS, Bancroft Library, Berkeley, Calif.

57. See Iris H. W. Engstrand, "John Sutter: A Biographical Examination," in *John*

Sutter and a Wider West, ed. Kenneth N. Owens (Lincoln: University of Nebraska Press, 1994), 76–92.

58. John Yates, "Sketch of a Journey in the Year 1842 from Sacramento California through the Valley by John Yates of Yatestown," MS, Bancroft Library, Berkeley, Calif.

59. Wilbur, *Pioneer at Sutter's Fort*, 61–62.

60. See also Heinrich Lienhard, *From St. Louis to Sutter's Fort, 1846*, trans. and ed., Erwin G. Gudde and Elizabeth K. Gudde (Norman: University of Oklahoma Press, 1961), 184; Walter Colton, *Three Years in California* (1850; reprint ed., Stanford: Stanford University Press, 1949), 277–78; Lafayette Houghton Bunnell, *Discovery of Yosemite and the Indian War of 1851*, 4th ed. (Los Angeles: G. W. Gerlicher, 1911), 3–4.

61. Hurtado, *Indian Survival on the California Frontier*, 211–18.

CHAPTER 3

1. Edward J. Pettid, S. J., ed., "Olive Ann Oatman's Lecture Notes and Oatman Bibliography," *San Bernardino County Museum* 16, no. 2 (February 1969), 1. Emphasis in original, paragraphing and punctuation added.

2. Biographical note, John H. Beeckman Collection, California Room, State Library, Sacramento, Calif. (hereafter cited as Beeckman Collection).

3. Beeckman to Dearest Wife, Feb. 13, 1849, Beeckman Collection.

4. Henry Livingston Beeckman to Aunt [Mrs. Henry Beeckman], Apr. 30, 1850, Beeckman Collection. Henry's relationship to John is unclear. He may have been a cousin or a brother, although the former relationship seems more likely.

5. Beeckman to dearest wife, Feb. 27, 1849, Beeckman Collection.

6. Beeckman to wife, Mar. 8, 1849, Beeckman Collection.

7. Beeckman to wife, Mar. 17, 1849, Beeckman Collection.

8. Beeckman to dearest wife, Feb. 27, 1849, Beeckman Collection.

9. Beeckman to wife, Mar. 17, 1849, Beeckman Collection.

10. Beeckman to wife, Aug. 7, 1849, Beeckman Collection.

11. Beeckman to wife, Jan. 20, 1850, Beeckman Collection.

12. Henry Livingston Beeckman to Gilbert L. Beeckman, Apr. 27, 1850, Beeckman Collection.

13. C. V. Anthony, *Fifty Years of Methodism: A History of the Methodist Episcopal Church within the Bounds of the California Annual Conference from 1847 to 1897* (San Francisco: Methodist Book Concern, 1901), 98–99.

14. Henry B. Sheldon to My Dear Parents, Apr. 6, 1852, Henry B. Sheldon Collection, California Room, State Library, Sacramento (hereafter cited as Sheldon Collection).

15. Sheldon to My Dear Friends, Apr. 10, 1852, Sheldon Collection.

16. Sheldon to My Dear Friends, Apr. 30, 1852, Sheldon Collection.

17. Sheldon to My Dear Friends, Apr. 30, 1852, Sheldon Collection.

18. Frémont quoted in JoAnn Levy, *They Saw the Elephant: Women in the California Gold Rush* (Hamden, Conn.: Archon Books, 1990), 41.

19. Brooks quoted in Levy, *They Saw the Elephant*, 46.

20. Ibid., *They Saw the Elephant*, 47.

21. Jane Cleveland Burnett, "Memories of Early California Days," Wellington C. Burnett Collection, Box 1, folder 6, Henry E. Huntington Library, San Marino, Calif. (hereafter cited as Burnett Collection).

22. Winthrop D. Jordan, *White over Black: American Attitudes toward the Negro, 1550–1812* (New York: W. W. Norton, 1977), 136–78.

23. Ibid., 142.

24. Ronald T. Takaki, *Iron Cages: Race and Culture in Nineteenth-Century America* (Seattle: University of Washington Press, 1982), 115.

25. On southern honor, race and sexuality, see Bertram Wyatt-Brown, *Honor and Violence in the Old South* (New York: Oxford University Press, 1986), 85–115.

26. John Mack Faragher, *Women and Men on the Overland Trail* (New Haven: Yale University Press, 1979), 66–109, passim. For a general study of the overland trail, see John D. Unruh, *The Plains Across: The Overland Emigrants and the Trans-Mississippi West, 1840–60* (Urbana: University of Illinois Press, 1979).

27. Wilson quoted in Lillian Schlissel, *Women's Diaries of the Westward Journey* (New York: Schocken Books, 1982), 28.

28. Schlissel, *Women's Diaries*, 10–16.

29. Olive Wellington Burnett to Lester Burnett, Oct. [20?] 1843, Burnett Collection, Box 1, folder 10.

30. Olive Wellington Burnett to Lester Burnett, Oct. [20?] 1843, Burnett Collection, Box 1, folder 10.

31. Burnett Collection, Box 1, folder 13.

32. Glenda Riley, *Women and Indians on the Frontier, 1825–1915* (Albuquerque: University of New Mexico Press, 1984), 83–93.

33. Ibid., 17–20, 209–10; Richard Slotkin, *Regeneration through Violence: The Mythology of the American Frontier, 1600–1860* (Middletown, Conn.: Wesleyan University Press, 1973); James Axtell, *The Invasion Within: The Contest of Cultures in Colonial North America* (New York: Oxford University Press, 1985), 304–5.

34. For example, Harper M. Workman, "Early History of Lake Shetek County," Minnesota Historical Society, St. Paul, contains graphic descriptions of rapes that occurred during the 1862 Sioux uprising. Workman recorded the testimony of several women who described their ordeal some years later.

35. Virginia Reed Murphy, "Across the Plains in the Donner Party (1846): A Personal Narrative of the Overland Trip to California," *Century Magazine* 42 (July 1891), 409.

36. The best full-length account of the Donner Party is George R. Stewart, *Ordeal by Hunger: the Story of the Donner Party*, new ed., with a supplement and three

accounts by survivors (Boston: Houghton Mifflin Co., 1960). Unless otherwise noted, my account of the Donner Party is based on Stewart. Still useful is C. F. McGlashan's account based on interviews with survivors, *History of the Donner Party: A Tragedy of the Sierra*, ed. George H. Hinkle and Bliss McGalshan Hinkle (Stanford: Stanford University Press, 1960), reprinted from the second edition published in 1880.

37. McKinstry to Kern, Mar. 4, 1847, Fort Sacramento Papers, MS 115, Huntington Library, San Marino, Calif.

38. Sutter, "Reminiscences."

39. See an 1849 account, J. Quinn Thornton, *The California Tragedy* (Oakland, Calif.: Biobooks, 1945), 130. Thornton got the numbers slightly wrong, but calculated the difference in male and female mortality rates.

40. Table 3.1 and statistical analysis based on Donald K. Grayson, "Donner Party Deaths: A Demographic Assessment," *Journal of Anthropological Research* 46 (Fall 1990), 223–42. Table 3.1 is based on Grayson's Table 6, p. 234.

41. This analysis of male leadership mortality is based on the data presented in Grayson, "Donner Party Deaths," 223–42, but the conclusions are my own. Grayson did not consider the mortality of male heads of households in his analysis.

42. This table includes only those men who made the winter camp at Donner Lake. Consequently, James Reed is not included, nor are a few men who died on the trail before reaching the Sierra Nevada.

43. Reed letter quoted in Stewart, *Ordeal by Hunger*, 361.

44. Thornton, *California Tragedy*, 131.

45. Caroline Bullard to Julia Bullard, ca. 1855, William Green Bullard Collection, California Room, State Library, Sacramento (hereafter cited as Bullard Collection).

46. Unruh, *Plains Across*, 403.

47. Richard White, "Trashing the Trails," in Limerick, Milner, and Rankin, *Trails*, 26–39.

48. Unruh, *Plains Across*, 124, 408–9.

49. Benjamin Bullard to Silas Bullard, Jan. 13, 1854, Bullard Collection.

50. Unruh, *Plains Across*, 185.

51. Kathryn Zabelle Derounian-Stodola, "The Indian Captivity Narratives of Mary Rowlandson and Olive Oatman: Case Studies in the Continuity, Evolution, and Exploitation of Literary Discourse," *Studies in the Literary Imagination* 27 (Spring 1994), 33–46; Richard Dillon, "Tragedy at Oatman Flat: Massacre, Captivity, Mystery," *The American West* 18, no. 2 (March/April 1981), 46–54, 59.

52. Derounian-Stodola, "Indian Captivity Narratives," 34; Dillon, "Tragedy at Oatman Flat," 49.

53. Royce Oatman to the honorable commandant of Fort Yumas, Feb. 15, 1851, quoted in Alice Bay Maloney, ed., "Some Oatman Documents," *California Historical Society Quarterly* 21 (June 1941), 109.

54. R. B. Stratton, *Captivity of the Oatman Girls: Being an Interesting Narrative of Life among the Apache and Mohave Indians*, 3d ed. (New York: Carlton and Porter, 1859).

55. Kenneth M. Stewart, "Mohave," in Alfonso Ortiz, ed., *Handbook of North American Indians*, vol. 10, *Southwest* (Washington, D.C.: Smithsonian Institution, 1983), 63.

56. Los Angeles *Star*, Apr. 19, 1856, quoted in William B. Rice, "The Captivity of Olive Oatman: A Newspaper Account," *California Historical Society Quarterly* 21 (June 1941), 102–3.

57. Quoted in A. L. Kroeber, "Olive Oatman's Return," *Kroeber Anthropological Society Papers* 4 (1951), 2.

58. Stratton, *Captivity of the Oatman Girls*, title page, 5–16.

59. Derounian-Stodola, "Indian Captivity Narratives," 35–36.

60. Stratton, *Captivity of the Oatman Girls*, 280.

61. Ibid. On Mohave marriage practices, see Stewart, "Mohave," 64–65.

62. Stratton, *Captivity of the Oatman Girls*, 283.

63. Ibid., 285–86; the emphasis is Stratton's.

64. Hurtado, *Indian Survival on the California Frontier*, 180–87.

65. Stratton, *Captivity of the Oatman Girls*, 285.

66. See Oatman's brief answers to questions about her captivity in A. L. Kroeber and Clifton Kroeber, "Olive Oatman's First Account of Her Captivity Among the Mohave," *California Historical Society Quarterly* 41 (December 1962), 311–12.

67. Oatman quoted in Pettid, "Olive Ann Oatman's Lecture Notes," 1.

68. Unidentified woman quoted in Riley, *Women and Indians*, 210.

69. Dillon, "Tragedy at Oatman Flat," 59.

70. Stratton, *Captivity of the Oatman Girls*, 271.

CHAPTER 4

1. C. T. H. [Casper T. Hopkins], "Our Divorce Law," *The Pioneer*, vol. 1, April 1854, pp. 213–20.

2. Ibid.

3. Ibid. For a particularly bitter outburst against divorce, see "Concerning Divorce," *Alta*, Jan. 26, 1851, p. 2.

4. Woods quoted in Sandra Sizer Frankiel, *California's Spiritual Frontiers: Religious Alternatives in Anglo-Protestantism, 1850–1910* (Berkeley: University of California Press, 1988), 2.

5. Kevin Starr, *Americans and the California Dream, 1850–1915* (New York: Oxford University Press, 1973).

6. Statistics derived from J. B. D. DeBow, *Statistical View of the United States* (Washington, D.C.: A. O. P. Nicholson, 1854), 200–201, 394; Joseph C. G. Kennedy, *Population of the United States in 1860* (Washington, D.C.: Government Printing Office, 1864), 22–23.

7. Paul Veyne, "Homosexuality in Ancient Rome," in Ariès and Béjin, *Western Sexuality*, 32–33; Jacques Roossiaud, "Prostitution, Sex and Society in French Towns in the Fifteenth Century," in Ariès and Béjin, *Western Sexuality*, 76–94; Ruth Rosen, *The Lost Sisterhood: Prostitution in America, 1900–1918* (Baltimore: Johns Hopkins University Press, 1982), 2.

8. Peter Gay, *The Bourgeoise Experience: Victoria to Freud*, vol. 1, *Education of the Senses* (New York: Oxford University Press, 1984), 333, 335.

9. Anne M. Butler, *Daughters of Joy, Sisters of Misery: Prostitutes in the American West, 1865–1890* (Urbana: University of Illinois Press, 1985), 7–11.

10. Butler, *Daughters of Joy, Sisters of Misery*, 1–16; Marion S. Goldman, *Gold Diggers and Silver Miners: Prostitution and Social Life on the Comstock Load* (Ann Arbor: University of Michigan Press, 1981), 73–99; Robert Dykstra, *The Cattle Towns* (New York: Atheneum, 1972), 126–27, 259–60; Joel Best, "Careers in Brothel Prostitution: St. Paul, 1866–83," typescript MS, Library of the Kinsey Institute for Sexual Research, Indiana University, Bloomington; Mary Murphy, "Private Lives of Public Women: Prostitution in Butte, Montana, 1878–1917," *Frontiers* 7, no. 3 (1984), 30–35; Paula Petrick, "Strange Bedfellows: Prostitution, Politicians and Moral Reform in Helena, 1885–1887," *Montana, The Magazine of Western History* 35, no. 3 (1985), 2–13; Ruth Rosen, "Go West Young Woman? Prostitution on the Frontier," *Reviews in American History* 14 (1986), 158–71.

11. Vicente Pérez Rosales, "Diary of a Journey to California," in *We Were 49ers: Chilean Accounts of the California Gold Rush*, ed. Edwin A. Beilharz and Carlos V. López (Pasadena, Calif.: Ward Ritchie Press, 1976), pp. 3–4, 6, 11, 20.

12. *Alta*, May 7, 1850, quoted in Jacqueline Baker Barnhart, *The Fair but Frail: Prostitution in San Francisco, 1849–1900* (Reno: University of Nevada Press, 1986), 15.

13. John Paul Dart to Brother, Dec. 26, 1850, John Paul Dart Collection, California Room, State Library, Sacramento, Calfiornia (hereafter cited as Dart Collection).

14. Brigham D. Madsen, *The Shoshone Frontier and the Bear River Massacre* (Salt Lake City: University of Utah Press, 1985), 33.

15. Wayman, *A Doctor on the California Trail: The Diary of Dr. John Hudson Wayman from Cambridge City, Indiana, to the Gold Fields in 1852*, ed. Edgely Woodman Todd (Denver: Old West Publishing Co., 1971), 70.

16. H. B. Sheldon to Dear Friends, June 25, 1852, Sheldon Collection.

17. H. B. Sheldon to Dear Friends, May 12, 1852, Sheldon Collection; H. B. Sheldon to Dear Friends, May 31, 1852, Sheldon Collection.

18. William Taylor, *Seven Years' Street Preaching in San Francisco, California*, ed. W. P. Strickland (New York: Carlton and Porter, 1856); William Taylor, *California Life Illustrated*, rev. ed. (London: Jackson, Walford, and Hodder, 1867).

19. Taylor, *Seven Years' Street Preaching*, 81–85, 312–13; Frank Soule, John H. Gihon, and James Nisbet, *The Annals of San Francisco* (1855; repr., Palo Alto: Lewis Osborne, 1966), 670–72.

20. Soule, Gihon, and Nisbet, *Annals of San Francisco*, 666.

21. Sheldon to My Dear Friends, May 12, 1852, Sheldon Collection.

22. H. B. Sheldon to Dear Friends, June 25, 1852, Sheldon Collection; emphasis in original.

23. Sheldon to Dear Friends, with a section addressed to Mother, Sept. [?], 1852, Sheldon Collection.

24. Sheldon to My Dear Friends, July 26, 1852, Sheldon Collection; emphasis in original.

25. Butler, *Daughters of Joy, Sisters of Misery.*

26. Sarah Royce, *A Frontier Lady: Recollections of the Gold Rush and Early California* (1932; repr., Lincoln: University of Nebraska Press, 1977), 114.

27. Mrs. D. B. Bates, *Incidents on Land and Water, or Four Years on the Pacific Coast* (Boston: Mrs. D. B. Bates, 1860), 317–18.

28. Ibid., 330.

29. Levy, *They Saw the Elephant,* 170, asserts that Sarah Royce was describing the 1855 altercation of Richardson and Cora. However, Royce's description of the episode, which she dates as 1850, differs from the Richardson-Cora feud in several respects. Moreover, the 1856 vigilance movement was so traumatic and famous that it is hard to imagine that Royce would not have mentioned it in association with the events that she narrated, or that she would have somehow gotten the date wrong by five years.

30. Robert M. Senkewicz, S. J., *Vigilantes in Gold Rush San Francisco* (Stanford: Stanford University Press, 1985), 5–7.

31. Richard Maxwell Brown, *Strain of Violence: Historical Studies of Violence and Vigilantism* (New York: Oxford University Press, 1975), 306–7, enumerates California's vigilante episodes. See also Robert Utley, *High Noon in Lincoln: Violence on the Western Frontier* (Albuquerque: University of New Mexico Press, 1987), 171–79.

32. The creation of vice districts is best understood in San Francisco. See Neil Larry Shumsky and Larry M. Springer, "San Francisco's Zone of Prostitution, 1880–1934," *Journal of Historical Geography* 7, no. 1 (1981), 73–77; Herbert Asbury, *The Barbary Coast: An Informal History of the San Francisco Underworld* (New York: Alfred A. Knopf, 1933), 98–101; Roger Lotchin, *San Francisco, 1846–1856: From Hamlet to City* (New York: Oxford University Press, 1974), 256; Benson Tong, *Unsubmissive Women: Chinese Prostitutes in Nineteenth-Century San Francisco* (Norman: University of Oklahoma Press, 1994), 93–125. On mining-town zones of prostitution, see Ralph Mann, *After the Gold Rush: Society in Grass Valley and Nevada City, California, 1849–1870* (Stanford: Stanford University Press, 1982), 56–67. On Sonora Town, see Richard Griswold del Castillo, *The Los Angeles Barrio, 1850–1890: A Social History* (Berkeley: University of California Press, 1979), 70, 141.

33. Hurtado, *Indian Survival on the California Frontier,* 169–92.

34. Herman Francis Reinhart, *The Golden Frontier: The Recollections of Herman Francis Reinhart, 1851–1865* (Austin: University of Texas Press, 1962), 45.

35. W. P. Crenshaw to Thomas J. Henley, Dec. 16, 1854, enclosed with letter of

Dec. 16, 1862, Office of Indian Affairs, Letters Received, California Superintendency, National Archives Microfilm M234, reel 34.

36. Hurtado, *Indian Survival on the California Frontier,* 180–82.

37. San Francisco *Bulletin,* Sept. 13, 1856, quoted in Robert F. Heizer, ed., *The Destruction of the California Indians* (Santa Barbara: Peregrine Smith, 1974), 278.

38. Sacramento *Union,* Oct. 1, 1858, quoted in ibid., 279–80.

39. This is a condensed version of an argument I made in *Indian Survival on the California Frontier,* 182–87.

40. Groth, *Men Who Rape,* 60–61.

41. Ageton, *Sexual Assault among Adolescents,* 111–12.

42. Fattah, "Use of the Victim," 105–29; Schwendinger and Schwendinger, *Rape and Inequality,* 201–4.

43. Sacramento *Daily Democratic State Journal,* Sept. 1, 1855, quoted in Robert F. Heizer, ed., *They Were Only Diggers: A Collection of Articles from California Newspapers, 1851–1866, on Indian and White Relations* (Ramona, Calif.: Ballena Press, 1974), 29.

44. Butte *Democrat,* Sept. 24, 1859, 3.

45. See, for example, newspaper articles reprinted in Heizer, *Destruction of the California Indians,* 278–83.

46. Hurtado, *Indian Survival on the California Frontier,* 169–92.

47. Sutter to Thomas J. Henley, Feb. 9, 1856, Letters Received, Office of Indian Affairs, California Superintendency, 1849–1880, National Archives, RG 75, Microfilm Publication M234, reel 35; Albert L. Hurtado, "Indians in Town and Country: the Nisenan Indians' Changing Economy and Society as Shown in John A. Sutter's 1856 Correspondence," *American Indian Culture and Research Journal* 12, no. 2 (1988), 31–51.

48. Hurtado, *Indian Survival on the California Frontier,* 63.

49. William T. Sherman, *Memoirs of General William T. Sherman,* 2 vols. (1875; repr., Bloomington: Indiana University Press, 1957), 1:33.

50. Warren Saddler, undated entry [1849 or 1850], MS Journal, vol. 2, Bancroft Library, University of California, Berkeley.

51. Tong, *Unsubmissive Women,* 3–12; Curt Gentry, *The Madams of San Francisco: An Irreverent History of the City by the Golden Gate* (Garden City, N.Y.: Doubleday, 1964), pp. 50–59; Goldman, *Gold Diggers and Silver Miners,* pp. 93–98; Elmer Clarence Sandmeyer, *The Anti-Chinese Movement in California* (1939; repr., Urbana: University of Illinois Press, 1973), pp. 52–54; and Lucie Cheng Hirata, 'Free, Indentured, Enslaved: Chinese Prostitutes in Nineteenth Century America," *Signs* 5 (Autumn 1979), 3–29.

52. Tong, *Unsubmissive Women,* 69–77, 94, 95, 98; Gentry, *Madams of San Francisco,* 50–59; Goldman, *Gold Diggers and Silver Miners,* 93–98; Sandmeyer, *Anti-Chinese Movement in California,* 52–54; and Hirata, "Free, Indentured, Enslaved," 3–29.

53. Kennedy, *Population of the United States in 1860*, 30.

54. William Bullard to Julia Bullard, Mar. 5, 1862, Bullard Collection.

55. Benjamin & Eleanor Bullard to Silas & Diantha Bullard, June 15, 1854, Bullard Collection.

56. Mary Bullard to Dear Aunt, May 28, 1855, Bullard Collection; Mary Bullard to Dear Aunt, June 3, 1857, Bullard Collection.

57. Caroline Bullard to Julia and Edward Bullard, Oct. 29, 1853, Bullard Collection.

58. Caroline Bullard to Julia Bullard, ca. 1855, Bullard Collection.

59. Cordelia Bullard to Aunt Diantha, May 14, 1854, Bullard Collection.

60. Mary Bullard to Dear Aunt, June 3, 1857, Bullard Collection.

61. Caroline Bullard to Julia, Jan. 13, 1856, Bullard Collection.

62. Caroline Bullard to Julia A. Bullard, Feb. 12, 1855, Bullard Collection.

63. Caroline Bullard to Julia Bullard, Nov. 18, 1857, Bullard Collection.

64. William Bullard to Dear Cousin [Julia], Apr. 1, 1859, Bullard Collection.

65. William Bullard to Miss Julia Bullard, June 16, 1859, Bullard Collection.

66. William Bullard to Dear Uncle & Aunt, June 15, 1855, Bullard Collection.

67. Mary Bullard to Dear Aunt, May 28, 1855, Bullard Collection.

68. Mary Bullard to Dear Aunt, June 3, 1857, Bullard Collection.

69. William Bullard to Silas Bullard, July 1, 1858, Bullard Collection.

70. William Bullard to Julia Bullard, Mar. 5, 1862, Bullard Collection.

71. William Bullard to Dear Cousin [Julia], Apr. 1, 1859, Bullard Collection.

72. William Bullard to Julia Bullard, June 29, 1862, Bullard Collection.

73. William Bullard to Cousin Julia Phillips, Dec. 21, 1862, Bullard Collection.

74. William Bullard to Cousin Julia, Oct. 12, 1862, Bullard Collection.

75. Collection Description, Bullard Collection.

76. Sheldon to Dear Friends, Sept. 28, 1852, Sheldon Collection; Sheldon to Dear Friends, Sept. [?], 1852, Sheldon Collection.

77. Sheldon to Dear Father, Mar. 9, 1854, Sheldon Collection; Sheldon to Dear Mother, Sept. 12, 1854, Sheldon Collection.

78. Sheldon to Father, July 5, 1854, Sheldon Collection.

79. John Paul Dart to [?] Oct. 22, 1853, Dart Collection.

80. John Paul Dart to Brother, Dec. 7, 1853, Dart Collection.

81. John Paul Dart to Brother, Dec. 7, 1853, Dart Collection.

82. John Paul Dart to Brother, Dec. 7, 1853, Dart Collection.

83. William M. Stewart, *Reminiscences of Senator William M. Stewart of Nevada*, ed. George Rothwell Brown (New York: The Neale Publishing Company, 1908), 64.

84. Ibid., *Reminiscences*, 64–65.

85. Ibid., *Reminiscences*, 65.

86. C. T. H., "Our Divorce Law," 213–20.

87. Griswold, *Family and Divorce in California*, 18–20, 28, 30–31.

88. Stewart, *Reminiscences*, 66.

89. Ibid., *Reminiscences*, 67.

90. "Concerning Divorce," *Alta*, Jan. 26, 1851, 2.

91. Ibid., 2.

92. "The Divorce Law of California," *Alta*, Feb. 25, 1854, 2.

93. [Untitled], *Alta*, June 12, 1854, 2.

94. Carl I. Wheat, ed., *The Shirley Letters from the California Mines, 1851–1852* (New York: Alfred A. Knopf, 1949), xv–xvi; Rodman Wilson Paul, "In Search of Dame Shirley," *Pacific Historical Review* 33 (May 1964), 127–46.

95. Paul, "In Search of Dame Shirley," 132–33. See also letters to Smith in the Shirley Papers, California Room, State Library, Sacramento (hereafter cited as Shirley Papers). Except for the famous *Shirley Letters*, and a few other published pieces, none of Smith's correspondence has been found. The Shirley Papers contain letters to Smith.

96. Alexander Hill Everett, *Prose Pieces and Correspondence*, ed. Elizabeth Evans (St. Paul, Minn.: The John Colet Press, 1975), ix–xv.

97. Louise Smith, "Leverett: An Epistle from a Lady in the Country to a Distant Friend," *United States Magazine and Democratic Review* 15 (October 1844), 360–62; Everett to Louise Smith, Oct. 4, 1844, Shirley Papers.

98. Everett to Louise Smith, Oct. 5, 1841, Shirley Papers.

99. Everett to Louise Smith, Jan. 26, 1842, Shirley Papers.

100. Ibid.

101. Everett to Louise Smith, June 18, 1842, Shirley Papers.

102. Everett to Louise Smith, Nov. 25, 1844, Shirley Papers.

103. Everett to Louise Smith, Dec. 28, 1844, Jan. 1, 1845, Apr. 17, 1845, May 26, 1845, Mar. 3, 1846, Feb. 2, 1847, Shirley Papers.

104. Everett to Louise Smith, Jan. 1, 1845, Shirley Papers.

105. Everett to Louise Smith, Mar. 3, 1846, Shirley Papers.

106. Everett to Louise Smith, Feb. 2, 1847, Shirley Papers.

107. Everett to Louise Smith, Feb. 2, 1847, Shirley Papers.

108. Emma Talbot to Louise Smith, Sept. 16, 1840, Shirley Papers.

109. Shirley [Louise A. K. S. Clapp], "Superstition," *The Pioneer* 2, no. 6 (December 1854), 344.

110. Paul, "In Search of Dame Shirley," 137.

111. Wheat, *Shirley Letters*, 4, 10–11, 51.

112. Ibid., 11, 27.

113. Ibid., 46.

114. Ibid., 88.

115. Shirley, "The Equality of the Sexes," *The Pioneer* 1 (1854), 85–88.

116. Everett to Louise Smith, Sept. 13, 1839, Shirley Letters; Alexander H. Everett, *Critical and Miscellaneous Essays* (Boston: James Munroe and Company, 1845), 515–17.

117. Paul, "In Search of Dame Shirley," 140–44; Viola Tingley Lawrence,

"Dame Shirley, the Writer of These Letters: An Appreciation," in *The Shirley Letters from California in 1851–52, Being a Series of Twenty-Three Letters from Dame Shirley . . .*, ed. Thomas C. Russell (San Francisco: Thomas C. Russell, 1922), xxx.

118. "Divorce Business," *Alta*, Apr. 5, 1857, 1.

119. Paul, "In Search of Dame Shirley," 140.

120. Lawrence, "Dame Shirley," xxxi.

121. Ibid., xxx–xxxi.

122. Paul, "In Search of Dame Shirley," 146.

123. Ibid., 145.

124. Polly Welts Kaufman, *Women Teachers on the Frontier* (New Haven: Yale University Press, 1984), 8–11.

CHAPTER 5

1. Inquest on Amelia Kuschinsky, Mar. 15, 1860, Shasta County, Records of the Clerk, Coroner's Inquests, Shasta College Museum, Redding, Calif. (hereafter cited as Coroner's Inquest).

2. Coroner's Inquest. Kuschinsky's exact age at death is unknown. It was reported as "about" sixteen in the Coroner's Inquest, and as fifteen in "A Case of Abortion and Death," *Shasta Courier*, Mar. 17, 1860, p. 2, col. 3.

3. "Case of Abortion and Death," *Shasta Courier*, Mar. 17, 1860, p. 2, col. 3.

4. Mildred Brooke Hoover, Hero Eugene Rensch, and Ethel Grace Rensch, *Historic Spots of California*, 3d ed., ed. William N. Abeloe (Stanford: Stanford University Press, 1966), 487; Erwin G. Gudde, comp. *California Gold Camps: A Geographical and Historical Dictionary of Camps, Towns, and Localities Where Gold Was Found and Mined*, ed. Elizabeth K. Gudde (Berkeley: University of California Press, 1975), 160–61; Erwin G. Gudde, *California Place Names: The Origin and Etymology of Current Geographical Names*, 3d ed. (Berkeley: University of California Press, 1969), 146.

5. Coroner's Inquest.

6. Sworn statement of Jacob Lacinsky, Coroner's Inquest.

7. Federal Manuscript Census, 1860, Trinity County, Evans Bar, California State Archives, Sacramento (hereafter cited as Manuscript Census, County). Unfortunately, the census was taken several months after Kuschinsky's death.

8. Ibid.

9. Woman quoted in Sandra L. Myres, *Westering Women and the Frontier Experience, 1800–1915* (Albuquerque: University of New Mexico Press, 1982), 152.

10. Manuscript Census, Trinity County.

11. Unless otherwise stated, details about the Stillers, Kuschinsky, and her death come from Coroner's Inquest.

12. Buck to his sister, July 30, 1859, in Franklin A. Buck, *A Yankee Trader in the Gold Rush: The Letters of Franklin A. Buck*, comp. Katherine A. White (Boston: Houghton Mifflin Company, 1930), 178–79.

13. Buck to his sister, Oct. 29, 1859, in Buck, *Yankee Trader*, 179; Buck's emphasis.

14. Tansy (*Tanasetum vulgare*) is an herb that was often prescribed to produce abortion in combination with gin, rum, and other substances. James C. Mohr, *Abortion in America: the Origins and Evolution of National Policy, 1800–1900* (New York: Oxford University Press, 1978), 61–62.

15. "An Act Concerning Crimes and Punishments," *Statutes of California*, 1850, Chapter 99, section 45.

16. Mohr, *Abortion in America*, 119–46; Donna C. Schuele, "Community Property Law and the Politics of Married Women's Rights in Nineteenth-Century California," *Western Legal History* 7 (Summer/Fall 1994), 245–81.

17. *Statutes of California*, 1858, Chapter 242.

18. "The Abortion Case," *Shasta Courier*, Mar. 24, 1860, p. 2, col. 2.

19. Manuscript Census, Shasta County.

20. Buck to his sister, Sept. 23, 1855, in Buck, *Yankee Trader*, 152, says that "Doctor Bates of Shasta" was elected treasurer.

21. Quoted in R. A. Burchell, *The San Francisco Irish, 1848–1880* (Berkeley: University of California Press, 1980), 128. See also David A. Williams, *David C. Broderick: A Political Portrait* (San Marino, Calif.: The Huntington Library, 1969), 90–91.

22. Bancroft, *History of California*, 6:617–19.

23. "The Abortion Case," p. 2.

24. Raymond F. Dasmann, *The Destruction of California* (New York: Collier Macmillan, 1966), 67; Robert Kelley, *Battling the Inland Sea: American Political Culture, Public Policy, and the Sacramento Valley, 1850–1986* (Berkeley: University of California Press, 1989), 80.

25. William H. Brewer, *Up and Down California in 1860–1864: The Journal of William H. Brewer, Professor of Agriculture in the Sheffield Scientific School from 1864–1903*, 3d ed., ed. Francis P. Farquhar (Berkeley: University of California Press, 1966), 299.

26. Hoover, Rensch, and Rensch, *Historic Spots of California*, 487; Gudde, *California Gold Camps*, 160–61; Gudde, *California Place Names*, 146.

CHAPTER 6

1. *Thirteenth Census of the United States Taken in the Year 1910 Abstract of the Census . . . with Supplement for California* (Washington: Government Printing Office, 1913), 599.

2. Malcolm Rohrbough, *Days of Gold: The California Gold Rush and the American Nation* (Berkeley: University of California Press, 1997), 172–84; Levy, *They Saw the Elephant*, 91–107.

3. Anne Crampton to "Dear Brothers," July 19, 1854, Johnson Beal Papers, California Room, State Library, Sacramento (hereafter cited as the Beal Papers).

4. Ann Crampton to Johnson Beal, June 17, 1861, Beal Papers.

5. Ann Crampton to Johnson Beal, Oct. 8, 1861, Beal Papers.

6. Anne Crampton to Brother and Sister, Nov. 6, 1865, Beal Papers.

7. Mary Bullard to Dear Aunt, June 3, 1857, Bullard Collection.

8. Mrs. S. A. Downer, "What California Wants," *Pioneer* 2 (July 1854), 80.

9. Dale Morgan, "Through the Haze of Time: The California Gold Rush in Retrospect," in Howard C. Gardiner, *In Pursuit of the Golden Dream: Reminiscences of San Francisco and the Northern and Southern Mines, 1849–1857*, ed. Morgan (Stoughton, Mass.: Western Hemisphere, 1970), vii–xlii; Starr, *Americans and the California Dream*, 50.

10. Starr, *Americans and the California Dream*, 115–16.

11. Hubert Howe Bancroft, *The Works of Hubert Howe Bancroft*, vol. 36, *Popular Tribunals*, vol. 1 (San Francisco: The History company, 1887), vii.

12. For some firsthand accounts, see D. P. Barstow, Statement of Recollections of 1849–51 by D. P. Barstow, Bancroft Library; George Barton, "A Double Tragedy in the Mines: Hanging of Mexican Woman, Juanita, at Downieville, Sierra County, in 1851," *The Grizzly Bear* (November 1923), 4; Milt Gotardi, ed., "The Hanging of Juanita," *Sierra County Historical Society Bulletin* 2, no. 3 (Dec. 20, 1970), 13–31.

13. "A Woman Hung at Downieville," *Daily Alta* (July 9, 1851), 2; "The Hanging at Downieville," *Daily Alta* (July 14, 1851), 2; "The Downieville Tragedy," *Daily Alta* (Jan. 29, 1852), 2.

14. Barton, "Double Tragedy," 4; Barstow, Statement of Recollections.

15. Josiah Royce, *California, from the Conquest in 1846 to the Second Vigilance Committee in San Francisco* (Boston: Houghton, Mifflin and Company, 1886), 368–74; *Illustrated History of Plumas, Lassen, and Sierra Counties* (San Francisco: Fariss and Smith, 1882), 445–47; Leonard Pitt, *The Decline of the Californios: A Social History of the Spanish-Speaking Californians, 1846–1890* (Berkeley: University of California Press, 1966), 73–74; Levy, *They Saw the Elephant*, 85–88.

16. Bancroft, *Popular Tribunals*, 1:577.

17. Ibid., 1:578.

18. Ibid., 1:577.

19. Ibid., 1:578–79.

20. Richard O'Connor, *Bret Harte: A Biography* (Boston: Little, Brown and Company, 1966), 18–38, 52.

21. William F. Strobridge, *Regulars in the Redwoods: The U.S. Army in Northern California, 1852–1861* (Spokane, Wash.: Arthur H. Clark, 1994), 204–5.

22. Harte quoted in O'Connor, *Bret Harte*, 45.

23. Ibid., 40; Owen C. Coy, *The Humboldt Bay Region, 1850–1875* (Los Angeles: the California State Historical Association, 1929), 144, 160, 165, 180.

24. Whipple quoted in O'Connor, *Bret Harte*, 47.

25. O'Connor, *Bret Harte*, 97.

26. Bret Harte, "The Luck of Roaring Camp," in Bret Harte, *The Luck of Roaring Camp and Other Tales* (New York: Dodd, Mead and Company, 1961), 1–14.

27. Gary Scharnhorst, ed., *Selected Letters of Bret Harte* (Norman: University of Oklahoma Press, 1997), 3; Paul, "In Search of Dame Shirley," 145.

28. Paul, "In Search of Dame Shirley," 145–46; Scharnhorst, *Selected Letters*, 20, n. 4.

29. George Plimpton, "Introduction," in Mark Twain, *Roughing It*, The Oxford Twain (New York: Oxford University Press, 1996), xxxv–xlii.

30. Mark Twain, *The Celebrated Jumping Frog of Calaveras County, and Other Sketches*, The Oxford Twain (New York: Oxford University Press, 1996), 7–19.

31. Mark Twain, "The Pioneers' Ball," in Mark Twain, *Mark Twain, Collected Tales, Sketches, Speeches, and Essays, 1852–1890*, 2 vols. (New York: The Library of America, 1992), 1:184–85.

32. Carey McWilliams, *Ambrose Bierce, A Biography with a New Introduction* (Hambden, Conn.: Archon Books, 1967), 28–93.

33. Ambrose Bierce, "The Haunted Valley," in *The Collected Writings of Ambrose Bierce* (New York: The Citadel Press, 1946), 451–60.

34. Fuentes, *The Old Gringo*, 1985), 161.

Index